began Dr. Stosny's program, all of my FM pain and symptoms have gone. My doctors are amazed and so am I. Thank you, Dr. Stosny!"

—*Joan B.*

"Dr. Stosny's CompassionPower Boot Camp gave me the tools to take charge of my emotions, quit blaming others, and begin rebuilding my self-esteem. Anyone who puts his program into practice can't help but become a better, more peaceable person."

—*Daleen R. Berry*

"Attending Dr. Stosny's Stop Walking on Eggshells Workshop was a life-changing experience. First, I learned that my husband and I were *both* walking on eggshells, and this class was applicable to both of us. Though the abuse was his problem, we both were angry and resentful towards each other. We arrived fairly hopeless and unsure of what to expect. Since the workshop, we have a newfound peace in our home and appreciation for each other. We have rediscovered compassion for each other. I have learned how to stop walking on eggshells. I have learned how to care for myself which allows me to care for others. Thank you, Dr. Stosny. I can't recommend this program enough!"

—*Boot Camp participant*

"It should be mandatory reading prior to saying marriage vows in order to get off to the right start! And it should be mandatory for everyone before they can graduate from high school! Then we'd know we are getting our kids off to the best start possible in life!"

—*Mary Anderson*

"I found in this work one of the 'missing pieces' to my puzzle. I did have a lot of history hit me all at once, and was quite tearful for hours afterward. (Even now I am still tearful as I recall my feelings.) I just wanted to thank you for your incredible work."

—*Debra Foote*

"Everyone could benefit from Dr. Stosny's methods. . . . Especially couples who have tried conventional marriage counseling and given up. His methods teach an entirely different approach to anger management and understanding what is really going on beneath the surface, an eye-opening experience!"

—*Matt Vinkler*

"I went to the seminar hoping my husband could change. . . . I left realizing it I was who had the power to change, it was I who needed to have compassion, not only for my husband but mostly for myself. Thank you, Dr. Stosny, for showing me there is so much life to live. Now even the smallest things I see mean so much, realizing that I have been created to enjoy this and so much more. Because of you I am slowly realizing the value in so so much. . . more important, the value in myself."

—*Jovanna Dunham*

"Dr. Stosny's approach to changing the patterns of emotional and verbal abuse works; regardless of the role you have in the relationship. I have hope for the first time in many years. He gave me practical tools to apply to my relationship."

—*Katie Simoneit*

" I came to the realization that verbal/emotional abuse toward me by my spouse was the reason for the problems in our marriage. I have since then visited Dr. Stosny's website for information many times. My spouse has finally given up the denial and is ready to accept help with changing his behavior. It would be an answer to my prayers if a CompassionPower program is available in our area for him to attend."

—*Janet*

"Dr. Stosny taught us how to *stop the abuse* as well as how to open the door to a happier, healthier, and more compassionate relationship with our loved ones and with everyone else in our lives. I witnessed and experienced, firsthand, the success of Dr. Stosny's brilliant program. I recommend Dr. Stosny's program to anyone and everyone."

—*Boot Camp participant*

"My husband and I attended the Chicago Boot Camp this past January and it was an amazingly positive experience. Our marriage/relationship has made quantum leaps in the areas of respecting and valuing each other and our children. The 'reconnection' aspect of the program has been awesome. There's so much more fun, connectedness, and compassion in our relationship. Everyone in our family is a 'happier camper.' Dr. Stosny is a genius. I recommend his Boot Camp to every couple."

—Boot Camp participant

"I am so grateful to Dr. Stosny. You were able to reach my husband in a way no one ever has before, and he said so. And I am working on my approaches from new ways that you taught."

—Boot Camp participant

"I just want to say that I believe in what you are doing! I believe that this was the only way to help my husband. He had gone to two different anger management counselors (court ordered for a year at a time). They never helped. The counseling we started would always end when it seemed like the counselor would start to deal with him and what he needed to change and work on. It was a venting session and he would try to portray me as the villain and it was all my fault—he had reasons to justify his actions. I have gotten an extra book and given it to my counselor. I am reading the information over and over and pick up some more every time. Thank you for all that you did and have done. May God bless you greatly!"

—J. Schreiner

"Dr. Stosny has a brilliant program. He is a dynamic and fascinating lecturer, with a strong knowledge base in psychology, neuropsychology, anthropology, and animal behavior. His program for abusers is the work of a genius . . . and it is proving to be the most successful program for the abusers out there."

—Boot Camp participant

"I think this program is excellent. I have referred many to it. Dr. Stosny's willingness to share your own experiences and conversational approach made me feel at ease and less intimidated. The written materials are very useful for at-home study."

—Boot Camp participant

_f_**P**

You Don't Have to Take It Anymore

Turn Your
Resentful, Angry, or
Emotionally Abusive Relationship
into a Compassionate, Loving One

STEVEN STOSNY, PhD

Free Press
New York   London   Toronto   Sydney

FREE PRESS
A Division of Simon & Schuster, Inc.
1230 Avenue of the Americas
New York, NY 10020

FREE PRESS and colophon are trademarks of Simon & Schuster, Inc.

For information about special discounts for bulk purchases, please contact Simon & Schuster Special Sales: 1-800-456-6798 or business@simonandschuster.com.

Designed by Elliott Beard

Manufactured in the United States of America

10 9 8 7 6 5 4 3 2 1

Library of Congress Cataloging-in-Publication Data

Stosny, Steven.
    You don't have to take it anymore: Turn your resentful, angry, or emotionally abusive relationship into a compassionate, loving one / Steven Stosny.
        p. cm.
    Includes index.
    1. Marital conflict. 2. Psychological abuse. 3. Abusive men—Rehabilitation. 4. Psychologically abused women—Rehabilitation. 5. Resentment. 6. Anger. 7. Self-help techniques. I. Title.
    HQ728.S856 2006
    306.872—dc22   2005053134

ISBN-13: 978-0-7432-8469-1
ISBN-10:   0-7432-8469-0

A Note to Readers

The names used in this book are fictitious and, in most instances, identifying characteristics have been changed. The cases described are mostly composites drawn from many different situations. The dialogue represents either the gist of what was actually said or a typical representation of what is said in the vast majority of similar cases. None of the cases presented is exclusively about particular clients, insofar as the topics discussed and the underlying dynamics of the cases are universal in families who walk on eggshells around an adult who regularly displays anger and resentment and who is also sometimes emotionally abusive. The important thing here was not to tell the stories of individual clients, fascinating though they may be, but to point out universal truths about overcoming the harmful effects of walking on eggshells.

Contents

PART III

The Boot Camp

PART IV

Resurrection for Your Marriage

You Don't
Have to
Take It
Anymore

Introduction

The Hidden Epidemic

This book will teach you how to heal a specific kind of unhappiness that occurs in relationships—the unhappiness that comes from resentment, anger, or emotional abuse. It will also teach you how to prevent unhappiness. In treating some 4,500 clients over the years, I have been struck by one fact: Even though couples are unhappy for hundreds of different reasons, my primary target of treatment for all of them is more or less the same—the resentment they all feel. Not depression, anxiety, anger, or abuse—just plain, ordinary resentment. Because all treatment also aims to prevent relapses, the strategies I use to *prevent* unhappiness are ultimately the same as those I use to treat advanced stages of it. Whether I am treating an unhappy couple or trying to keep one from veering into chronic unhappiness, whether I am attempting to undo an entrenched pattern of abusive behavior or trying to keep a dangerous one from developing, my primary target is always their *resentment*. None of the many different kinds of unhappiness can improve in the face of constant resentment.

If you suffer from resentment or live with a resentful man, you will one day have an unhappy marriage, if you do not already. If this sounds like your situation, this book is for you. If your partner is resentful, he will almost certainly have occasional angry outbursts and, sooner or later, engage in some form of emotional abuse. Once he crosses that line, you are at a much higher risk of getting pushed, grabbed, shoved, slapped, or worse, especially if he has been violent in the past or if he grew up in a violent family. While it's true that not every resentful person becomes angry, emotionally abusive, or violent, it's also true that every angry, abusive, and violent person starts out with resentment. If this sounds like your husband, the Boot Camp section at the end of this book is for him.

Conscious Intention versus Motivation

If you live with a resentful, angry, or abusive partner, you know that he often gets worse if you show that you're hurt. "I'm not *trying* to hurt you," he might say, "I'm just pointing out facts." Although there is some denial of responsibility here, he really is confounded by your normal response to his behavior. He confuses conscious intention with unconscious motivation.

Conscious intention is the goal—what we try to do with a given behavior. For instance, your husband might have a *goal* of discussing a budget with you. But if he feels devalued in any way, by anything at all—the bills, the kids, his job—his unconscious *motivation* may be to *devalue* you, by implying that you are stupid or irresponsible for not seeing the issue exactly like he does. It's an unconscious motivation, by which I mean he's not aware of it. So when you react with hurt or defensiveness, he accuses you of evading the facts.

Resentful behavior is certainly different from abusiveness, and both differ from just being angry. You can definitely have one or two of these three relationship demons without the others. But the deeper, unconscious *motivation* of all three emotional states is to *devalue*—to lower the value of the other person, either by dismissing, avoiding, or attacking. And the devaluer does this even though he may still love his wife. Examples of devaluing behavior are stonewalling, criticizing, belittling, and implying superiority. And devaluing can be implied by tone even when the words seem to be positive. You can say, "I love you," for instance, with an inflection that implies that, "You're not worthy of the love I'm giving you." Devaluing behavior can often be barely perceptible in the tone of a voice, or a closed-off body posture or facial expression, or a silent disregard.

Not surprisingly, all three demons—resentment, anger, and abuse—damage the bonds of love in the same way, for all three feel like betrayal. All *are* a betrayal of the implicit promise your loved one made you when you formed your emotional bonds. You both agreed to care about how each other feels, especially when one of you feels *bad*. The implicit betrayal that occurs when your partner doesn't seem to care about you is why a slap to the heart hurts more than a punch to the face and a cold shoulder harms as much as a screaming tirade.

This book will help you if you are being abused or if you are an abuser yourself. It will help if you live with an angry man or woman or if you have trouble with your own anger. Most importantly, it will *prevent* problems of anger, abuse, physical battering, and just plain unhappiness by eliminating the *resentment* that leads to all of them, through enhanced compassion for yourself and everyone you love.

The Universality of Walking on Eggshells

Research shows that no social or economic class, race, or gender-orientation is spared the corrosive effects of walking on eggshells. Although the external pressures on different groups vary greatly, the way they suffer is the same. The fact is *anyone* can fall into walking on eggshells in a relationship. In my practice I have worked with many bright, competent, and accomplished women from all walks of life—business, academia, and the upper echelons of government. From their social and professional identities, you would never suspect that they walk on eggshells at home. Yet these successful, powerful women are as tormented and stressed in their relationships as their poorer, less accomplished sisters. They have just as much self-doubt and anxiety when it comes to love, and in some ways are even more isolated by their embarrassment.

"This doesn't happen to women like me," one executive of a marketing firm told me.

"If the world only knew," sighed a high-ranking official in the U.S. State Department.

"How can I be so good at work and such a failure at love?" asked a partner in a leading law firm.

"Nothing has ever been really hard for me," said one brilliant college professor, "and now I can't figure out Marriage 101."

Their considerable achievements notwithstanding, these women experience the low self-esteem of all women who walk on eggshells in their love relationships. Self-esteem rests predominantly on two factors: competence/mastery (work) and intimate relationships. To maintain realistically high self-esteem, you have to feel adequate in both areas. Unlike work, where your own effort, talent, and skills largely determine success, relationships do not rely on just one person supplying love and compassion. If your partner blames you for his own feelings of inadequacy, you are as likely as anyone to buy into it, due to the way love is mirrored or reflected back to us by our partners. (We'll discuss this further in Chapter 3.) And don't pretend, as so many assertive women have, that your *anger* at him is proof that you *don't* buy into it. Anger protects you from vulnerability, but the anger itself is evidence that you've internalized at least some of what he has said. If you had not, you would be able to dismiss your husband's implication that you're unworthy of love as easily as if he were to accuse you of having green hair.

We can all become resentful, angry, or emotionally abusive toward the people we love when our *core hurts*—guilt, shame, and anxiety *about* the *self*—obscure our *core value*, our innate humanity, from which our sense of self-value arises. The treatment outlined in these pages enhances universal core values to heal core hurts and, therefore, has been highly effective in helping people of all races, economic classes, and gender orientations. For shorthand, I'll refer to "husband" and "wife" throughout the book, but all observations about husbands and wives apply equally to *any* love relationship.

Visceral Fear of Harm

In general, this book will help you come to trust the messages that your emotions send you, but there is one that I want you to be aware of even before you start reading: For your own safety and for the safety of everyone you love, you must learn to trust your *visceral* reactions to *fear of harm*. That's a feeling in your muscles and in your gut that you will be physically injured. A visceral feeling comes over you more abruptly and with greater intensity than mere anxiety about having a bad evening or even dread of betrayal, depression, and other worries about conflict and emotional abuse. Your visceral fear of harm is not cognitive; you sense aggressive impulses in others *before* your brain can formulate thoughts about possible danger. That's why you get tense in certain situations, like walking down darkened sidewalks or seeing suspicious strangers, without knowing why. Women have a heightened sense of this early-warning system, which is why your husband remains perfectly calm and might even get annoyed with your nervousness as you walk together in a darkened parking garage.

The Most Dangerous Kind of Self-Doubt

Although visceral fear of harm is compelling, many women start to doubt it when the physical threat comes from someone they love, and when they have learned to walk on eggshells. In that case powerful emotions, such as love, guilt, shame, and abandonment anxiety that keep you attached to people you love, can easily cause you to doubt the internal alarm system meant to keep you from harm. For instance, you may feel guilty or ashamed if you admit to fear of your husband, as if your involuntary reaction to threat were a betrayal of him. Or your dread of losing him might exceed your fear of him, which, you are likely to rationalize, only happens when he "gets a certain way." Or your love for him might be so strong that you want to believe that your fear could not possibly be real, that it's all in your head. Actually, it's just the opposite; love, guilt, shame, and abandonment anxiety are more in your head, while fear of harm resides in your body and reflexes.

This book will help you sort out these complex, confusing emotions. But your safety must always come first, even before a deeper understanding of yourself. Get used to monitoring your body; be aware of how you feel around your eyes, in your neck, shoulders, back, chest, arms, hands, stomach, gut, thighs, and knees. These are the most reliable indicators of whether your husband poses a threat to your physical safety.

If your body tells you that you are in danger, you must always put your physical safety first, even if he has never been violent in the past. I have seen too many cases of women who ignored their visceral fear of harm and were badly hurt. Please do not ignore yours.

If you are afraid of being physically harmed, call the National Domestic Violence Hotline (for U.S. and Canada) 1-800-799-SAFE. You can get local referrals from this clearinghouse.

Think of a time when you might have felt *afraid* of your partner. Try to imagine the incident in detail. Write what it felt like in each of the following parts of your body.

Head   Shoulders

Eyes   Chest

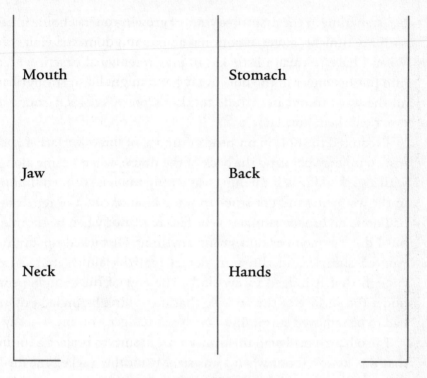

Mouth	Stomach
Jaw	Back
Neck	Hands

How to Use This Book

If you are *not* experiencing visceral fear, here is the best way to use this book to heal yourself and to improve your relationship.

- Read the whole book yourself.
- Go back and do all the exercises, including those in the Boot Camp section.

When you feel able, compassionately insist that your husband read the *entire* Boot Camp section and Resurrection sections and do *all* the exercises therein.

Self-Disclosure and Dedication

My interest in the pain that comes from walking on eggshells is not purely professional or academic. It began before I can remember, sometime in the first three years of growing up in a home filled with resentment, anger, emotional abuse, and domestic violence. When I have to treat a little kid in my professional practice, I let him put his finger in the hole in my head—a small finger can turn all the way around in it. Kids think it's pretty cool. Of course I don't tell them how I got it.

I acquired the hole in my head at the age of three. My father had just completed painting the back of the house, when I came along with a stick. (I knew something was wrong when it stopped sliding in the wet paint and got stuck in some kind of dry-wall repair he had done on broken shingles.) His face reddened when he saw me, but I don't remember him saying anything. He picked up an un-painted shingle and threw it, not *at* me he claimed, but close enough that it lodged in my skull. The end of the shingle bent under the surface of the bone so that it couldn't be pulled out; it had to be removed surgically.

I also have a bridge in the front of my mouth to replace a tooth that was knocked out when I was six. My mother picked me up—that usually calmed him down when he got aggressive, but not this time. He swung at her as she held me. He missed her.

I have only the vaguest memories of these and other incidents. All I remember about the head injury is the shocked and panicked looks on the adult faces in the hospital emergency room. It must have been ghastly seeing a three-year-old with part of a shingle sticking out of his head and blood all over his face. But that's all I recall—no pain, no trauma, just scared adults. The same is true of the punch that dislodged my newly grown-in second tooth. I re-member my mother holding me in fear, and then later sitting in a big chair as the dentist tried to force in the plastic false tooth.

I do have vivid memories of my mother being hit and beaten. That's typical, based on everything we know about the effects of family abuse on children. More surprising (only because the effects of verbal abuse haven't been studied as much as physical abuse), my memories of him insulting and yelling at her—and of her in-sulting and yelling back—are as vivid as the violence. And just as hurtful to recall are images of her sitting tearfully on the sofa while he refused to talk to her or even look at her—"getting the cold shoulder," she called it. She always said that the cold shoulder hurt more than the bruises.

My mother left my father for the last time (there had been 13 prior separations and reunions), when I was 11 years old. She married a gentle man six years later and had a wonderful life as a respected member of her church and community. We never really talked about our past, not until I started graduate school and began researching the causes of family abuse. Then one summer night, while relaxing on her front porch, I asked her opinion, as someone who had lived through all forms of abuse, of what I'd been reading in the research literature. At the time, the research suggested that abusers had dysfunctional attitudes about *male privilege* and the inferiority of women, and used abuse to control and oppress what they regarded as the weaker sex. Although the research showed that abusers were angrier than nonabusive men, advocates argued that they merely used anger to control their wives. In other words, they didn't abuse because they were angry; they were angry because they were abusive. It sounded right to me. But my mother would have none of it.

"The bad attitudes and anger aren't the point," she said. "Everybody wants to control their spouses when you come right down to it. What stops most people is compassion—you couldn't stand to see someone you love feeling bad. Find out why these men and the women who do it can't feel enough compassion. Figure out how to make them more compassionate, and you'll really have something."

Of course she was right. You cannot be resentful, angry, or abusive if you are compassionate. You cannot develop negative attitudes about women (or anyone else) without a failure of compassion. Any couple now walking on eggshells has lost touch with the compassion that probably brought them together in the first place.

The success of our intensive Boot Camps and our Compassion-

Power workshops over the years is a direct result of my mother's words on that night in the late 1980s. This book, like all the work I've done on the subject, has to be dedicated to her. From her suffering and her wisdom and her compassion, this treatment was born.

PART I

Walking on Eggshells

One

Why You Have Thorns in Your Heart

It's not breaking the eggs that does the lasting harm; it's the continual walking on eggshells. Emotional damage has a way of lingering in the times *between* resentful, angry, or abusive flare-ups. The empty, dull ache of unhappiness is most accurately measured in the accumulative effect of these small moments of disconnection, isolation, and dread.

The following quiz reveals what it feels like to walk on eggshells day after day. Read it aloud—the objectivity in hearing your own voice say the words, especially your answers, is the first step toward healing.

Walking on Eggshells Quiz

Please put a checkmark next to your answer.

Am I anxious, nervous, or worried about my partner's:

Attitude

Never _____ *Sometimes* _____ *Most of the time* _____

Resentment
Never _____ *Sometimes* _____ *Most of the time* _____

Anger
Never _____ *Sometimes* _____ *Most of the time* _____

Sarcasm
Never _____ *Sometimes* _____ *Most of the time* _____

Criticism
Never _____ *Sometimes* _____ *Most of the time* _____

Glares
Never _____ *Sometimes* _____ *Most of the time* _____

Frowns
Never _____ *Sometimes* _____ *Most of the time* _____

Gestures (like finger-pointing)
Never _____ *Sometimes* _____ *Most of the time* _____

Chilly moods
Never _____ *Sometimes* _____ *Most of the time* _____

Cold shoulders
Never _____ *Sometimes* _____ *Most of the time* _____

Stonewalling
Never _____ *Sometimes* _____ *Most of the time* _____

Do I edit my thoughts before I speak and second-guess my behavior before I do anything, in fear that it might set him off or cause the silent treatment?
Never _____ *Sometimes* _____ *Most of the time* _____

Is he fine one minute and into a tirade the next, all seemingly over nothing or about the same thing over and over?
Never _____ *Sometimes* _____ *Most of the time* _____

Do I feel tense when I hear the door open or when he comes into the room? When I walk by him, do my shoulders tense, until we get past one another?
Never _____ *Sometimes* _____ *Most of the time* _____

Do I think that if I just tried harder things might be all right?
Never _____ *Sometimes* _____ *Most of the time* _____

Do I feel that that nothing I do is good enough?
Never _____ *Sometimes* _____ *Most of the time* _____

Is my marriage in a cold standoff (disagreements are minimal, but there's a chilly wall between us)?
Never _____ *Sometimes* _____ *Most of the time* _____

Are my defensiveness and other reactions to him on automatic pilot; they just seem to happen on their own?
Never _____ *Sometimes* _____ *Most of the time* _____

If you live with a resentful, angry, or abusive partner, you probably have a vague feeling, at least now and then, that you have lost yourself. In your constant efforts to tiptoe around someone else's moods in the hope of avoiding blow-ups, put-downs, criticism, sighs of disapproval, or cold shoulders, you constantly edit what you say. You second-guess your own judgment, your own ideas, and your own preferences about how to live. You begin to question what you think is right and wrong. Ultimately, your perceptions of reality and your very sense of self change for the worse.

The cold fact is that it's hard *not* to lose yourself in the morass of what you *should* say or what you *need* to do (to keep things peaceful) and how you're *supposed* to be at any given moment. If you have to be one thing one minute and behave a different way in another (depending on your partner's moods), your confidence and sense of self can seem to disappear. You begin to feel that you cannot reclaim yourself or begin to feel better until *he* changes and starts treating you better.

The understandable but tragic expectation that you are dependent on him for your emotional well-being is the first thing you must change. You must heal and grow, whether or not he changes. Even when your inborn sense of fairness and justice tells you that he ought to be the one to make changes, your pain tells you that *you* need to become the fully alive person you are meant to be. This means that you have to remove the focus from him and put it squarely on you. Happily, that is also the best thing you can do to help him and your relationship. This book will help you reclaim your true sense of self. That is its primary goal. But it will also help change your relationship.

All the tools you need to heal are in these pages. All the tools that he needs to replace resentment, anger, or abusive behavior with compassion are also in these pages. The first part of the book is about reintegrating your deepest values into your everyday sense of self. This will make you feel more valuable, confident, and powerful, regardless of what your partner—or anyone else—says or does. As you read these pages and reconnect to your deepest values, you will naturally, forcefully, and compassionately demand value and respect from your partner. Your compassionate demand for change is likely to be the only thing that will motivate him to once again be the man you married. But whether or not *he* changes, you must connect with your enormous inner value, resources, and personal power to stop walking on eggshells and to emerge as the richly creative, beautiful whole person you truly are.

The Worst Things

One of the worst things that can happen to your health and happiness is to live with a resentful, angry, or abusive partner. The worst thing you can *do* to your soul is *become* a resentful, angry, or abusive partner. And the worst thing you can *develop* in a love relationship is an identity as a *victim*, which destroys your personal power and solid sense of self. The cry I hear over and over again from women who walk on eggshells is, "I don't like the resentful, angry person he's made *me*."

You Don't Have to Take It Anymore is about overcoming abusiveness and victim identity. My emphasis on healing, growth, and empowerment means that you will not see in these pages lengthy checklists of behaviors that qualify you as a victim or lengthy descriptions of resentful, angry, or abusive behavior and attitudes. The book does not offer detailed descriptions of angry, abusive men or explorations of how bad they are. You know better than anyone else that your relationship has put thorns in your heart. You don't need a description of the thorns to know how much they hurt or how bad it is for you to keep them. You need to learn how to take them out and how to heal the wounds in ways that prevent scarring.

Checklists and bullets about the behaviors or attitudes that qualify as resentful, angry, or abusive would distract you from your most important task. The true issue at stake is *your* core value—the most important things about you as a person—not his behavior or your reaction to it. As you reinforce and reconnect with your core value, you are far less likely to be a victim. As you experience the enormous depth of your core value, the last thing you will want to do is identify with being a victim, or with the damage or bad things that have happened to you. In your core value you will identify with your inherent strengths, talents, skills, and power as a unique, ever growing, competent, and compassionate person. You want to *outgrow* walking on eggshells, not simply survive it, and you do that only by realizing your fullest value as a person.

The renewed compassion for yourself that you learn in these pages will lead directly to a deeper compassion for your resentful, angry, or abusive partner. With that compassion you will demand meaningful, lasting change, for you will appreciate the enormous harm he does to himself when he hurts you. One of two things is likely to result from your reclamation of self and your compassionate demands of him. You may be able to stop walking on eggshells and walk into a deeper, more connected relationship with a more compassionate, loving partner. It might not seem so now judging from his attitudes and behavior, but your husband wants that as much as you do. If you were to ask, he would probably tell you that deep in his heart he wants to be a compassionate, loving husband, even if he'd blame you for why he isn't. The Boot Camp section of this book will free him from blame and help him become the person he really wants to be. But if he chooses not to do the hard work that reclamation of his true self requires, for his sake, for the sake of your children, and for your own sake, you can no longer tolerate his resentful, angry, or abusive behavior. From your core value, you will stop walking on eggshells, one way or the other.

You Both Walk on Eggshells

If you feel that you are walking on eggshells, you probably do not realize that your partner is, too, though in a different way. He is so reactive to you and so unable to regulate his reactions that he constantly expects you to say or do something that will push his buttons and make him withdraw or attack. He feels that you are totally in control of his emotions, and all he can do is pout or shout like a defiant child. He feels that *you* control *him,* you "push his buttons." Almost every abusive person I've ever worked with felt that *he* walked on eggshells, in constant dread that his partner would do something to "set him off."

The Pendulum of Pain

Please do not make the mistake of thinking that you can heal yourself simply by getting in touch with your understandable resentment and anger and leaving your relationship. Most of the women who leave (or nearly leave) out of resentment and anger end up returning out of guilt, shame, and anxiety, when they see how lost their husbands seem without them. They enjoy a brief honeymoon period following the reunion, until the tension returns and the resentment and anger get overwhelming. So they leave again (or withdraw emotionally from their husbands), only to face renewed guilt, shame, and abandonment anxiety, once the resentment and anger subside. Sometimes economic considerations drive women to return to these relationships, but they are not the most compelling factor. Research shows that women with means return to walking-on-eggshells relationships as often as women who are financially dependent. My own mother, like many of my clients, was the sole support of our family, yet she returned to my *unemployed*, resentful, angry, and abusive father 13 times in my first 11 years of life.

This pattern of leaving (or nearly leaving) out of anger and resentment, only to return out of guilt, shame, and anxiety is a hallmark of walking on eggshells. I call it a *pendulum of pain*. It has nothing to do with your indecisiveness or your personality. It follows from the strengths of your emotions, from your attachment to your husband, which we'll explore more in the next chapter. Resentment and anger at loved ones always dissolve into guilt, shame, and abandonment anxiety. These painful, completely irrational emotions keep you attached to your husband no matter how bad the relationship is—these emotions developed in our brains at a time when leaving the tribe meant certain death on your own by starvation or saber-toothed tiger.

As long as you love someone, the only way to keep resentment and anger from turning to guilt, shame, and anxiety is to stay resentful and angry all the time. It might be safer if you did stay resentful and angry all the time, but that is probably not your nature. When your resentment subsides and your anger is exhausted, the pain of seeing someone you love in distress can become overwhelming and make you return to your now remorseful, if not helpless, partner. However, if he does not learn to regulate his resentment, anger, or abusive behavior with compassion for himself and for you, the pendulum will swing back and forth, again and again.

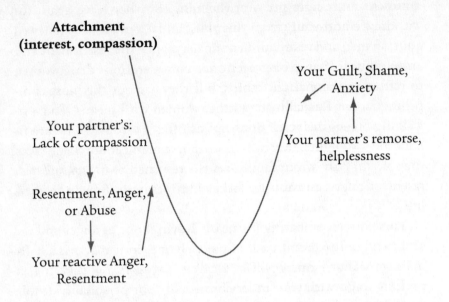

**Attachment
(interest, compassion)**

Your Guilt, Shame,
Anxiety

Your partner's:
Lack of compassion

Your partner's remorse,
helplessness

Resentment, Anger,
or Abuse

Your reactive Anger,
Resentment

Reacting in kind to a resentful, angry, or abusive partner can keep you forever swinging on the pendulum of pain—I've seen this dynamic go on for 30 years. More than anything else, *resentment* keeps you stuck in this pain.

Precursor to Anger and Abuse: How Resentment Works

Describing what resentment feels like can be difficult. People often say vague things like, "I'm in a sour mood," or "I'm really irritable." If someone acts or sounds defensive or aggressive, you might describe him as having a chip on his shoulder. Bad as these terms sound, they just scratch the surface of resentment, the most complex of all emotional states.

To begin with, resentment is more of a mood than a discrete emotion. Emotions occur like waves that rise and fall, usually within a few minutes. Moods are more like a steady current flowing underneath the surface. Moods determine emotions more than emotions influence moods. For instance, if your present mood is positive, you are most likely feeling interest, enjoyment, compassion, or love, which motivate caring, playful, romantic, supportive, or cooperative behavior. But if your underlying mood is resentful, it's most likely causing visible waves of anger, anxiety, jealousy, or envy, which motivate behavior that is controlling, dominating, compulsive, possessive, confrontational, dismissive, or rejecting.

Resentment usually includes an obsessive stage that both agitates and energizes you. Your heart rate increases and blood vessels expand. Thoughts race through your mind about how unfair things are, how wrong someone's behavior is, how much better treatment you deserve, how it *should* be this way or *shouldn't* be that way, and how you'd like to set things right or at least get even. You fantasize about embarrassed opponents backing down, admitting they were wrong, and apologizing with great deference. (In response, you would probably be magnanimous and forgiving.) This arousal stage prepares you for confrontation, but consumes most of the energy for it. So you'll stay up thinking of what you're going to say or do when you get the chance, but then sleep fitfully or eat and drink too much or too fast or hardly at all. By the time the moment of confrontation comes, you're just too tired. "Ah, the hell with it, it's not worth arguing about."

In its post-obsessive stage, resentment completely drains you. It dampens alertness and saps your energy, which would otherwise go into something you're interested in or enjoy. If you're walking on eggshells, your life has become a joyless drive to get things done. You'll do everything you have to do—take the kids to the dry cleaners and drop off the clothes at the soccer game. But you aren't usually interested in anything and don't enjoy anything without alcohol or drugs. Chronic resentment creates a dull, unpleasant feeling, and the only relief from it for many people, comes from that emergency store of energy called anger. Resentful people get angry a lot and mostly over little things. Many have to smoke or drink to calm down.

Resentment also increases error rates, impairs concentration, diminishes fine motor skills, and lowers overall performance competence. You certainly won't drive or work well if you're chronically resentful, and you wouldn't want to be operated on by a resentful doctor.

The Unfairness of Fairness

One thing is certain, if you live with a resentful person, you know the meaning of unfairness. But here's the surprise, your husband truly believes that he is *more* than fair, even if he occasionally overreacts to you because, he says, of *your* unfairness. People by and large attribute their resentment to the unfairness, untrustworthiness, or unreliability of others, who will not give them the understanding, respect, help, appreciation, sympathy, affection, consideration, love, or reward they think they deserve. They tend to feel like victims. From their perspective they swallow a lot and put up with a lot, and go along with a lot, until they can't *stand* it anymore and have to lash out or retreat into a prolonged sulk.

No, he's not crazy for thinking that he's always fair. Research tells us that we tend to judge others by the fairness of their behavior, while we judge our own behavior by its *utility*—whether it works for us. I'm sure you've noticed that your resentful partner can find a way to live with himself doing the same behaviors that he cannot tolerate from you or the kids. In fact, we tend to use the concept of fairness to *justify* our own unfairness, rather than inspire us to fairer or more moral behavior. The resentful person who cuts in front of you in the checkout line thinks, "On top of everything I have to put up with, I shouldn't have to wait in line, too." Cain would argue today, in a lawsuit no doubt, that he slew his brother because of God's unfairness in rejecting his sacrifice.

At heart, your husband's concept of fairness is less about right and wrong than a way of avoiding his own core hurts, which he tries to do by controlling you. (Now you know why negotiating doesn't work—it's not about reasoned fairness; it's about emotional avoidance and control.) He says to you and the kids, "Cross the line of what I say is unfair (make me feel something I can't handle) and you deserve all the contempt I can muster."

The Sheer Complexity of Resentment

The many dimensions of resentment make it easy to get lost in the blind alley of "fairness." the following example is a composite of a great many of my clients; I'll call him Carl.

Carl leaned forward, well away from the back of his chair. His head hung slightly—he looked exhausted, with puffy eyes and a wan complexion. He had not glanced around my office when he walked to his seat and had barely glanced at me when I introduced myself; the new environment held little interest for him. I took the chair facing his and asked what he would like to accomplish in this, our first session. He had prepared what he was going to say but hesitated enough to make it seem spontaneous—a tall order after obsessing about the problem for several days.

He started nodding in the silence, as if agreeing with some inner advice-giver. When he spoke, he was far more animated than earlier.

"I agreed to have my brother-in-law, who I don't like, move in with us, because my wife wanted it. I knew it wouldn't work out, but I went along, just to keep the peace. Now I keep noticing things about him that irritate me. I mean, it's one of those things where almost everything he does gets on my nerves. He snores, he doesn't comb his hair right. He bangs things around, plays his music when I'm trying to read the paper, that kind of crap. I swear that sometimes he's *trying* to get on my nerves." He started to put his hand on the side of his head, but decided to use it instead for a broad gesture to underscore his complaint. "And his sense of humor bites. He gets an attitude, just because I make jokes about guys not getting jobs. I mean, they're funny jokes." During his monologue, Carl was looking upward and to the left, as people do when trying to recall something. Now he looked straight into my eyes, as if to convince me of how funny his jokes were. "This one I told, that he got all out of joint with, was about this guy who's getting interviewed for a job, and the person doing the interviewing asks him, 'What's this you put under *disability*?' And the guy gets all defensive. 'I put *lazy*. What worse disability is there for working?'" I smiled a little, but not enough to satisfy him. Although it would have given us some rapport, reinforcing his sarcasm with a laugh would have been a poor choice. Feeling rejected by my lack of laughter, Carl protested, "I work hard, I shouldn't have to put up with this crap in my own house."

When I said nothing, he slumped back in the chair, his puffy eyes looking at the tips of his shoes, as if his stream of thought had completely escaped him. This new position concealed the dark lines of sleep deprivation. His neck seemed limp, as if his head had become a little too heavy to hold up. The tension in his body was gone. He was ashamed.

"Then I take it out on my wife," he said softly. But in just a second or two, his body stiffened once more. Just as suddenly as the shame had overtaken him, he raised his head with the renewed energy of anger. "If it wasn't for her, I wouldn't have to put up with him. She knew I didn't want him there. She knew I just went along to keep the peace, because I didn't want a big argument."

At last, the blame turned to his wife, as I knew it would.

There are two laws of chronic resentment. The first is, *"Nothing is too petty to resent."* But the second, more damaging law is, *"Resentment always winds its way, in some form or other, to the wife or husband, no matter what stimulates it in the first place."* Carl was living in accord with both laws.

Resentment arouses the entire central nervous system and, unlike most emotional states, *keeps* it aroused. This means that you can't be resentful about just one thing or toward just one person. (If you encounter a jerk on the road, you will not be so sweet to your children when you get home.) So even though Carl's resentment had nothing to do with his wife, it inevitably turned against her, driving him to devalue the most important person in his life. The resultant war with his own emotions drained his life of meaning, conviction, and passion. He started drinking every night to relieve what he referred to vaguely as the stress. He became easily insulted and aggressive in traffic. He always had to be right. He was constantly amazed at the incompetence and unfairness in the world and shocked whenever *he* was accused of being unfair. It seemed to him as if people at work, home, and on the road were in a conspiracy to irritate him. His kids had lost their caring father. His wife, Sherry, did not recognize the man she married. Resentment had all but killed his capacity for interest and enjoyment and impaired his health, relationships, sex life, job performance, and driving safety. Sherry had finally gotten fed up with walking on eggshells, and that was the real reason Carl was in my office. But the only solution he could see regarding his brother-in-law—throwing him out—would increase the already high level of bad feelings in the household.

Why was it so hard for Carl to see the truth about himself? More importantly, why couldn't he see that his insensitivity to Sherry's perspective had created a marriage in which she had to walk on eggshells?

One reason is the sheer complexity of resentment. Even in highly diluted forms, resentment includes regret, remorse, anger, irritability, shame, and anger at oneself. Just look at the components of Carl's resentment about his brother-in-law:

- He *regrets* his brother-in-law moving in. "I knew it wouldn't work. . . . It's even worse than I thought it would be."
- He's *sorry* about his part in it. He had a few drinks and told Sherry that, although he wasn't thrilled about it, he would make the best of his brother-in-law moving in, if it would make her happy.
- He's *angry* at *Sherry* for not appreciating how much of a bother this would be and for not understanding him, for not

wanting what he wanted, for not feeling the way he did, and for not agreeing with him.

- He's *angry* at *other people* because he gets irritable about little things, like traffic, the news, his team losing, the baby crying, the phone ringing.
- He's *angry* at *himself* for failing to realize how much bother it would be, for not being assertive about his true feelings, and for utterly failing his wife.
- He's *ashamed* of how petty he could be and for taking it out on his wife.

The sheer complexity of resentment makes it difficult to resolve. You might hide a few of the pieces under the carpet, but there's always another bit or two sticking out of a corner somewhere.

Resentment Is Not about Attitudes or Content

The driving force behind resentment is *emotional.* Resentment is *not* an "attitude problem." And it's never about content—the *things* you resent, like brothers-in-law or "nagging wives." It's about using blame in an effort to reduce guilt, shame, and anxiety. That's why trying to resolve the issues you resent in a love relationship never reduces the overall level of resentment; you'll feel guilty about the resentment itself, so you'll just shift it to something else. When Sherry tried to pay more attention to Carl and less to her brother, Carl resented that he had to *ask* her for the attention.

Many therapists confront resentful, angry, or abusive clients about their dysfunctional attitudes. This is a mistake that usually backfires. Negative beliefs and attitudes are a function of an inability to regulate guilt, shame, and anxiety. A person who cannot relieve these painful emotions without blaming them on someone else will certainly develop all sorts of dysfunctional attitudes and distorted beliefs. A man who feels inadequate because he doesn't know how to give emotional support is liable to say that his wife is

too emotional, or too needy, or too selfish. He may very well gener-
alize his pejorative attitudes to include all women. Confronting
such attitudes and beliefs in therapy, without teaching your husband to *regulate* his guilt, shame, and anxiety, will make things
harder on you. If he has been to a confrontational therapist or
worse, a group for abusive men, you know well who bears the brunt
of the blame for whatever shame is invoked in the therapy or
group. Think of how often he has come home and taken it out on
you, especially if the therapist or group leader believes that he or
she won by making your husband back off some point of his belief
system. We'll talk more about this in the chapter on why therapy,
anger-management, and abuser groups actually keep you walking
on eggshells.

In CompassionPower programs we pretest the dysfunctional attitudes of men toward women. Once clients gain a vocabulary of
their own core hurts (feeling powerless, inadequate, or unlovable)
and a sense of their core value—what they acknowledge as the *most
important* things about them, usually protecting and caring for
their families—they can give up their addiction to blame. This en-
ables them to relinquish their negative attitudes, one by one, *without* confrontation.

The crucial point for you to remember is that your husband's
resentment, anger, and abuses are about his inability to live up to
his core value, not about the content of his complaints or the fairness of his attitudes.

The Emotional Costs to You and Your Children

Carl ran the gamut of resentful, angry, and abusive behaviors, although he never hit his wife. He criticized, demeaned, belittled,
withdrew, ranted, gave the silent treatment, sulked, and shut down
(he "leaves the planet," as Sherry put it). Like most couples, Carl
and Sherry went through bouts of anger, depression, anxiety, and
low self-esteem. Like a great many men, Carl concealed his symptoms with bravado and a grandiose sense of self. They both had

trouble with overeating, impulsive behavior, chronic boredom, and occasional alcohol abuse.

Waking Up in the Middle of the Night

Carl and Sherry also had trouble sleeping. Between them, they suffered all three forms of insomnia. Carl sometimes had *near-term* insomnia—taking at least 90 minutes to two hours (a whole sleep cycle) to fall asleep. More often he had *end-term* insomnia—waking up a couple of hours before he needed to get out of bed. He didn't have enough energy to get up nor enough tranquility to fall back to sleep. Typically he'd start to doze about the time his alarm went off, so he would feel tired and cranky the whole day.

Sherry woke up in the middle of the night, almost every night, for at least a couple of hours. Although the resultant level of fatigue, especially in the afternoon, is no worse than that felt from the other two forms of sleep disturbance, *mid-term* insomnia has a more powerful effect on mood. Just a couple of weeks of this interrupted sleep pattern can produce biological depression, most likely because it inhibits the neurotransmitters in your brain that are responsible for balancing moods and feeling good.

When she woke up in the middle of the night, Sherry thought about Carl's frequent withdrawal and emotional shut-downs. Like so many women who walk on eggshells, she found his silent abuse more hurtful than his angry tirades. The message she got from the more subtle forms of abuse was: "You're not worth my attention." It made her feel unseen, unheard, and unattractive, "Like I didn't count." She felt "alone, like a single parent." She thought, with loads of self-recrimination, how hard it was to keep from pushing Carl's buttons. She second-guessed herself so much that for a while she lost herself "in a deep hole."

No One in the Family Escapes the Effects
of Walking on Eggshells

Families do not communicate primarily by language. That might surprise you, until you consider that humans bonded in families for millennia before we even had language. Even today, the most sensitive communications that have the most far-reaching consequences to our lives occur between parents and infants through tone of voice, facial expressions, touch, smell, and body posture, *not* language.

Though less obvious than interactions with young children, most of your communications with your older children and with your husband also occur through an unconscious process of emotional *attunement*. You psychologically and even physically tune in your emotions to the people you love. That's how you can come home in one mood, find your husband or children in a different mood and, bam!—all of a sudden, out of nowhere, you're in their mood. Quite unconsciously, you automatically react to one another.

Emotional attunement, not verbal skills, determines how we communicate, from our choice of words to our tone of voice. If attuned to a positive mood, you are likely to communicate pleasantly. If you're in a negative mood, your words will be less than pleasant.

Now here's the really bad news. Due to this unconscious, automatic process of emotional attunement, your children are painfully reactive to the walking-on-eggshells atmosphere between your husband and you, even if they never hear you say a harsh word to one another.

Everyone in a walking-on-eggshells family loses some degree of dignity and autonomy. You become unable to decide your own thoughts, feelings, and behavior, because you are living in a defensive-reactive pattern that runs largely on automatic pilot. No fewer than half the members of these unfortunate families, including the children, suffer from clinical anxiety and/or depression. (*Clini-*

cal doesn't mean feeling down or blue or worried, it means that the symptoms interfere with normal functioning. You can't sleep, can't concentrate, can't work as efficiently, and can't enjoy yourself without drinking.) Most of the adults lack genuine self-esteem (based on realistic self-appraisals), and the children rarely feel as good as other kids. They are ten times more likely to grow up to be resentful, angry, or abusive adults. If the family is violent, children are ten times more likely to become abusers or victims of violence as adults. They are also at increased risk of alcoholism, criminality, mental health problems, and poverty.

The most common symptom of children in families who walk on eggshells is depression. But the signs can fool you; childhood depression looks different from the weeping, withdrawn, or sullen adult version. In children the disorder resembles chronic boredom. Children normally have high levels of interest, enjoyment, and excitement. If your child is not interested in the things in which children are normally interested, lacks enthusiasm, and is seldom excited, he or she is probably depressed. Another common symptom of these children is anxiety, particularly worry about things that children do not normally worry about, like how their parents are going to get through the evening with each other. Many kids have school problems, show aggressive tendencies, hyperactivity, and either over-emotionality—anger, excitability, or frequent crying that seem to come out of nowhere—or the polar opposite: no emotions at all. In the latter condition, they can look like little stone children; you could slice up a puppy in front of them and they wouldn't care. They have turned off all emotion to avoid the pain of walking on eggshells.

One piece of research on children in abusive families might startle you. Witnessing a parent victimized is usually more psychologically damaging to children than injuries from direct child abuse. In my own family, that was certainly true. I have only the faintest memories of child abuse—a small hole in my skull and a knocked-out front tooth—but I have vivid nightmares of seeing my mother ignored and dismissed as well as demeaned and terrified.

Seeing a parent abused is the more profound form of child abuse.

When it comes to the more severe forms of destructiveness, purely emotional abuse is usually more psychologically harmful than physical abuse. There are a couple of reasons for this. Even in the most violent families, the incidents tend to be cyclical. Early in the abuse cycle, a violent outburst is followed by a honeymoon period of remorse, attention, affection, and generosity, but not genuine compassion. (The honeymoon stage eventually ends, as the victim begins to say, "Never mind the damn flowers, just stop hitting me!") Emotional abuse, on the other hand, tends to happen every day. So the effects are more harmful because they're so frequent.

The other factor that makes emotional abuse so devastating is the greater likelihood that victims will blame themselves. If someone hits you, it's easier to see that he or she is the problem, but if the abuse is *subtle*—saying or implying that you're ugly, a bad parent, stupid, incompetent, not worth attention, or that no one could love you—you are more likely to think it's your problem.

All Forms of Abuse Have in Common
a Failure of Compassion

Whether overt or silent, all forms of abuse are failures of compassion; he stops caring about how you feel. Compassion is the lifeblood of families and failure of compassion is the "heart disease" of a family's emotional life. It actually would be less hurtful if your husband *never* cared about how you feel. But when you were falling in love, he cared a great deal, so now it feels like betrayal when he doesn't care or try to understand. You feel as if he's not the person you married.

It may not seem so from your day-to-day interactions, but your husband probably loves you. His emotional reactivity indicates that a strong bond still stirs the guilt and shame that, tragically, he blames on you. The fact that he loves you is both good news and bad news. Love by itself is so focused on how we feel that it masks the differences between people. The very intensity of love can make the person you love seem like little more than a *source* of strong emotions. In other words, it seems to him that you *cause* his emotions. If he feels good, you're on a pedestal; but if he feels bad, you're a demon.

Compassion makes us sensitive to the individual strengths and vulnerabilities of other people. As he learns to feel compassion under stress, your husband will see that you are different from him, with your own temperament, sensibility, experiences, longings, hopes, and dreams—all of which he probably *did* see when you were falling in love and his level of compassion was naturally high. Love by itself buries differences in the shadows of how strongly we feel. Compassion shines light on our differences and lets us appreciate and sympathize with loved ones. Love without the sensitivity of compassion is *rejecting* of who you really are as a person, *possessive, controlling,* and *dangerous.*

Clearly, walking-on-eggshells relationships create gifts of pain that keep on giving throughout the generations. To understand how to reverse these corrosive effects on you and your children, we need to understand how relationships between lovers, parents, and children *should* function. The next chapter shows how they're meant to go and how they go wrong.

Two

How Love Is Meant to Work and Why It So Often Doesn't

Anyone can fall into walking on eggshells in a relationship. In my practice, I work with women from all sorts of backgrounds—professional women, stay-at-home moms, politicians. The financially successful, powerful women seem on the surface to have it all and to have their whole acts together, but they, too, are suffering from their partners' anger, resentment, and emotional and verbal abuse. They are as upset by what has happened to their relationships as women with a little less money or a lot less money. *All* women who walk on eggshells have abundant self-doubt and anxiety at home, although they may not have always had these feelings of inadequacy about work. If you've been walking on eggshells like most of these women, you must have wondered over and over: How did it get this way? He seemed so wonderful, how did he get so critical, blaming, resentful, angry, and nasty?

It's actually very easy for *any* kind of love relationship to go wrong; our great susceptibility to rejection, emotional pain, and abuse begins at *birth*. Let's look more at how this emotional feedback system works.

We come out of the womb completely helpless, except for one quality: our drive to love. The only thing infants can do to ensure their survival is to love someone who will take care of them. We have an innate drive to attach emotionally to someone who will value and care for us as we value and learn to care for them. Aptly enough, psychologists call this drive to attach—to forge and maintain emotional bonds—our *attachment system*.

The attachment system gives babies various inborn ways to signal their needs for care. The distressed wail of an infant is unmistakable in message and unequaled in emotional power, especially for the parents, but not *just* for them. The wail of the infant sets off a painful internal alarm in all adults. If you are near an infant who is letting out a cry of distress, you will experience a sharp rise in heart rate, blood pressure, and muscle tension, and you will not be able to focus on much besides the crying child. If you cannot comfort the child—or get away from the crying—you may become physically ill.

When your baby cries, you experience a terrible kind of distress. The *only* thing that will make you feel better is to make your child feel better.

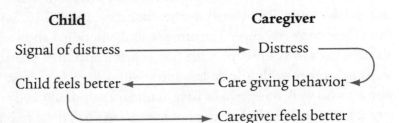

For years, scientists have described the attachment system as a series of actions or behaviors, all but ignoring the deeper emotional significance that would be apparent to any mother. It is not just *behavior*—feeding, changing, calming—that makes both the child and parent feel better. If you just shove a bottle in the mouth of your crying baby while reading a magazine or otherwise ignoring her, will she stop crying? No. Will you be able to concentrate on what you're trying to do? Not likely. Once children are in distress, no matter what the cause, they need to feel *valued* to feel better. The valuing emotions that motivate caregiving—interest, compassion, love—matter at least as much as the caregiving behavior itself. You have a better chance of calming your hungry child with loving caresses and no bottle than with a bottle and warm blanket but no love. The *attunement* of caring between you and your child calms both of you. If the infant could verbalize what's happening, he or she would say something like, "You care about me and so I feel better."

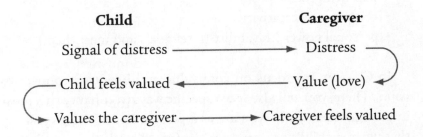

Each time this distress-love-care sequence is repeated, both parent and child become more secure in their attachment. Parents grow more confident in their ability to nurture, and children learn that they are valued and have value even when they feel distressed. Eventually these securely attached children learn to regulate their own distress, fear, and shame *internally*. They associate value with the unpleasant emotion, feel bad for a while, and then start to think of what they can do to *improve, appreciate,* or *connect to others.* The well-nurtured child who is startled in the night has learned enough confidence to regulate his distress, fear, and vulnerability. He'll think of something he values, like his baseball team or his video game. Or he'll think of his parents down the hall who will protect him. Or, if he has learned words, he might say to himself, "The shadows moving on the wall are just reflections of the moonlight on the branches of a tree waving in the breeze outside my window."

Self-Building

The child's emotional expectation that someone will meet his or her needs implies a kind of *core value* or worthiness of affection and care. As children mature, core value tells them how important, valuable, loving, and lovable they are as well as the kind of treatment they can expect from attachment figures, as it forms the foundation of personal

- security
- well-being, self-esteem
- competence, creativity
- personal power (the ability to set goals and meet them)

In Chapter 5, I focus on core value and how to reconnect to yours. There, you will also learn specific ways to enhance this most important part of who you are as a person. For now, let's just say that when a child's core value is reinforced by the compassionate behavior of caregivers, his or her emotional experience can develop into a strong, stable sense of self. Thus compassionate behavior *builds* the sense of self. For such a fortunate person, emotions guide and enrich life with high levels of interest and enjoyment.

The crucial elements of *self-building* in attachment relationships are unconditional safety and security for all parties, and high levels of compassion. If a relationship consistently fails at compassion, it loses its self-building function and does more harm than good. If it falls below the threshold of safety and security, it becomes *self-destroying*.

How It Goes Wrong

Sometimes the child's cries of anguish go unanswered, or worse, are *punished:* "Stop that damn crying!"

A child consistently treated this way is less likely to associate self-value with distress; when he feels bad, he is liable to feel inadequate or unworthy. Instead of motivating him to improve or connect, his distress makes him feel bad about *himself* and *powerless* over his emotions.

Child	**Caregiver**
Signal of distress ⟶	Distress
Child feels devalued, rejected, ⟵ Ignore/reject/punish	
powerless, unlovable	

These children grow up feeling less than important, valuable, and lovable, at least when they're stressed. When bad things happen to them or emotional demands are made on them, they feel like, "I can't handle it." When a gesture of love is made to them, they feel like, "I don't deserve it." They develop alternative ways to deal with stress: Some withdraw, some become emotionally needy, some try to manipulate and control their environments, and some attempt to substitute power for love—they want to feel more worthy of love but choose power instead. It's a tragic substitution. Power can get you compliance, sometimes fear, always resentment, but never love.

No matter how well these children adapt, they grow especially sensitive to certain attachment vulnerabilities that we can all feel from time to time. I call them *core hurts,* which are feeling unimportant, devalued, rejected, powerless, and inadequate or unlovable.

By the time we're adults, we've all developed internal strategies to numb or avoid core hurts. Some of these are beneficial, like talking to friends, exercising, or creating something. But some devastate relationships, like blame, resentment, anger, aggression, obsessions, addictions, compulsive behavior, or couch-potato numbness.

Insecurely attached children who do not develop their core value often have trouble regulating their negative emotions. As a result, they themselves often become parents who ignore, reject, or punish their own children for displays of distress. They interpret the child's distress to mean that they are failures as parents. Thus, crying becomes a signal not of the child's needs but of the parents' inadequacy. (The inability of some adults to stop a baby from crying—and turn off their own painful internal alarms—is the leading cause of child abuse, shaken baby syndrome, and infanticide.) Make no mistake, all parents feel inadequate as parents sometimes, so we're all likely to get angry at our children for reminding us of that. I used to tell myself that my own low-grade anger and resentment at my own child were helping to guide her behavior and helping her to learn. But we use most of our anger at our children to punish them for making us feel like failures as parents. The caregiver side of the equation really looks like this:

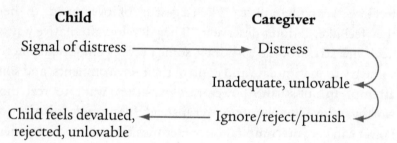

Child	Caregiver
Signal of distress ⟶	Distress
	Inadequate, unlovable
Child feels devalued, ⟵ rejected, unlovable	Ignore/reject/punish

Research shows that little boys are more likely to be ignored, rejected, or punished for showing distress. To understand why, take a moment to imagine a little girl feeling shame. She feels so bad about herself that she can't even look at you; her sobbing face is buried in her little hands as she quivers with the pain of rejection and isolation. Your every impulse is to take her in your arms and comfort her; whatever she might have done is forgiven and she is reaccepted in the attachment bond. Clearly, the social purpose of the classic display of shame—lowered head, pained expression, feeling of anguish or loss of hope—is to regain reattachment.

When addressing a group of people, I often ask the men in the audience to think of when they were very young boys and showed that they felt bad about themselves in the same way their sisters did. "What happened when you tried crying like that?" I ask.

Almost every man says that he was teased, rejected, or hurt more. "Are you a sissy?" or, "Crybaby!" or, "Come on, be a man!" or, as my father would say, "I'm going to give you something to really cry about, boy!"

Little boys have as much of an instinct to cry in shame as little girls, with the same instinctive desire for reattachment. Girls, for the most part, get comforted for doing it, while boys get rejected. To attain the closeness they want, women have learned to expose vulnerability; men have learned to hide it.

Unable to soothe their core hurts with feelings of value, boys (and poorly nurtured girls) are far more likely to numb or avoid their core hurts with blame, resentment, anger, aggression, emotional shut down, or substance abuse, or any combination of the above.

To Love Adequately, You Sometimes *Have* to Feel Inadequate

If you continually avoid or numb core hurts, you strip your emotions of their self-correcting messages. In a love relationship, a stab of inadequacy motivates you to do something that will make you feel more adequate. The inadequacy you felt when you first heard your infant cry was a powerful motivation to help, which was the *only* way you could feel adequate; it snapped you into a gut-level compassion and desire to help, which overcame your feeling of inadequacy. If you had numbed or suppressed your own core hurt, you would not have felt that same urge to provide care. Studies of primates show that the typically hysterical response that occurs in both mothers and infants when they are separated is completely eliminated after shots of morphine, which numb the distress and, presumably, the underlying urge to connect and give care. With their core hurts numbed by drugs, addicted human mothers are likely to neglect or abandon their newborns. Volunteers at urban hospitals hold "boarder babies," who were abandoned by addicted mothers and need to be held and to feel valued at least a little bit to maintain their physical and psychological health.

If you thought the parent-child bond was difficult to maintain, consider this. Most of us enter love relationships in adulthood without an inkling of how to make them work. When it comes to love, we're *all* inadequate. But if you do not allow yourself to feel inadequate for even a moment, your emotional energy will go to *avoiding* that which makes you feel inadequate, namely relationship skills. You will have little motivation to become adequate in the only way possible: by giving care, compassion, and love. *To love adequately, you have to tolerate feeling inadequate.*

Your husband's inability to tolerate occasional feelings of inadequacy is why he becomes resentful, distant, angry, or abusive when you express some desire or emotional need or say anything that he can remotely construe as criticism. The vast majority of people who are resentful, angry, or abusive fail to tolerate feelings of inadequacy long enough to motivate behavior that will allow them to reconnect and reattach to loved ones. Instead, they blame their feelings of inadequacy on their loved ones.

Clearly, your husband's resentment, anger, or abuse is not your fault. In his heart, even *he* doesn't believe that it is, as he will readily admit after he completes the Boot Camp section of this book. But right now, he's simply addicted to *blame*. He blames you in his efforts to numb his feelings of inadequacy—the very feeling he needs to kindle his gut-level desire to care for you. Even when he recognizes his anger—which he usually denies—he'll blame *that* on you: "You push my buttons," or, "I might have over-reacted, but I'm human, and look what you did!" Most of the time, all you did was ask for compassion.

You must always remember that the sole purpose of your husband's resentful, angry, or abusive behavior is to defend *him* from feeling *inadequate*, especially as a protector, provider, lover, and parent.

My client Mike complained because his wife Cindy wasn't walking with him in the mall. She had gotten into the habit of lagging a few steps behind him. For one thing, he had longer legs and took larger strides, making it hard for her to keep up. She also liked to window-shop, which put her even farther behind. But eventually she would yield to his complaints and catch up, as she did on this day. So what do you think happened when she dutifully walked beside him? He didn't even *notice*. His anxiety wasn't caused by her not walking with him, so it wasn't relieved when she did. He muttered something to himself about how much money she spends, without even looking at her.

It's easy to see how Cindy could think that nothing she did was right, as long as she agreed with Mike that *her* behavior, and not *his* anxiety and blame, made him feel bad most of the time. His anxiety was about his status as a provider. When she didn't walk beside him, he felt rejected *because* he felt like a failure as a provider. But when she did walk beside him, he still felt like a failure as a provider, so he turned his complaints against her "overspending," even though she mostly window-shopped in the mall and actually spent very little.

Your husband had these vulnerabilities to feeling like a failure as a protector, provider, lover, and parent before he met you and, unless he undergoes the kind of changes outlined in the Boot Camp section of the book, he will have them long after your relationship ends. You cannot protect him from his feelings of failure because only he can make them better. And he can make them better only by being a more protective, supportive, and loving husband and a better parent.

The tragedy of walking on eggshells is that both of you feel inadequate and unlovable. The resentful, angry, or abusive partner has chosen a tragic substitution of power for value. The choice is entirely self-destructive, for in the history of humankind, no one has ever felt more lovable by hurting someone he loves.

Control Freaks: The Response to Feeling Inadequate

Resentful, angry, or abusive husbands are often very anxious by temperament. In other words, they were *born* that way. From the time they were young children, they've had a continual dread that things will go badly and that they will *fail* to cope. As a result, they expend enormous amounts of emotional energy trying to *avoid* terrible feelings of failure and inadequacy. Unfortunately, they waste most of that energy trying to control other people.

Controlling men and women are usually not into control for its own sake. (After all, it's awfully hard work, it's *never* finished, and no one ever appreciates it.) They just want to keep their environment from making them feel bad. The problem is they're trying to regulate an *internal* system—their emotions—by controlling *external* conditions. That's like a thermostat trying to keep it comfortable in the room by blowing warm air around the outside perimeter of the building. (No wonder controlling people seem hassled and tired all the time.) Although living with a controlling husband can feel like you're getting a constant message that you're inadequate, the truth behind his message is, "Don't make me feel something I can't handle, because *I'm* inadequate!" If he responds to his sense of inadequacy by devaluing you, he begins to slide down a long, reckless slope toward self-destruction. Unless you take steps to reassert your own core value, you and your children can easily slide along with him. The next several chapters will help you see how to prevent that from happening and how to reverse the slide if it has already begun.

Three

The Mirror of Love

You've probably wondered how your husband's emotions and moods can have such powerful effects on you. How is he able to live rent free in your head and control how you think, feel, and behave? Is his personality that strong? Is yours that weak? Is he that much more certain and decisive than you? Do you just *let* him walk all over you?

The answer to all of these nagging questions is a flat-out *no*. The emotional power of love has more to do with the *biology* of attachment than the *psychology* of relationships or of individual personality, character, moral certainty, or assertiveness. (Remember, *he* feels controlled by *you*.) Your husband draws his enormous power over your thoughts, feelings, and behavior from the same source that you draw your power over his—from the *mirror of love*.

The Hidden Power of the Mirror of Love

If your boss reads the newspaper while you're talking to him, you're not likely to get upset, though on a bad day you might feel disappointed, or on a really bad day you could feel insulted. But if your *husband* reads the paper when you're trying to talk to him, you're likely to feel rejected, inadequate, or unlovable—though these might be hidden under a veneer of resentment or anger.

Why is it so much worse when your husband does the same thing your boss does? Well, your boss is one of the few people in the world who can make you feel bad. He or she—along with a few other people—can make you feel incompetent about your skills and deficient in your performance of particular tasks. Your boss can make you feel disappointed and sad or resentful and angry, but he or she can't make you feel bad about *yourself*. Only those you love can do that. Conversely, your boss and a few other people in the world can make you feel good, competent, and efficient, but hardly anyone can make you feel good about *yourself* as a loving and compassionate person in the way your husband once did. His ability to do so was a large part of why you fell in love with him in the first place.

Intimate relationships have enormous power to reach deeply into the sense of self because they serve as *mirrors* of the *inner self*. We learn how lovable we are and how valuable our love is to other people only by interacting with the people we love. We don't learn those things in school, from books, or from interactions with people we don't love. We are programmed from birth to believe in the accuracy of the reflection we see in the mirror of love—young children never question the impressions of themselves they get from their parents. They do not think that their stressed-out mothers or their raging fathers are having a bad time or trying to recover from their own difficult childhoods. Children invariably blame themselves and attribute negative reflections of themselves from their parents to their own inadequacy and unworthiness.

The instinct to believe the information about ourselves that our loved ones reflect to us weakens as we grow older, but it remains the baseline sense of self on which we draw throughout our life span. You would laugh at someone who implied that you have a hump on your back, but if your husband says it, you are likely to run to a mirror. Your assumption is, if he's displeased, there must be *something* wrong with you. No matter how much you might argue with him about his criticisms and put-downs, you are likely to believe them, at least on an unconscious level. You might not agree with the particular defect he's pointing out, but you will, on some deep level, agree that you're defective. Some part of you buys into the flaws that he reflects back to you, even though you know intellectually that he's distorting who you are and what you're doing. This hidden power of the mirror of love is why successful, powerful women are just as likely as anyone else to walk on eggshells in their intimate relationships.

Of course the mirror of love also reflects good news. If you learn how lovable you are and how valuable your love is from compassionate parents, you will naturally have a more realistic view of yourself in love relationships. You'll be disappointed and saddened sometimes, but you will hardly ever feel inadequate, unworthy, or unlovable, because you have internalized solid images of your own self-worth from your parents' compassionate mirror of love. Just as important, when you do feel sad or disappointed, you will know that you can do something to improve your condition and your situation. Your sadness will be short-lived; you'll feel bad for a while, then regroup and start to feel valuable once again. *The mirror of love generates energy when it reflects value, and depletes energy when it doesn't.*

Internalized Images

The self-image you have *internalized* from your loved ones makes all the difference in your emotional well-being. That's why some people who had abusive or neglected childhoods have trouble in their current relationships even though their spouses are loving and compassionate. If in your heart you feel unlovable, you won't really believe someone who says she loves you, and you won't feel deserving of her compassion.

Suppose you had internalized your body image based on the reflection from a fun house mirror that made your hips look a mile wide. You would think you were in deep trouble and that no diet could possibly help. And you probably would not have questioned the validity of the image by simply looking down at your own hips. When people see distorted reflections of themselves in experimental mirrors, they do not trust the contradictory evidence they get by looking down at their hips—they see themselves as having gained too much weight. And once you've internalized a negative image, you distrust even accurate mirrors—people who are gaunt from eating disorders actually see themselves as fat when they look in a mirror that reflects little more than skin and bones. Even people who do not have eating disorders but who were told repeatedly as children that they were too thin are likely to see themselves as thin adults, despite mirror reflections that show a few extra pounds.

When it comes to your physical appearance, at least you have lots of other mirrors to compare to the distorted funhouse reflection; this gives you a chance to overcome an internalized negative image about your body. But there are no reflections of your adequacy in a love relationship, other than those you get from people you love. If you judge how lovable you are by the reflections of someone who cannot love with compassion, you have a distorted view of yourself, which greatly increases your risk of walking on eggshells. And if your husband has been conditioned to believe that he is unlovable, he is more likely to act in ways that cause you to walk on eggshells.

Filling Out the Sense of Self

Reflections from the mirror of love give us a fuller sense of ourselves in relation to the rest of the world. This is similar to the way we use other people's opinions about our appearance, work strategies, and parenting goals to improve ourselves. We ask, Which dress looks better in this light, Should I ask the boss for a raise, or How do I get my kids to do their homework? The big difference in these kinds of feedback is that we're not programmed to accept their validity without question. If you don't agree with your friend's opinion about the dress, you ask someone else or make the decision on your own, just as you'd eventually make the decision about the boss and your kid's homework, based on what you think is right. But when it comes to how loving and lovable you are, it's extremely hard to know what is right when it goes against the reflection you see in the mirror of love. The lack of objective certainty about love is also why there are no *neutral* reflections in the mirror. In other words, you can accept that your friends might not have an opinion about the dress or can't grasp the complexity of asking the boss for a raise or that they have no idea of how to motivate kids to do homework. But your husband ignoring you, not seeing you, or not hearing you—which he might regard as neutral—gives the same negative feelings about yourself as him criticizing, dominating, or yelling at you.

Our instinct to use our loved ones' attitudes toward us to fill out our sense of self is why it can feel as if you've lost part of yourself—and much of your identity—when you lose a love relationship. This fear of losing yourself can be debilitating, and it is one reason that you continue to walk on eggshells.

As we go through the stress of daily living, we tend to interact with one another on a superficial level. We aim to get things done; we try to deal with everyone's everyday needs, like trash that needs emptying, homework that has to be done, cars that have to be serviced, and birthday cards for in-laws that have to be bought, signed, stamped, and mailed. Living within this busy schedule can work fine, if family members are able to stay in touch with their core value. When everyone's actions mirror love to each other, everyone will have the energy they need to deal with life's demands.

In families walking on eggshells, mostly flaws and defects are reflected back at each member in the form of criticism, resentment, and anger. As a result, they quickly begin to confuse "function" with value and "errands" with love. When you're walking on eggshells, it's never just about the facts—no matter how he puts it, you hear: "If you don't do this, I can't value you. And if I can't value you, you are not worth loving." This is the message he reflects back at you, no matter how much he says he is talking "facts" or "logic."

However, it is most likely *not* the message he intends to give.

Most men do not want to make their wives feel flawed or defective and are surprised to learn that they do feel that way. Even then, they often don't believe it and say things like, "You're making too much of it," or "You're too sensitive." Your husband probably does not grasp that he has such great power over your emotional well-being, indeed your entire sense of self. He doesn't understand that he has that power, whether he wants it or not and whether he consciously tries to use it or not. He can be made to understand this and other laws of attachment, however, in the Boot Camp section of this book.

Why We Hurt the Ones We Love: Blaming the Mirror

Just as a distressed or misbehaving child can make us feel like failures as parents and thoroughly inadequate, and just as a raging parent can make a child feel powerless, inadequate, and unlovable, a distracted lover can make us feel disregarded, devalued, and rejected. After working for many thousands of hours with people trying to overcome painful relationship problems, I'm convinced that we use resentment and anger to punish loved ones, not so much for their behavior as for the pain we feel from our reflections in the mirror of love. In other words, it's what we take their behavior to *mean* about us that causes us distress, resentment, and anger. "If he treats me that way, I must be unworthy of love, and damn it, he's not going to get away with *reminding* me!"

We want to attack the mirror because we don't like the reflection.

How We Become *Like* the Reflection in the Mirror

A dynamic in human relationships called *projective identification* helps us understand what's happening with anger and resentment. *Projection* is what we do when we attribute our own emotional states or attitudes to others. If your husband feels irritable, for instance, he will accuse you of being irritable. If he feels guilty about his attraction to an actress on TV, he might say that you're attracted to the leading man. Projective identification occurs when we identify with the projection—you get irritable when your husband accuses you of being irritable and you notice for the first time how hot the actor is, after he mentions it. Similarly, children can easily identify with adult projections about them being "bad kids."

Projective identification happens so often in daily living that we hardly notice it. If a girlfriend believes that you gossip about her, you have an urge to let another girlfriend know that she feels that way. If someone believes you don't like her, you start to notice things about her that you really don't like. But fortunately, projective identification also works in a positive way. It's hard not to like people who like you or to be compassionate to someone who truly believes that you are compassionate.

Of course, projective identification works strongest in reflections in the mirror of love. If you project your confidence onto your children, you will help them gain confidence, and if you project your distrust of them, they will likely become sneaky. Frequent criticism makes loved ones feel incompetent and make mistakes. Resentment makes them feel less lovable and behave less lovingly.

Now, here's the ultimate irony. Although we become resentful and angry when we internalize distorted reflections from our partners, the reflections *become* accurate when we get resentful and angry; we become *like* the distortions in the mirror. That's because it's not possible to feel loving or worthy of love at the same time that you feel resentful or angry—they are incompatible emotional states; you can feel one and then the other, but not both at once.

Your Reflection in the Mirrors of Love

Use the following scale to rate the qualities that your parents reflected to you.

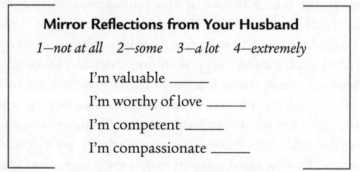

Mirror Reflections from Your Parents

1—not at all   2—some   3—a lot   4—extremely

I'm valuable _____

I'm worthy of love _____

I'm competent _____

I'm compassionate _____

Use the following scale to rate the reflections that your husband mirrors to you.

Mirror Reflections from Your Husband

1—not at all   2—some   3—a lot   4—extremely

I'm valuable _____

I'm worthy of love _____

I'm competent _____

I'm compassionate _____

Of course you want to reflect the best qualities for your children to internalize and emulate. The following can help.

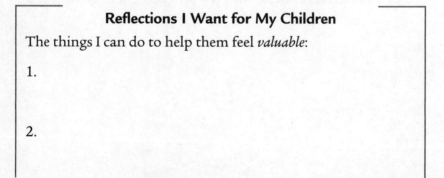

Reflections I Want for My Children

The things I can do to help them feel *valuable*:

1.

2.

3.

The things I can do to help them feel worthy of love:

1.

2.

3.

The things I can do to help them feel competent:

1.

2.

3.

The things I can do to help them feel compassionate:

1.

2.

3.

In Part II of this book, you will learn that reflections of your value as a person—of how lovable you are and how valuable your love is—must come from *your* core value, not from the impressions you've internalized from distorted mirrors of love. The following exercise can serve as a preview of that transformation.

Reflections from *Your* Core Value

The things that *I* do to prove to myself that I am *valuable*:

1.

2.

3.

The things that *I* do to prove to myself that I am worthy of love:

1.

2.

3.

The things that *I* do to prove to myself that I am competent:

1.

2.

3.

The things that *I* do to prove to myself that I am
compassionate:

1.

2.

3.

Note: If you get stuck, you probably answered these questions
in part in describing the reflections you want for your children.

Four

Why Marriage Counseling, Psychotherapy, Anger-Management, and Abuser Treatment Made It Worse

Chances are you have already tried marriage counseling and individual psychotherapy. You may have tried sending your husband to anger-management or some kind of abuser treatment. Let me guess your experience: Your personal psychotherapy did not help your relationship, marriage counseling made it worse, your husband's psychotherapy made it still worse, and his anger-management or abuser classes lowered the tone but not the chronic blame of his resentment, anger, or abuse. As if that weren't disappointing enough, you probably bought self-help books, which either told you that you lacked the skills to be assertive and set limits on your husband or that you are a hapless victim of a power-hungry, controlling aggressor, whom you have the misfortune to love but really *shouldn't*.

Fortunately, you can learn something about healing from each one of these failed treatments, which we examine next, one by one.

Why Marriage Counseling Fails

By the time most of my clients come to see me, they have already been to at least three marriage counselors, usually with disastrous results. A major reason for their disappointment is that marriage counseling presupposes that both parties have the skill to regulate guilt, shame, and feelings of inadequacy without blaming them on one another. If your husband could reflect on the motivations of his behavior—what *within him* makes him act as he does—he might then disagree with you or feel he can't communicate with you or feel incompatible with you for any number of reasons, but he wouldn't yell, ignore, avoid, devalue, or dismiss you in the process. If your husband were able to regulate his own emotions, your marriage counseling might have been successful.

Another strike against marriage counseling is manifest in an old joke among marriage therapists: We all have skid marks at the door where the husband is being dragged in. As you well know, men do not go voluntarily to therapy as a rule. So therapists tend to go out of their way to engage the man because he is 10 times more likely to drop out than his wife. If the therapist is sufficiently skilled, this extra effort to keep the man engaged isn't a problem, in *normal* relationships. But in walking-on-eggshells relationships it can be disastrous, because the therapist unwittingly joins with the more resentful, angry, or abusive partner in trying to figure out who is to blame in a given complaint. Of course he or she won't use the word, *blame.* Most marriage counselors are intelligent and well-meaning and really want to make things better. So they couch their interventions in terms of what has to be done to resolve the dispute, rather than who is to blame. Here's an example of how they go wrong.

THERAPIST: Estelle, it seems that Gary gets angry when he feels judged.

GARY: That's right. I get judged about everything.

THERAPIST: (to Estelle) I'm not saying that you *are* judging him

GARY: (interrupting) Oh *yes* she is. It's her *hobby*.

THERAPIST: (to Estelle) I'm saying that he *feels* judged. Perhaps if your request could be put in such a way that he wouldn't feel judged, you would get a better reaction.

ESTELLE: How do I do that?

THERAPIST: I noticed that when you ask him for something, you focus on what he's doing wrong. You also use the word *you* a lot. Suppose you framed it like this: "Gary, I would like it if we could spend five minutes when we get home just talking to each other about our day." (to Gary) Would you feel judged if she put it like that?

GARY: Not at all. But I doubt that she could get the judgment out of her tone of voice. She doesn't know how to talk any other way.

THERAPIST: Sure she does. (to Estelle) You can say it without judgment in your voice, can't you?

ESTELLE: Yes, of course I can. I don't mean to be judgmental all the time.

THERAPIST: Why don't we rehearse it a few times?

So now the problem isn't Gary's sense of inadequacy or his addiction to blame or his abusiveness, it's Estelle's judgmental tone of voice. With this crucial shift in perspective introduced by the therapist, Estelle rehearsed her new approach. Gary responded positively to her efforts, while the therapist was there to contain his emotional reactivity. Of course at home, it was quite another matter, despite their hours of rehearsal in the therapist's office.

In a less reactive relationship, the therapist's advice wouldn't be so bad. It's questionable whether it would help, but it wouldn't do any harm. If Gary could regulate his emotions, he might have appreciated Estelle's efforts to consider him in the way she phrased her requests; perhaps he would have become more empathic. But in the day-to-day reality of this walking-on-eggshells relationship, Gary felt *guilty* when Estelle made greater efforts to appease him. Predictably, he blamed it all on her—she wasn't doing it right, her

"I-statements" had an underlying accusatory tone, and she was trying to make him look bad.

By the way, research shows that therapists behave in their own relationships pretty much the same way that you do. In disagreements with their spouses, they fail just as often as you in trying to use the communication-validation techniques they make you do in their offices. They find it as tough as you and your husband do to put on the brakes when their own emotions and instinct to blame are going full throttle. After all, how is Mr. Hyde supposed to remember what Dr. Jekyll learned in marriage counseling?

Even highly skilled marriage therapists don't quite get the dynamics of walking on eggshells. For example, one popular and otherwise excellent marriage therapist and author has written that women in abusive marriages have to learn to set boundaries. "She needs to learn skills to make her message—'I will not tolerate this behavior any longer'—heard. [The] hurt person [must] learn how to set boundaries that actually mean something." This is the therapeutic equivalent of a judge dismissing your lawsuit against vandals because you failed to put up a "Do not vandalize" sign. You have to wonder if this therapist puts Post-its on valued objects in her office that clearly state, "Do not steal!"

Putting aside the harmful, inaccurate implication that women are abused because they don't have the "skill to set boundaries," this kind of intervention completely misses the point. Your husband's resentment, anger, or abuse comes from *his* substitution of power for value. It has *nothing* to do with the way you set boundaries or with what you argue about. It has to do with *his* violation of his deepest values. As we'll see in the chapter on removing the thorns from your heart, you will be protected, not by setting obvious boundaries that he won't respect, but by reintegrating your deepest values into your everyday sense of self. When you no longer internalize the distorted image of yourself that your husband reflects back to you, your husband will clearly understand that he has to change the way he treats you if he wants to save the marriage.

At least one of the reasons marriage therapy fails to help walking-on-eggshells relationships is that it relies on egalitarian principles. As noble an idea as it is, this approach can only work in a relationship in which the couple see each other as equals. Remember, *your* husband feels that *you* control his painful emotions and, therefore, feels *entitled* to use resentment, anger, or abuse as a defense against you. He will resist any attempt to take away what he perceives to be his only defense with every tool of manipulation and avoidance he can muster. In other words, he is unlikely to give up his edge of moral superiority—he's right, you're wrong—for the give-and-take process required of couples therapy. And should the therapist even remotely appear to side with you on any issue, the whole process will be dismissed as sexist psychobabble.

Many men blame their wives *on the way home* from the therapist's office for bringing up threatening or embarrassing things in the session. Two couples I know were seriously injured in car crashes that resulted from arguments on the way home from appointments with therapists they worked with before I met them. I'm willing to bet that if you've tried marriage counseling, you've had a few chilly, argumentative, or abusive rides home from the sessions.

The trap that many marriage counselors fall into (taking you with them) is that resentment—the foundation of anger and abuse—can *seem* like a relationship issue. "I resent that you left your towel on the bathroom floor, because it makes me feel disregarded, like my father used to make me feel." But as we have seen, the primary purpose of resentment is to protect the vulnerability you feel (or he feels) from your low levels of *core value*. Please be sure you get this point: *Low core value is* not *a* relationship *issue.* You each have to regulate your own core value *before* you can begin to negotiate about behavior. In other words, if self-value depends on the negotiation, you can't make true behavior requests—if your request isn't met, you will retaliate with some sort of emotional punishment: "If you don't do this, I'll make you feel guilty (or worse)." Merely teaching the couple to phrase things differently reinforces the false and damaging notion that your partner is responsible for your core value and vice versa.

Many women live with resentful, angry, or abusive men who seem to the rest of the world to be charmers. I've had cabinet secretaries, billionaires, movie stars, and TV celebrities for clients, all of whom could charm the fur off a cat *in public*. Before they were referred to me, each one of these guys had been championed by marriage counselors who concluded that their wives were unreasonable, hysterical, or even abusive. They have no trouble at all playing the sensitive, caring husband in therapy. But in the privacy of their homes they sulk, belittle, demean, and even batter with the worst of them.

These men have gotten so good at charming the public, including their marriage counselors, because they've had lots of *practice*. Since they were young children, they've used charm and social skills to *avoid* and *cover up* a monumental collection of core hurts. Though it can be an effective strategy in social contexts, this masquerade falls flat on its face in an intimate one. If your husband is a charmer in public, his resentment, anger, or abuse at home is designed to keep you from getting close enough to see how inadequate and unlovable he really feels. In fooling the marriage counselor and the public at large, he makes a fool of you but an even bigger fool of himself.

Why *Your* Psychotherapy Did Not Help Your Relationship and *His* Made It Worse

Research and clinical experience show that women in therapy tend to withhold important details about their walking-on-eggshells relationships. Most say that they're embarrassed to be completely honest with their therapists. One woman told me that she was convinced that her therapist, whom she thought was "awesome," wouldn't like her if she knew about the harsh emotional abuse at home. Though it is incredibly hard to believe, she saw that same therapist for five years without ever mentioning her husband's severe problems with anger and abuse. By the time I was called in, the woman was suffering from acute depression and anxiety that were destroying her physical health. When I spoke to the therapist, however, she had no clue about the abuse.

When therapists *are* aware that their clients are walking on eggshells at home, they feel almost bound to persuade the woman to leave the relationship. The most frequent complaint I hear from women who have undergone this kind of advocacy therapy is that they were reluctant to reveal the depth of their guilt, shame, and fear of abandonment to their disapproving therapists. Some have reported that their counselors would say things like, "After all he did to you, and you feel *guilty*?" I have heard hundreds of women report this kind of pressure from their therapists and have heard hundreds of therapists at conferences express exasperation about their clients' reluctance to leave their walking-on-eggshells relationships. While training therapists worldwide, I always emphasize the utter necessity of compassion for their clients' enormous burden of guilt. Making hurt women feel ashamed of their natural (albeit irrational) feelings of guilt is intolerably bad practice. Compassion for her core hurts is the healthy way to help her heal her pain.

Despite these problems, your psychotherapy probably helped you a little, even though it did not help your relationship. Whether *your husband* is helped at all is another matter.

The goal of traditional psychotherapy is to reprocess painful experience in the hope of changing the way the client sees himself and his loved ones. If your husband's therapy unearthed painful experience from his past, without first teaching him basic emotional self-regulation, he most likely dealt with that pain in the only way he knew how—by taking it out on you. He either seemed more entitled to display resentful, angry, or abusive behavior or used the pain of his past as an excuse for it. Here are the sort of things women hear from resentful, angry, or abusive men who are in therapy:

"With all I've had to put up with, don't you hassle me, too!"

"It's so hard being me, I shouldn't have to put with your crap, too!"

"I know I was mean to you, but with the pain I've suffered, you have to cut me some slack."

In defense of your husband's therapist, this approach is designed to make him more empathic to you *eventually*. But it takes a long time—a great many weekly one-hour sessions—before his sense of entitlement gives way to an appreciation of your feelings. And once he reaches that point, he has to deal with the guilt of how he's treated you in his "pre-empathic" years. For at least a few more months of slow-acting therapy, he'll feel guilty every time he looks at you. Without the skills offered in the Boot Camp section of this book, he'll either lash out at you for making him feel guilty or distance himself from the wrongly perceived source of his pain—*you*.

As we've already seen, marriage counselors have to make special efforts to build working alliances with reluctant male clients. That formidable task is all the harder in the more intimate context of individual psychotherapy with a man who dreads exposing vulnerability, as just about all resentful, angry, or abusive men do. To establish and nurture this tenuous alliance, therapists will often employ a joining technique. He or she may validate your husband's feelings about your behavior, both for the sake of the therapeutic alliance and out of fear that he'll drop out of therapy, as most men do before making any real progress. Your resentful, angry, or abusive husband will likely interpret the best joining efforts of his therapist as reinforcement that he has been mostly right all along and you have been mostly wrong. To make matters worse, most therapists have a bias to believe what their clients tell them, even when they know that they're getting only half the story and a distorted half at that. This is a bit hard to swallow when you consider that many resentful, angry, or abusive men make their wives sound like Norman Bates's mother—they're just minding their own business, when she comes screaming out of nowhere wielding a bloody knife.

If you were lucky enough to communicate with your husband's therapist—and that's something that most resentful, angry, or abusive men will not allow—you probably heard things like this:

"He's really trying, give him credit for that."

"As you know, he has so many issues to work through."

"We're starting to chip away at the denial."

The message to you is always, "Continue to walk on eggshells and hope that he comes around."

Why Anger-Management Didn't Work

Research shows that anger-management programs sometimes produce short-term gains, and that these all but disappear when follow-up is done a year or so later. That was almost certainly your experience if your husband took an anger-management class. They are especially ineffective with men whose wives have to walk on eggshells.

The worst kind of anger-management class teaches men to "get in touch with their anger" and to "get it out." The assumption here is that emotions are like nineteenth-century steam engines that need to let off steam on a regular basis. These kinds of classes include things like punching bags and using foam baseball bats to club imaginary adversaries. (Guess who would be the imaginary victim of your husband's foam-softened clubbing.) Many studies have shown conclusively that this approach actually makes people angrier and more hostile, not to mention more entitled to act out their anger. Participants are *training* their brains to associate controlled aggression with anger. Could the designers of these programs really think women would be pleased that their men learned in anger-management class to fantasize about punching them with a foam bat?

Of course, there is a much better alternative to both "holding it in" and "getting it out." In the Boot Camp section of this book, your husband will learn to replace resentment, anger, and abusive impulses, with compassion for you.

Hopefully, your husband did not attend one of these discredited classes on anger expression. But you might not have been so lucky when it came to the second worse form of anger-management: desensitization. In that kind of class your husband would mention your behaviors that push his buttons, things like you nagging him. The instructor would then work to make those behaviors seem less provocative to him. The techniques include things like ignoring it, avoiding it, or pretending it's funny. Didn't you always dream that one day your husband would learn to be less angry by ignoring you and avoiding you or thinking that you're funny when you ask him about something serious?

Core hurts, and not specific behaviors, trigger anger. If the class succeeds in making your husband less sensitive to you nagging him, he will nevertheless get irritable when you tell him you love him, as that will stir his guilt and inadequacy. Most important, you don't *want* him to become less sensitive to core hurts. Quite the opposite, as he becomes *more* sensitive to them, he will be more sensitive to you, provided that he learns how to regulate his feelings of inadequacy by showing compassion and love for you, which the Boot Camp section will help him to do.

Desensitizing doesn't work at all on resentment, which is the precursor to most displays of anger. Resentment is not simply a reflexive response to a specific event, to something you say or do. Resentment arouses the entire nervous system and works like a defensive *system* itself. That's why you don't resent just one or two or two hundred things. When you're resentful, you are constantly scanning the environment for any possible bad news, lest it sneak up on you. Anger-management classes try to deal with this constant level of arousal with techniques to *manage* it, that is, to keep your husband from getting so upset that he feels compelled to act out his anger. "Don't make it worse" is the motto of most anger-management classes. If he was aggressive they taught him to withdraw. If he shut down, they taught him to be more assertive. What they *didn't* teach him was how to stop blaming his core hurts on you and act according to his own deeper values. If attempts to manage anger don't appeal to core values, resentful men begin to feel like they're "swallowing it," or "going along to avoid an argument." This erodes their self-esteem and justifies, in their minds, occasional blow ups: "I am sick and tired of putting up with your crap!" Then they can feel self-righteous: "I'm mad as hell and I'm not going to take it anymore!"

In a love relationship, managing anger is not the point. You need to promote compassion, *which is the only reliable prevention of resentment, anger, and abuse.*

Why Abuser Groups Didn't Work

Most abuser groups confront men with, as one advocate wrote, "the full spectrum of male abuse of women." These include all imaginable forms of controlling behavior—including financial, sexual, social, and political—and every imaginable form of dominating, demeaning, or belittling behavior. They call this approach "education," on the assumption that men are ignorant of how abusive they are and of the negative effects of their abuse on their families. To a certain extent this is true. But when coupled with the other major assumption of this approach—that men *want* to control and abuse women—it's a disastrous formula for intervention.

Abuser groups teach that our patriarchal culture has fostered the dominance and oppression of women since the beginning of history. Books written by advocates detail the many benefits that men reap from their abusiveness. One recent example describes a client who threw an abusive tantrum when his wife and daughter asked him to help with the dishes, making such a fuss that they never asked again. According to this author, the man benefited enormously from his abusiveness, because he was able to enjoy his evenings at home without having to do the dishes. You have to wonder just how much he enjoyed his evenings with a resentful, hostile wife and child, while having to continuously regulate his own guilt and inadequacy.

The problem I've always had with the benefits analysis of resentful, angry, or abusive behavior is its implicit suggestion that these guys are basically happy campers as long as their victims go along with what they want. The thousands I have treated live in a festering self-loathing that lies just beneath the surface, although they can hide it behind a wall of bravado and entitlement from some abuser group leaders. The more their victims comply, the guiltier and more unlovable, resentful, angry, and abusive they feel.

The fatal flaw of traditional abuser groups is that the assumptions on which they base their therapy are partially right. Many men do not understand how much of their behavior is abusive and they certainly do not grasp the full effects of their resentment, anger, and abuse on loved ones. And many men *are* conditioned to dominate women, influenced in part by the remnants of a culture that has historically oppressed women. But educating these types of men on the many and varied kinds of abuse can only teach them how to be *more abusive* or how to be abusive in different ways. Many graduates of such programs have boasted to me of the new ways they learned "to get back" at their wives. "It never occurred to me not to have a joint-checking account before the group," one guy boasted. Economic abuse is a favorite group topic. "I don't have to give her a credit card at all." Another graduate put it more chillingly: "They teach you to beat up your wife without leaving marks."

Research on traditional abuser groups show that they stop violence only a tiny bit more than doing nothing at all, and that they often *increase* emotional abuse, even if they change the form of it. "Don't yell, *leave*," was written on a three-by-five card one abuser-group graduate showed me. They were trying to promote time-outs, but they ignore the fact that *you* will feel unseen, unheard, unimportant, and unlovable when he walks out on you while you're trying to resolve something. Some research on abuser groups shows that the time-outs they teach actually *increase* abuse and violence. That's what happened to the man who was sent to me with the "Don't yell, *leave*," three-by-five card still in his pocket. He started to walk out on his wife while she was desperately trying to make her feelings known to him. She grabbed his arm and said,

"You're not leaving until we talk about this!" But he felt justified in getting away from her, because that's what the group leader told him to do. So, without bothering to turn and face his distraught wife, he smacked the back of his free hand across the bridge of her nose.

Traditional abuser groups view dysfunctional attitudes as a primary cause of abuse. Even if that were true (we'll see in a bit that it isn't), abusers are fully capable of putting on a show about attitudes. Barry echoed so many abuser group graduates when he said: "If you're halfway intelligent you figure out the party line about power and control and tell them what they want to hear."

Here's a common example of why confronting attitudes—as opposed to identifying the core hurts that cause them—is too superficial a strategy to produce change. A man slaps, demeans, or silently rejects his wife because she refuses to make his dinner. The leader of his abuser group would dutifully confront his *attitude* about "male privilege." The argument would go like this: "She doesn't *have* to make your dinner. Your expectation that she *should* is oppressive, controlling, abusive, and sexist." The abuser would probably agree that he retaliated against his wife because she didn't defer to him as the head of the household. But that attitude, though certainly dysfunctional, is just a way for him to avoid his core hurts, his feelings that he is inadequate or unlovable. The problem is that abuser group leaders are all too happy to let him continue avoiding core hurts. They fail to understand that, had the man felt adequate and lovable, he might have been disappointed that his wife didn't make his dinner, but he wouldn't have attacked her for it.

This abuser would learn in our Boot Camp that his reaction stemmed from the fact that he felt *unlovable* when his wife wouldn't make his dinner. Once he understood this crucial point, he'd realize that no one could possibly feel more lovable by hurting someone he loves; if he wants to feel lovable, he has to become more compassionate. His developing *compassion* would then make him see that his wife would have felt used, unappreciated, taken for granted, and unlovable, if she *had* to make his dinner. With compassion, he could negotiate with his wife about what *every* couple needs to negotiate: division of labor.

Abuser groups fail because they focus on negative attitudes, rather than the core hurts that cause them. They fail to put men in touch with their compassion, which can eliminate their negative attitudes and, more important, their resentment, anger, and abuse. Because of this misguided philosophy, your husband probably came home from his group sessions defensive, resentful, and irritable, and regulated his core hurts in the only way he knew how, by blaming you: "Because of *you*, I have to go to that group and be treated like an abuser or a criminal!"

You do not *want* your husband to feel guilty and ashamed, for these painful emotions focus attention on how bad *he* feels. You want him to be compassionately concerned about *your* well-being. Think about it, do you feel valued when your husband feels bad about himself or when he feels compassion for you? Is he more likely to hurt you if he feels valuable or if he feels devalued by guilt and shame?

Finally, traditional abuser groups inadvertently reinforce two assumptions that drive abusive behavior. The first is: *The one with the most power wins.* The group leaders have power over your husband's legal status, just as he has power over your emotional well-being. As they use—or threaten to use—their power over him, they unwittingly sanction, even justify in his mind, his use of power over you. The second way abuser groups reinforce abusive assumptions is by trying to invoke guilt, shame, and fear to control your husband's behavior. Doesn't that sound exactly like what he tries to do to you and your children?

The failure of traditional abuser groups is due in no small part to their shaming approach and their complete ignorance of how people change. You do not change someone by confronting him with your superior values. You change him by appealing to *his* deepest values. This is the core-value approach that underlies the Boot Camp featured later in these pages.

Why Self-Help Books Didn't Help

A lot of self-help books are written for women on the subject of angry and abusive men. Some are better than others, but most make crucial mistakes that limit their helpfulness. They start out by inadvertently making their readers *identify* themselves as victims, with lengthy descriptions of the many ways they can be abused and explanations of how resentful they should be about it. The problem with victim-identity is that it keeps you perpetually *reactive* to your resentful, angry, or abusive partner, instead of *proactive* in accordance with your deepest values. As a result, you can easily revert to the negative identity of adolescence—teenagers don't know who they are but they know who they're *not* and they're *not* whatever their parents want. Many women have come to me in desperation, carrying an armful of self-help books, because they felt as powerless in their victim-identity as they felt as teenagers in their parents' homes.

Worst of all, victim-identity makes your husband's resentment, anger, or abuse—and your reaction to it, whether you *survive* it or not—the most important things about you. Please understand that *what other people do to you is not about you.* You heal and grow by acknowledging that the most important things about you are your inherent value as a person, along with your strengths, talents, skills, competence, resilience, compassion, and personal power.

Finally, self-help books about angry or abusive relationships tend to demonize the man you love. The authors don't seem to understand that abusive behavior is only part of what you see in your husband. It's intolerable to be sure, but it is not *all* that he is and certainly not what you love about him. Describing him as nothing more than resentful, angry, manipulative, deceptive, or abusive *has* to seem shallow to someone who lives day after day with that man. A book that focuses on overt behavior, without explaining the pervasiveness of resentment, the depth of core hurts, and the necessity of compassion and core value, can scarcely help you reclaim your true self.

•   •   •

It greatly saddened me to write this chapter and say explicitly what you probably have already learned from your noble but failed attempts to change your relationship: You're unlikely to get help from marriage counseling, psychotherapy, anger management, abuser groups, and most self-help books. The good news is that meaningful help *is* available. It comes from *within you*. You can draw on your great inner resources by reintegrating your deepest values into your everyday sense of self. This will make you feel more valuable, confident, and powerful, regardless of what your husband does. From this position of strength, you can look at your resentful, angry, or abusive partner *compassionately*, and see that every harsh word he says to you and every cold shoulder he turns toward you makes him hate himself a little more. If he cannot make the changes that your recovery of your core value requires, you will be able to leave him without guilt—for his own sake—and finally escape the pendulum of pain. To stop walking on eggshells, you need to accept your true self, which has been obscured by pain. Your *true* self emerges from your *core value*.

PART II

Reclaiming the Self

Five

Recovering Your Core Value

At one time in your life, you were probably more familiar with your innate gifts and strengths than you are right now. And if your marriage had developed normally, you would have matured with a regular awareness of your inherent value as a person, a wife, mother, and whatever public role you have chosen to play. This chapter will help you regain that internal experience of your core value, from which arises your ability to love, achieve, and create value in your external life.

The first step you need to take is to recognize that you were born with a core value and that you never lose it, though walking on eggshells in your relationship has probably made you lose touch with it. To help you remember that it is always within you, you will learn to pack your environment with daily reminders of it—when you see a sunset or your child's smile, you will remind yourself of your core value. Almost everything you do has the potential to become an expression of the deep sense of value you've had since the day you were born.

The Innate Drive to Love and Create Value

Babies who are unloved fail to thrive, even when given food and medical care. Some don't even metabolize food given to them intravenously; they lose the will to live and in some cases they actually die from lack of love. Research shows that, if given the choice between food or loving care, children will always take loving care, even if they have to be hurt to get it—abused children form fierce loyalties to abusive parents who, despite their abusive actions, also love them. I once had an eight-year-old client who felt particularly bad about himself because his mother had broken her foot by kicking him in the head. Yet he angrily defended her against anything that remotely sounded like criticism.

A more recent discovery in child development suggests that being loved isn't enough. Children also need to *love back,* as research with severely depressed mothers indicates. The mothers in these studies were able to love and care for their children and meet most of their needs to be loved. Yet, because of their deep depression, they felt uncomfortable receiving love *from* their babies. It's easier to understand their dilemma if you think of times when you've felt down or blue or even just slightly depressed. At those times when your self-esteem was low, perhaps you felt uncomfortable holding eye contact. And it was a bit harder to accept compliments, praise, or affection from others. You felt like you were getting something you didn't deserve. Oh, you knew intellectually that you deserved it, but the subtle sense of unworthiness remained, just beneath the surface of your conscious awareness. This same basic sense of unworthiness, multiplied several times over by the severity of their depression, is what made the mothers in these studies turn away from their babies when they tried to express love. As a result, these loved infants, who were not allowed to love, became depressed.

From the beginning of life, and throughout the span of our lives, loving is just as important as being loved. The need to love and be loved *overrides* comfort and even the instinct to survive. We are born with the drive to create and experience *value*, to make someone or something *important* and worthy of appreciation, protection, time, energy, effort, and sacrifice. When you experience something you value, like your child's smile or a sunset or the moon rising over the ocean, your sense of self grows and makes you feel more alive. Most positive emotions and virtually all passion, purpose, and conviction come from creating value and staying true to it. On the other hand, most painful emotions, emptiness, and virtually all aggression rise from failure to create value or stay true to it.

I call this innate drive to create value, *core value*. Other writers have referred to it as the "life force" or the "human spirit"; for religious writers, it's the soul. Core value is your ability to create *and* experience value. It is the source of all that you value in life, including love and happiness. When you're in touch with core value, your life is enriched and you have a greater awareness of being alive. When you are not, your life is painful, empty, or numb. The greatest pain in your relationship is that it has too often cut you off from the *internal* source of your value and personal power.

Your Negative Emotions Are Signals to Value Yourself More

Your negative emotions are the best indicators of when you are cut off from your core value. Although your husband stimulates many of your negative emotions, they are really not about him; they are about your need to value yourself more. This may be hard to see now because the hurtful nature of your relationship has gotten you into the habit of perceiving your negative emotions as something to *avoid* by walking on eggshells. But in reality, your anxiety, distress, depression, feelings of isolation, resentment, and anger are internal alarms; they signal that you are, at that particular moment, disconnected from your core value. They tell you that you are ignoring or violating something important to you.

For example, Bettina's husband has so often criticized her for the way she parks the van in their garage that she finds herself backing out of the garage and pulling in, over and over again, to get it just right and possibly avoid criticism. Sometimes, she spends as much as a half hour doing this. As we've already seen, her husband's criticism reflects how he feels about himself far more than the way she parks. More importantly, Bettina's anxiety and distress tell her that she has placed her value as a person on something as trivial as parking the van in the garage. It's understandable that she feels that way, given the history of her relationship, but to heal and grow, she must make her core value more sacred to her, *regardless* of whether or not her husband ever understands.

Learn to view your anxiety, distress, depression, feelings of isolation, resentment, and anger like a gas gauge, telling you that your core value is running on empty and that you need to fill it up.

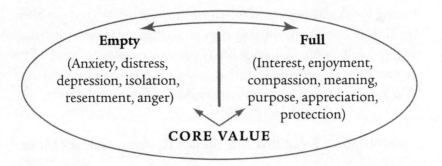

The rest of this chapter gives ways to help you fill up your core value and keep it full under stress. You will learn to remember your core value in every sort of environment and situation and feel a warm glow each time you do. This will give you perspective and free mental resources from the stringencies of walking on eggshells so that you can use them to solve the problems of your marriage in your long-term best interests.

What Core Value *Feels* Like

Imagine that you're in a desert so vast that it would take five days to walk out of it. You have enough water for only three days. In other words, you cannot save yourself. But you know that rescue teams are out looking for you, and there's a good chance you'll be rescued before you run out of water. You come across a young child, say less than three years old. The child is dying now, and *will* die now, unless you share your water. Of course there's a risk to that. If you share the water, you'll both die tomorrow, and you might have been rescued on the second day.

So what will you do? Share the water? Or watch the child die?

If you think that you might *not* share the water and give yourself an extra day to be rescued, the rule is that you cannot walk away— if you withhold the water, you must watch the child slowly die, lips cracked, eyes bulging, tongue swelling, skin parched and burned. Imagine how much you would have to fight off the humane instinct to give the child a drink of water.

Most people would share the water and hope for the best. (Even murderers in prison have said they would share the water if they couldn't walk away. I know that *you* would share the water, or you wouldn't have read this far about core value.) Imagine that you *have* shared the water. But now it's the second day, and the water is gone. The child is growing weak, trembling, whimpering, shivering with fear. What are *you* doing?

Of course you're comforting the child the best that you can. Close your eyes for a moment and imagine that you are trying to comfort this frightened child in this barren desert. You are the only person in the world who can make her feel better right now. You're hugging her, rocking her, whispering to her or singing to her, doing whatever you would do to comfort her. Making her feel better is the most important thing in your life at this moment. You're trying so hard to comfort this frightened child that you don't realize right away how well it's working. She *is* calming down. She's holding tightly onto you, feeling soothed, peaceful, and good, because of *you*. She feels secure and comforted, wrapped in your compassion.

To the extent that you can imagine saving and comforting this child, you experience your core value. That's what it feels like. It's an awesome light within you, the source of your ability to love, value, appreciate, form emotional connections, and experience compassion. It's your deepest humanity. It makes you recognize natural, artistic, and spiritual beauty. It makes you feel alive.

Remember this feeling of core value; we'll use it in the exercise at the end of this chapter.

The Common Experience of Core Value:
Improve, Appreciate, Connect, Protect

You can *feel* core value when you help children in danger or make a strong intimate connection to another person or appreciate a sweeping sunset or feel the beauty of a work of art or have a spiritual experience or become aware of your own humanity. But these wonderful happenings are relatively rare in normal day-to-day living. Core value more frequently occurs on a daily basis as an unconscious motivation to *improve, appreciate, connect,* or *protect.* Doing any one of these automatically activates your core value.

Not incidentally, these four basic motivations—improve, appreciate, connect, protect—have the power to change negative emotions into positive ones. No matter what the negative feeling—sadness, grief, loneliness, core hurts, resentment, or anger—acting on any one of these awesome motivations will make you feel better. If you do two at once, you will feel even better. Do three or more simultaneously, and you'll feel a lot better—close to euphoria, even joy. A description of each should make it clear why doing any *one* will make you feel at least a little bit better, no matter how bad the circumstance or how negative or painful the feeling.

Improve

Thanks to the powerful human motivation to improve, you don't necessarily have to fix the problem to feel better. You just have to make it a *little* better. If you're feeling bad and you just think about what you can do to make it a little better—you don't even have to do it, just *think* of it—you'll start feeling better. If you're upset at your husband, and you think of how you can make yourself feel a little better—take a leisurely bath, smell a flower, call a girlfriend—you start to feel better. Making things a *little* better frees more mental resources in the neocortex, the problem-solving part of the brain. These added mental resources allow you to make things *even* better, freeing more mental resources that enable you to improve yet a little more, and so on. It's worth repeating: *improve* does not mean fix; it means make things *a little better* at a time. Here's another composite case example.

Maggie was fed up with getting Tony's cold shoulder every time she didn't do something he wanted her to do. He never overtly criticized her; he would just sulk on the sofa for the rest of the night. Her usual pattern was to try to make conversation, but her efforts typically yielded only one-word responses. After a little of that, she'd start confronting him about his coldness, which, of course, he would deny, implying that she was too sensitive or too demanding. Then it would either turn into a fight or she would take her own silent position on the other end of the sofa, so that the two of them looked like sulking bookends. But on *this* night, Maggie tried to think of what would make her feel a little better while her husband was sulking. She got out their wedding pictures and paged through them. This made her feel more than a little better; as she paged through the album, she started to feel *happy*. She felt so good that she shared the pictures with Tony. Her genuine warmth about the pictures—very different from nagging him about his coldness—warmed him up. He too enjoyed the pictures. Before they were finished, he apologized for his sulking—the same sulking he had vigorously denied.

It's important to note that they would not have connected in this way had Maggie tried to think of a way to bring Tony around. Then she would have come off as manipulative. Sharing the pictures worked to warm up Tony *only* because it had genuinely warmed up Maggie; he merely reacted to her warmth. The change had to occur in Maggie first. Her intention was to make herself feel a little better, not share the pictures with Tony. Once her core value was activated, she naturally chose to *connect* with her husband by sharing the pictures with him.

The real shift in Maggie came less from the pictures than from her motivation to *improve*. She would have felt better looking at the pictures, or anything else she valued, regardless of whether she also chose to *appreciate* her marriage, *connect* with Tony and *protect* him from his self-destructive sulking. And she would have felt better acting on her motivation to improve even if Tony had chosen to go on sulking when she brought him the photos. She would not have allowed his resentful behavior to control her core value.

Briefly describe something that makes you feel anxious, sad, isolated, resentful, or angry.

List three things *you* can do to improve (a little bit) *your* experience of the above, regardless of what anyone else does.

1.

2.

3.

Appreciate

To appreciate something is to open yourself to certain qualities, behaviors, or creations of other people. For example, you can appreciate how loving your friends are, your partner's fine work on the yard, the effort your children made on their homework, the beauty of the sunset, the drama of the painting, the strategy of the game, all of which enhance your sense of self for as long as you appreciate them. Appreciation makes you feel more alert and alive; you increase the value of your life while you appreciate your child's joy, curiosity, or sense of wonder. If she *feels* your appreciation, you don't have to worry about whether you praise her enough. And if you *felt* your husband's appreciation, you wouldn't feel so bad that he doesn't think to compliment you.

The good news about appreciation is that its positive effects spread and multiply. Appreciating a sunset will make you appreciate your family more, and vice versa. That's why you wish that your husband would better appreciate objects of beauty—you intuitively know that if he did, he would appreciate you more, which would make it easier for you to appreciate him.

Briefly describe something that makes you feel anxious, sad, isolated, resentful, or angry.

List three things *you* can appreciate about someone or
something in your life.

1.

2.

3.

Resolve to actively appreciate those things. For instance, if you
wrote, "a mountain scene," go to the mountains as soon as
possible. If you wrote, "seeing my child asleep," look at your
child sleeping as soon as possible, and feel the glow of your
core value.

Protect

The instinct to protect people we care about is so strong that it
generally overrides self-protection. You would instinctively step in
front of a gun to protect your child. You might not do it if you
thought about it, but you would likely act on the instinct to protect *without* thinking about it. The instinct to protect is stronger in
humans than in any other animal in part because our offspring are
helpless and vulnerable for a much longer time. Animals with
weaker social bonds are on their feet and running 10 minutes after
birth. As you go up the food chain, the young are helpless for increasingly longer periods of time and therefore require stronger
emotional bonding to maintain prolonged stages of protection. By
the time you get to humans, well, these days our young are helpless
until about 35.

If you have a family, the instinct to protect controls your self-
value, regardless of how successful you might be at work. (Imagine

the emotional fate of a world-class CEO who lets go of his child's hand in traffic.) And if you feel that you can protect your family's well-being, your self value will be high, even if you fail in other areas of life. Research shows that getting fired from a job is more bearable for people more attuned to the protection of their families than their own ego. Protective people tend to search immediately for another job as a means of putting food on the table, while the ego-driven are likely to endure a few weeks of painful depression. It takes longer for them to recover because they misunderstand their pain, which is not telling them they are failures; it's telling them to protect their families. The pain will continue until they heed its message and resume protection of their families, at least emotionally if not financially.

Of course, protection of loved ones is different from doing what they want. You would not be protective of your children if you let them eat a bunch of junk, neglect their school work, and stay out to all hours of the night. And you are not protective of your husband by staying with him if he does not overcome his addiction to blame. As you learn to focus on protecting your children and your husband from the harmful effects of walking on eggshells, you will feel sufficiently empowered to demand compassionately that he treat you and them with value and respect. That is the only way he can respect himself.

Briefly describe something that makes you feel anxious, sad, isolated, resentful, or angry.

List three things *you* can do that will make you feel protective
of people you love.

1.

2.

3.

Connect

Emotional connection is a sense that you are in some way a part of
someone or something else. Research shows that people function
at their best and report the most happiness when they have *three*
levels of emotional connection: *intimate, communal,* and *spiritual.*
Love relationships tend to fall apart when they are the *only* source
of emotional connection. The expectation that your husband
should meet all your emotional needs or that you should meet all
of his puts more stress on your relationship than it is designed to
support. When couples become isolated in their "oneness," they
lose sight of reality. They tend to discount perspectives—as well as
reality checks—from other people who care about them. Isolation
in your walking-on-eggshells relationship can make you think that
resentment, anger, and even abuse are a normal part of love.

Intimate Connection
An intimate connection is a sense that an important part of your
emotional world is also an important part of someone else's. It requires at least an intuitive understanding of that person's core
hurts and core value, along with the knowledge that your emotional well-being is tied up together; in general, if he feels good,

you feel good; if he feels bad, so do you. Remember our discussion in Chapter 2 of why this kind of emotional interconnectivity is so powerful—it motivates the caring and cooperative behavior necessary for human survival. By virtue of our intimate connections, we are hard-wired to respond to the needs of loved ones, and we fail to do so at our emotional peril.

But, alas, the hard-wiring was completed many thousands of years ago in much simpler times. Modern families have developed a lot more emotional needs in trying to cope with an infinitely more complex world. And the burden of meeting those needs falls disproportionately on the shoulders of women. Most women these days are in a doublebind. To meet the increased emotional challenges of modern life, you need a solid sense of self—a pool of growth and emotional health from which you can draw buckets of nurturance to give to the people you love. Yet it's harder to develop a solid sense of self when you have to spend so much time meeting the needs of loved ones. It's a delicate balance, you can't sell out yourself for your relationships and you can't sell your relationships short for yourself.

As hard as this balance between self and family is to maintain, you were probably able to do it *before* you started walking on eggshells. Then it was easier to help your children, not just because they needed you, but as an expression of your core value. You could more easily express care for your husband because you felt a sense of caring from him. But now it all seems like so much work; there are days when you just feel too worn out to keep doing it.

Please understand that there *is* hope for the future. *Whatever you do from your core value generates energy; doing the same behaviors while* disconnected *from your core value depletes energy.* As you develop and reconnect with your core value, it will once again become easier for you make intimate connections with your children, your extended family, your close friends, and with your husband, if he changes. (Part IV offers potent reconnection exercises for the two of you to use, provided that he does the Boot Camp work necessary to ensure your safety and security.)

If you are thinking about leaving your walking-on-eggshells relationship, which you may have to do to get him to take on the hard work of change, don't worry that you will lose your only intimate connection. Research assures us that lover/partner relationships are not the only way to fill the need for this most personal form of emotional connection. Close friends and family can fill the bill nicely.

Briefly describe something that makes you feel anxious, sad, isolated, resentful, or angry.

List what you can do to feel more connected to:

1. Your children

2. Your extended family

3. Your close friends

Communal Connection

Communal connection is a sense of *belonging* to a group of people, based on shared values, beliefs, goals, or experience. For instance, in a church community you share faith and religious tenets with people you may not know individually. In a school community, like the PTA, you share a common interest in the welfare of your children. In a neighborhood you might share goals of making the block safer, cleaner, or a more pleasant place for everyone to live, and in a sorority you share common school experiences. Communal connections can form around social causes, special interests, or political groups. They come to life in organizations for the arts, athletics, or parenting, and in political or civic groups like the YWCA, Now, and Rotary, or in youth organizations, like the Girl/Boy Scouts and 4-H clubs.

Communal connection is almost always out of balance in families that walk on eggshells. Most are isolated, with little or no sense of community. But in many others, community activities loom more important than the intimate connections of family members. In the former case, you can improve your marriage by investing value (appreciation, time, effort, sacrifice) in any one of the examples of community connection just listed. In the latter, you need to cut back on social activities, including after school activities for your kids, in favor of more family dinners and quality time together.

Briefly describe something that makes you feel anxious, sad, isolated, resentful, or angry.

List three things *you* can do to enhance your sense of community.

1.

2.

3.

Spiritual Connection

Spiritual connection is a sense of attachment to something *larger* than the self. It can be God, nature, the cosmos, a social cause, or the sea of humanity. Spiritual connection has a way of making us humble, in the best sense of the word. Imagine standing on a cliff, staring up at a starry sky. You would feel a sense of awe because, unlike any other animal, you are able to grasp the vast beauty of what you see. A paradox about humans is that we become more significant when we realize how insignificant we are.

The importance of spiritual connection predates recorded history. Anthropological evidence suggests that the Neanderthals—the more primitive group of cave dwellers who predated and may have coexisted with our ancestors—buried their dead in what appear to have been religious ceremonies. Spiritual connection differs from mere superstition and from what I call "fear of consequences" or "give me this" theology, which is usually motivated by fear or greed. A psychological sense of spirituality is a feeling of union and transcendence, motivated by compassion, awe, or joy. If you want to experience spiritual connection, pray to be more compassionate, not to escape your emotions or win the lottery.

Briefly describe something that makes you feel anxious, sad, isolated, resentful, or angry.

List three things *you* can do to enhance your spiritual connection.

1.

2.

3.

Transcendence

An important characteristic of all forms of emotional connection is transcendence, which allows you to rise above purely selfish and petty concerns. Relationships automatically develop resentment when selfish and petty concerns become more important than the emotional connection between you. If your husband makes a fuss about shoes in the middle of the floor, the two of you are emotionally *disconnected*. Negotiating about the shoes will get you nowhere, until it becomes clear that your connection is more important than the shoes. Most fights between loved ones result from the pain of *disconnection*. (Part IV shows how to maintain your connection when negotiating about behavior.) Similarly, communities fall apart when the petty concerns of individuals interfere with the community's welfare. Spiritual connections disappear completely when marginalized by convenience and mood.

We Need All Three Levels of Connection

The best way I know to express the relative importance of the three levels of emotional connection is this: You can major in one, but you have to minor in the other two. That is, you can get away with putting 10 eggs in one basket, as long as you put one in each of the others. What you *cannot* do is put all your connection eggs in one basket. Many of the problems of intimate relationships stem from the expectation that they can fulfill not only every need for intimacy but all three levels of emotional connection. A love relationship that isolates one or both parties from parents, friends, community, and spiritual connection is doomed to failure.

Here is a simple but potent intervention that will help most intimate relationships. *Become more involved in your community and in your spiritual life.* You will be amazed at the results.

The *Most* Important Thing about You

Think of people you know who seem to have it together. They seem confident but not cocky, with their lives more or less in balance. They have ample energy to give to family, work, and community, yet they still have something left over for personal enjoyment. You've probably known at least a couple of people like that at some point in your life. Have you ever wondered what makes them different from everyone else? It might very well be that they *know* what is most important to them. The clichéd way to put it is, "They know how to set priorities." On a more profound level, their emotions keep them positively energized because their values are in their *natural* order, with the deepest ones counting the most. To overcome confusion and self-doubt, you have to stay true to your deepest values—the things that are *most* important *to* you and *about* you.

We acquire values in two ways: We're born with some, like forming attachment bonds, and others we internalize in the course of life, such as justice and honesty. Whether learned or innate, values have to be hierarchical because some things are necessarily more important than others. (If you don't believe it, think of putting a carrot down the garbage disposal and then a kitten and see if your brain doesn't make a distinction.) Your more important values make you who you are as a person. When true to them, you have a strong sense of self, and when untrue to them, you seem to become a different person. And now you know why your husband seems to have a Jekyll and Hyde personality. When he's in his core value, he's the man you married. But once it he leaves it, he becomes resentful, angry, or abusive. His emotions serve as guardians of his deeper values, prodding him with jabs of guilt, shame, and anxiety whenever he strays from them. Unfortunately, he blames his guilt, shame, and anxiety on you.

In a walking-on-eggshells relationship, the natural hierarchy of values is turned upside down. Less important things have become more important than the most important things. Preferences (such as how the house looks), tastes (what we should eat, where we should go), and division of labor (who should do what) seem more important than the deeper values of love, compassion, and connection.

The Most Important Questions

You can take the first step toward reintegrating your deepest values into your everyday sense of self by answering the following questions.

What is the most *important thing about you as a person?* There are a lot of important things about you, but this is the *most* important. You would be a different person without this quality. (To ensure that you get to the *most* important thing, ask yourself, "Why is this important to me?" Write down that answer, then ask the same question of your answer, "Why is *that* important to me?" Keep going until the question no longer makes sense. At that point you have arrived at the *most* important thing.)

What is the most *important thing about you as a wife?* (This is what *you* regard as the most important thing, not what you think he might say.)

What is the most *important thing about your life in general?* (This is what you would put in your eulogy if you were to write it at the end of your long life.)

Interestingly, the vast majority of men in my practice, most of whom have resentment, anger, or abuse problems, write something like the following: The most important thing about them as persons and husbands is their capacity to love, protect, and support their wives and children. They write that the most important thing about their lives in general is making the world a better place, at least in some small way, for the people they love. Some also write that they want to contribute some kind of legacy to their community, country, humanity as a whole, nature, or God. No one writes that the most important thing about him is his habit of shutting down emotionally, ignoring, resenting, or devaluing his wife.

The Most Important Things about Me

The *most* important thing about me as a person is:

The *most* important about me as a wife is:

The *most* important thing about my life in general is:

Your answers to the "most important" questions can form the foundation of understanding and accepting your true self. They do not depend on your husband or your parents or your boss or on anyone else. They are the source of your inherent value, your strength, your resilience, and your personal power.

You Must Control Your Core Value

Although it can seem temporarily diminished, your core value is *invincible*. The world can cause you expense and inconvenience; it can hurt your feelings and even your body, but it can *never* harm your core value. *Nothing your husband or anyone else says or does can lower your core value.* To help you internalize this vital truth, write the following and then read it out loud, with all the conviction you can muster:

> I am worthy of respect, value, and compassion, whether or not I get them from others. *If I don't get them from others, it is necessary to feel* more *worthy, not* less. It is necessary to affirm my own deep value as a unique person (a child of God). I respect and value myself. I have compassion for my hurt. I have compassion for the hurt of loved ones. I trust myself to act in my best interests and in the best interests of my children, which will ultimately be in the best interests of my husband.

Your Core Value Bank

The *Core Value Bank* on page 96–97 is designed as a repository of your core value, a kind of bank account of the most important things. You can think of each of the eight segments as a safe deposit box containing images of the most important things to and about you. The Core Value Bank is itself an image of your *internal* value. Its contents correspond to persons and things in the world, but it resides entirely *within* you. It's *always* there, ready to give you strength whenever you need it. Each time you see, hear, smell, touch, or taste something in the world similar to the contents of your Core Value Bank, it will remind you of your core value and thereby activate it within you. In other words, you will be motivated to improve, appreciate, connect, or protect. The next time you see a sunset, for example, it will not only seem beautiful, it will remind you of your core value. Put as much content as you can in your safe deposit boxes—you'll be amazed at how many reminders you'll start to find in your environment.

The best thing about the Core Value Bank is that you make deposits at the same time you make withdrawals. You will *never* run out of core value.

After you fill in the boxes, we'll put your Bank to use as a tool of emotional reconditioning. Get ready for magic.

Box 1: You've already filled in this box with the emotion you felt when you imagined helping and comforting the desperate child in the desert.

Box 2: Fill in:
1. The *most* important thing about you as a person.
2. The *most* important thing about your life in general. (Fast-forward 60 years and think of what you would want your eulogy to be.)

Box 3: Fill in the names of your loved ones. You're writing their names, but the emotional content of this box will be the actual love you feel for them.

Box 4: Fill in a symbol (a drawing, mark, or word will do) of something that has spiritual importance to you. It can be religious, natural, cosmic, or social—anything that connects you to something larger than the self, which, while you are connected to it, seems more important than your everyday, mundane, or selfish concerns.

Box 5: Name, draw, or describe a nature scene that you value—something that you feel is beautiful. It can be a sunset, valley scene, leaves turning, ocean view, and so on.

Box 6: Identify a piece of art, music, or other human creation that makes you feel value.

Box 7: Identify a sense of community connection, for example, a church, school, work, or neighborhood.

Box 8: List three compassionate things you have done. These do not have to be Mother Teresa kind of compassion. They can be relatively small gestures, when you helped or comforted someone else and received no material gain.

Core Value Bank

Box 1	Box 2
The emotions I felt as I imagined rescuing and comforting the child in the desert:	The most important thing about me as a person:

The most important thing about my life in general: |

Box 5	Box 6
Something beautiful in nature:	Something beautiful human made (art, music, architecture, furniture, etc.):

Core Value Bank

Box 3	Box 4
The people I love:	My spiritual connection:

Box 7	Box 8
My community connection:	Compassionate things I have done: 1. 2. 3.

Emotional Reconditioning

You can use your Core Value Bank to recondition your entire emotional system. It's a step-by-step process of associating core value with distress, the way that well-nurtured children learn to do early in life (Chapter 2). To get started, try using your Core Value Bank to regulate relatively minor resentments involving situations that occur in traffic.

1. You're running late, and the car ahead of you won't speed up or get out of your way. Imagine for a moment how irritating this would be when you have to get somewhere—feel the frustration of how *unfair* or *wrong* it is.

   Now experience your core value—helping and comforting the child in the desert, the most important things about you, the people you love, your spiritual and communal connections, something beautiful in nature and art—the items in your Core Value Bank. Feel the warm light of your core value.

2. Someone cuts you off—you have to hit the brakes hard. Imagine for a moment how irritating this would be—feel the frustration of how *unfair* or *wrong* it is.

   Experience your core value—helping and comforting the child in the desert, the most important things about you, the people you love, your spiritual and communal connections, something beautiful in nature and art—the items in your Core Value Bank. Feel the warm light of your core value.

3. The traffic totally jams up, nothing but gridlock for miles and miles. Imagine how irritating this would be—feel the frustration of how *unfair* it is when you have to get somewhere.

   Experience your core value—helping and comforting the child in the desert, the most important things about you, the people you love, your spiritual and communal connections, something beautiful in nature and art—the items in your Core Value Bank. Feel the warm light of your core value.

4. A guy in another car flips you the finger and yells at you. Imagine for a moment how irritating this would be—feel the frustration of how *unfair* or *wrong* it is.

   Experience your core value—helping and comforting the child in the desert, the most important things about you, the people you love, your spiritual and communal connections, something beautiful in nature and art—the items in your Core Value Bank. Feel the light of core value.

5. Somebody is tailgating you. Imagine for a moment how irritating this would be—feel the frustration of how *unfair* or *wrong* it is.

   Experience your core value—helping and comforting the child in the desert, the most important things about you, the people you love, your spiritual and communal connections, something beautiful in nature and art—the items in your Core Value Bank. Feel the warm light of your core value.

6. A jerk leans on the horn and *won't* stop! Imagine for a moment how irritating this would be—feel the frustration of how *unfair* or *wrong* it is.

   Experience your core value—helping and comforting the child in the desert, the most important things about you, the people you love, your spiritual and communal connections, something beautiful in nature and art—the items in your Core Value Bank. Feel the light of core value.

7. A van speeds by too close to you. Imagine for a moment how irritating this would be—feel the frustration of how *unfair* or *wrong* it is.

   Experience your core value—helping and comforting the child in the desert, the most important things about you, the people you love, your spiritual and communal connections, something beautiful in nature and art—the items in your Core Value Bank. Feel the light of core value.

Remember, anger, resentment, and distress work like a sensitive gas gauge, warning that your core value is running on empty and that you need to fill it up. You can fill it up to the high level you deserve in just one week, by following this formula: Every day, for the next seven days:

- Appreciate at least one thing about each person you love.
- Make at least one spiritual connection.
- Appreciate a new thing of beauty in nature, in art or music, and in your community.
- Do at least one compassionate thing for another person.
- Do at least one compassionate thing for yourself.

You will soon get into the habit of looking for aspects of value in everyone and in everything you see.

With your core value filled up, you can begin to remove the thorns from your heart.

Six

Removing the Thorns from Your Heart

If you walk on eggshells, you have no doubt developed a strong pattern of reactive resentment and anger. That is understandable and certainly not your fault. You have every right to be resentful and angry. You have every right to express your resentment and anger. You have every right to stay with your resentment and anger for as long as you want. But I am here to tell you that you have a more compelling right to heal the wounds that cause your resentment and anger. Although it may seem extremely unfair, you must choose between resentment and anger on the one hand and healing on the other; you *cannot* do both. Here's why.

Resentment and anger have amphetamine and analgesic effects. They provide an immediate surge of energy and numbing of pain— a feeling of physical power—to replace the powerlessness and vulnerability of whatever core hurts have been stimulated at the time. But as with any other amphetamine, you get a surge of energy and confidence from resentment and anger, but then you *crash*. They always drop you down lower than the point at which they picked you up. When you get resentful or angry, you get depressed afterward. Think about it, after your resentment and anger go away, your energy is lower, you have more self-doubt, and your mood is at least a little depressed. You have borrowed energy and the confidence it brings from the future, and you have to pay it back. And that's just the physiological response to the amphetamine—it does not include the added depressive effects of doing something while you're resentful or angry that you're later ashamed of, like hurting someone you love.

So here is what can easily happen: You get resentful or angry, then you get depressed. You get resentful or angry again, and you get depressed again. Pretty soon, your brain begins to look for things to get resentful about just to militate out of your depressed mood. To avoid feeling depressed, you'll have to be resentful most of the time. If this roller-coaster syndrome has happened to you, your life has become a joyless drive to get things done. You feel tense and irritable most of the time, and are not as sweet to your kids as you would normally be. It's impossible to feel lovable while you feel resentful and it's very hard to treat others lovingly.

Resentment and anger numb the pain of core hurts, but they also prevent healing. They function a lot like ice on a wound. Suppose you cut your hand and put ice on it to numb the pain. As long as you hold the ice on the wound, you won't feel pain, but the wound won't begin to heal, either. When you remove the ice and the pain comes flooding back into the wound, then the healing begins—and only then. If you use resentment or other low-grade anger to numb pain, you will feel the hurt (or emptiness) when you're not angry or resentful.

The Health Risk

You may have read headlines in the newspaper that medical studies show that anger has dangerous effects of on your health. Some have called anger the "heart-attack emotion," others have framed it as the "not-so-silent killer." The headlines usually don't tell you that it's not just *any* anger that does the damage; it's a specific kind of hostile anger that lasts for an extended period. Hostile anger has a revenge motive—you want to put someone down or get back at someone for a perceived injury. Most anger, like that triggered by loud noises, irritations, frustration, or unpleasant events, is not hostile. Although the headlines never quite get it right, the damage to your health is done by resentment. When resentful, you constantly think of how you've been wronged and how the offender should be made to pay. For example, you may get angry at your husband for not cleaning up his mess after making a sandwich for himself. If you're not feeling generally resentful, that anger will go away shortly, especially if he cleans it up when you point it out to him. But if you are resentful, you will continue to think about his offense, and fantasize about what you might do to get back at him, such as not cleaning up *your* mess. And isn't it true that whenever you do feel resentful, even if he does clean it up, you will still resent that you had to ask him to do it or that he hadn't done it sooner?

The other factor that makes anger so harmful to your health comes from *duration*—how long it lasts. Unhealthy anger lasts longer than a few minutes and long-lasting anger hurts you more than does getting angry a lot or even getting intensely angry. Once again, the true culprit is resentment, which, as you well know, can go on for days and weeks and even years.

Lingering anger and resentment present a great risk to your health, because our bodies weren't built to withstand the internal chemical effects these emotions cause. Resentment, anger, and hostility raise your blood pressure, damage the blood vessels in your heart and brain, constrict your muscles and cause chronic pain. As it goes on, the effects on health are many and severe.

Long-lasting resentment can easily cause:

- Chronic, low-grade depression
- Destruction of T cells (This lowers the *immune* system. If you're resentful you probably have lots of little aches and pains, get frequent colds or bouts of flu, headaches, muscle aches, stomachaches, and gastrointestinal problems.)
- Hypertension, which increases threat of stroke and heart attack

- Heart disease
- Cancer
- Addictions
- Shortened life span

Considering the high-risk behaviors that usually go with chronic resentment, such as smoking, drinking, poor diet, and impulsive behavior, some people can take three minutes off their lives for each minute they spend feeling resentful. You might think about that in your next weekend resentment binge, when you're not going to speak to anybody. You might want those six days back sometime.

As part of the fight-or-flight system common to all mammals, anger evolved to give us short bursts of energy for dealing with emergencies. It did not evolve to deal with the sustained stresses of daily modern life. For models of how anger is supposed to function, you need look no further than common house cats. When your cat gets angry, he'll arch his back, hiss, slash at the drapes, run through the house, or jump off the walls. But within five minutes, he's calmly licking himself like it never happened. If he was angry with you, he'll probably rub against your legs and purr. Like all mammals, he responds to his perception of a dangerous stimulus. Following his natural instincts, he either corrects his perception (there's not really a threat), manipulates the stimulus (attacks or runs away), or adapts to it ("Well, the dog has to live here, too"), all of which render the anger unnecessary. As quickly as it came over him, it's gone.

Humans are the only animals with anger-resentment problems because *we* don't do anger the right way. We go home and *think* about it. We think of how it *should* have been and how *unfair* it is that it wasn't that way. We think of how we were disregarded, devalued, disrespected, or rejected because things weren't the way they should have been. We'll fantasize: "When she said *that* to me, I should have said *this* to her. Then she would have said *that*, and I would have said *this*! She would have replied with . . . and I would have *screamed!*" This kind of imaginary dialogue can go on for hours and usually will, until replaced by something else to complain about. Nothing breeds resentment like resentment.

Resentment keeps you in a chronically devalued state of mind. When you feel resentful, you generally feel bad and, because you're hyperreactive to other people, you're not able to act according to your deepest values. If you stay mired in resentment long enough, you're sure to develop a *victim identity*, in which you identify with the damage done to you by someone else's bad behavior. Considering yourself damaged will have profoundly negative effects on your health, well-being, growth, and development. For one thing, it channels much of your emotional energy into fantasies of revenge rather than strategies for growth and healing. It keeps you obsessed with the person or persons who damaged you. Worst of all, your sense of self becomes a *monument* to someone else's bad behavior. It's no accident that people with victim identity so often feel empty when not resentful or depressed. Too much of their inner life has become a monument to other people's thoughtlessness, insensitivity, or abuse.

Responding to criticism about calling people victims, advocates have encouraged use of the word *survivor*. But this semantic change doesn't resolve the central problem. Your sense of self is still organized around your reaction to someone else's bad behavior, which still makes you susceptible to all the negative health effects of resentment. Think of it this way: Before you entered a resentful, angry, or abusive relationship, did you identify with being a loving and compassionate person or with being damaged or having survived someone's damaging behavior? To reverse the negative effects of walking on eggshells, you must reclaim the person you were and grow from there. The goal of healing is to have whatever harm you've suffered become the *least* important thing about you. Other people's behavior is not about you at all. Only your core value is about you.

Compassion for Yourself

It is not your fault that you have thorns in your heart that cause you resentment and anger. But it is your responsibility to remove the thorns and to heal the wounds before they leave scars. If that sounds unfair, think of it this way. If I were stabbed right now, my pain would be understandable and certainly not my fault as my assailant is to blame for my injury. But while I am not to blame, I am responsible to heal my own wound. My body, not my assailant, must do the healing. When you are psychologically injured, your mind, not your assailant, must do the healing, with compassion for yourself.

If you *choose* to heal—and it is certainly your choice—you make the choice out of compassion for yourself, with awareness that your emotional health and well-being are more important than anyone else's resentment, anger, or abuse.

Self-compassion is feeling sympathy for your hurt, with a desire to heal and improve. Your sympathy activates for your sense of *humanity*, which makes you human and allows you to love and create value. It may sound paradoxical, but the sympathy you feel makes you stronger and less vulnerable, even though it stems from your innate vulnerability. Here's an example: When you experience your husband's resentment, anger, or abusive behavior, you likely feel core hurts—rejected, devalued, powerless, inadequate, or unlovable. With self-compassion, you recognize your core hurts, without trying to ignore or avenge them. Because it comes from your deepest humanity, your *sympathy* for having been hurt *makes* you feel lovable! It is *proof* that you are lovable! The bad behavior of your husband clearly reflects *his* inability to hold onto compassion and respect, *not* your inability to love or your unworthiness to be loved. Of course, you will still feel sad and disappointed by his behavior, but you will not feel a core hurt. Thus your interaction with him will be purely about *his* behavior, not *your* core value. *People's behavior always reflects the current state of their core value.*

Do's and Don'ts of Self-Compassion

Respect for self and others

- *Do* treat yourself and everyone else with respect.
  Don't ridicule yourself or anyone.

- *Do* listen to your heart and choose in your short- and long-term best interests.
  Don't ignore inner longings.

- *Do* appreciate your uniqueness and that of others.
  Don't compare people.

- *Do* appreciate deeper commonalities with all people.
  Don't look to exclude yourself or others from essential humanity.

- *Do* listen to others.
  Don't interrupt.

- *Do* reflect.
  Don't react.

- *Do* talk.
  Don't yell, scream, or lecture.

Regulation of impulses, emotions

- *Do* consider the consequences of acting on impulse.
  Don't punish yourself about possible consequences.

- *Do* take other people's perspectives and compare them with your own.
  Don't get locked in your own perspective.

- *Do* express deeper feelings.
  Don't express symptoms/defenses, e.g., shaming anger, anxiety, obsessions.

- *Do* be flexible.
  Don't be rigid.

- *Do* empower the self and others.
  Don't engage in power struggles.

- *Do* express problems accurately.
  Don't exaggerate or minimize.

- *Do* praise your specific effort or behavior.
  Don't praise the self in general.

- *Do* teach yourself how to *do* better.
  Don't shame or humiliate yourself or others for mistakes.

- *Do* consider how you can prevent the mistake in the future.
  Don't threaten or punish.

- *Do* criticize specific *behavior* at specific times.
  Don't criticize or label yourself or others (lazy, dumb, liar, etc.).

- *Do* enhance your strengths.
  Don't focus on your weaknesses.

The yoke of human kindness and wisdom

- *Do* maintain core value.
  Don't limp over core hurts.

- *Do* continually strive to heal core hurts.
  Don't punish yourself for having them.

- *Do* deeply accept yourself, even though you have things you want to change.
  Don't reject yourself because of the things you want to change.

Solution finding

- *Do* stay focused on *solutions*.
  Don't blame self or others.

- *Do* consider alternative solutions.
  Don't suppose there is only one right way to solve problems.

- *Do* brainstorm possible solutions.
  Don't dismiss ideas out of hand.

Emotional Healing

Emotional healing occurs when we activate core value in the experience of core hurts. When you feel devalued, for instance, you do something that makes you feel valuable. Anything else will fail to heal the hurt. For example, suppose your husband disagrees with something you say. (That happens occasionally, right?) His reaction is so negative that he doesn't want to hear anything more from you on the subject. You're likely to feel *devalued*. You can numb the core hurt with resentment or anger: "Who the hell is he to dismiss me like that? He's so rude and nasty!" This strategy may make you feel more powerful, but not more valuable. If you say those things out loud you will likely have a fight, which will not make you feel valuable. You could also numb or avoid the core hurt by drinking, taking drugs, or becoming obsessed with something, but none of these will make you feel more valuable. You could blame yourself and think, "Why should he listen to me, I'm stupid." Although self-blame makes the pain worse, it does allow you at least to take control of your punishment—it doesn't hurt as much if you do it to yourself first—but it will definitely not make you feel valuable.

So what *will* make you feel more valuable? Let's look at the core-value motivations one at a time.

1. You can *improve* the situation a little by stating your position again to your husband or by stating it to a friend. The clearer you are, the more irrational his response will seem to you. You can improve your *experience* of the situation by recognizing that your opinion does not require his validation.

2. You can *appreciate* your own resilience, your line of thinking, the sunset, your child's smile, a work of art, or *anything* else.

3. You can *connect* to your husband, at least mentally, by thinking of times when he was tolerant and when you could feel close to him. (This does not justify his intolerance, but *you* will feel more valuable and in control of your self-value, which is the most important thing.)

4. You can *protect* him, by forgoing your instinct and your *right*, to retaliate.

Any one of the above will make you feel more valuable. You'll come up with many more possibilities yourself, as soon as you focus on making yourself feel more valuable rather than on your pain or revenge. Similarly, when you feel unlovable, you must do something that will make you feel lovable; for example, you must be compassionate. (If you think of the qualities that make an adult lovable, you'll see that most are aspects of compassion.) Your compassion need not necessarily be for the person who has harmed you, but if you want to feel lovable, the easiest way is to be compassionate to *someone*—a child, friend, stranger—anyone will do. Once you have reconnected to this core value, your compassion will become the best defense you can possibly have in protecting you from a resentful, angry, or abusive partner. The following, a composite of dozens of cases that mark the beginning of recovery for women, illustrates this point.

Helen had lived for several years with her resentful, angry, and emotionally abusive husband, Phillip. Though he never overtly called her names or described her as stupid, she felt continually belittled and put down by his holier-than-thou attitude. When I met Phillip I had to agree that he seemed pretty self-righteous. As he would have put it, he had a "duty to give criticism where it is due." Phillip tried to numb his sense of inadequacy by implying (although he never said it) that there was something wrong with his wife for having emotional needs.

When I first saw Helen, it was clear that she was convinced that he was right; she felt there *was* something wrong with her. A short, slightly overweight woman with tired eyes and a face that would be pleasant were it not so pinched with worry, she seemed to be asking why she was confused, why she couldn't just accept what he told her.

"After all," she said, "he never shouts or calls me names. And he's very supportive of my career."

"So?" I asked.

"So there must be something wrong with me."

"Because you want to love and be loved? If that's a disease, there's a lot of it going around."

"I don't want to love this much," she said tearfully.

"Then stop," I said with a shrug.

She looked shocked at first but then got a little annoyed with me. "I can't just *stop*."

"If you can't stop, it must be who you are as a person."

"To be hurt?"

"To love. Your love isn't what's hurting you; the person you love is hurting you."

She was quiet for a long time, before asking with dread in her voice, "So I should leave him?"

"What is your love telling you to do?"

She seemed bewildered, trying to think of what I wanted her to say—an unavoidable side effect of walking on eggshells. "Is it telling me to let him go on hurting me?" she asked somewhat timidly.

"Love makes you concerned about the best interests of the person you love. Isn't that right?"

"Yes," she said cautiously.

"Is it good for him to hurt you?"

"He seems to enjoy it."

"Does he like himself when he hurts you?"

"He blames it on me. He says I'm too needy."

"Does he like himself when he blames you?"

"No. He's miserable all the time, when he's not drinking or obsessing about something."

"So is your love for him telling you to let him go on doing things that hurt him?"

"But he says that he only hurts me because I make him miserable. You're saying that he's miserable because he hurts me?"

"How can he *not* be miserable when he hurts someone he loves?"

"But doesn't that mean that he doesn't really love me, if he hurts me?"

"Does he hurt everybody he doesn't love?"

"No, of course not. I'm the only one he hurts."

"So it can't mean that he hurts you because he doesn't love you or he would hurt other people he doesn't love."

"He hurts me because he loves me?"

"He hurts you because he loves you *inadequately*. When he senses your emotional needs, he feels like a failure as a husband. Instead of doing better he blames his failure on you. You remind him how much of a failure he is, just by having your own emotions."

"He says I'm too needy."

"Well, I guess if you haven't eaten for three weeks you could say that you're 'too hungry,' but would that accurately describe your condition?"

"You mean I'm starving?"

"You have a hungry heart. *Anyone* would in your situation."

"Why doesn't he?"

"Sometimes it seems like starving a hungry heart will make you stronger. That's probably what he thinks—if he starves himself of love and compassion, he'll get stronger."

She was staring at me. "Does anything get stronger from starvation?" She shook her head.

"The other mystery of the hungry heart is the very thing that has you in this bind. It makes you think that if you could convince yourself that you don't really *want* food, you won't feel hungry. If you don't love him, you won't have a hungry heart. Now that's a mystery."

Now she was downright incredulous. "You're not saying that I should love him *more?*"

"Love him enough to recognize that his hurting you is killing what little sense of adequacy as a husband he has left. Love him enough to demand that he find it in his heart to value and respect you, according to his deepest values. He seriously violates his deepest values when he fails to value and respect you."

She seemed confused. "I don't think those are his deepest values."

"Go home and ask him to write down the answers to this question: 'What is the absolute *most* important thing about you as a person, as a husband, and as a father?' I guarantee he won't write anything about resentment or always having to win the argument or having to criticize and feel superior to you."

"If those are his deepest values, why can't I get him to respect and value me?"

"More important than getting him to respect and value you is getting you to respect and value yourself. If you do that, he has to react differently to you. That's your best chance of getting him to honor his own deeper values and become the loving person he wants to be deep in his heart. Unfortunately, you can't rely on him being able to do it. You have to develop your own core value, regardless of what he does. As you build more value into your life, you'll naturally gravitate toward people who can return your value. Hopefully it will be him, but that's up to him. If he can't do it or won't try, you will not feel too needy, or like you're crazy because you're a human being with a hungry heart. You will feel sad and disappointed if he can't become the man he wants to be, but you won't internalize his resentment, anger, or abuse, and you won't feel inadequate and unlovable just because he does."

She looked increasingly sad. "I probably have to leave him," she said. "But then he'll fall apart."

"He might well fall apart at first. But every time he says a harsh word to you or gives you the cold shoulder, or simply fails to value and respect you, he hates himself a little more. If he can't find himself by loving you, he'll have to do it by losing you. If he won't change, your leaving him is his only hope."

To my pleasant surprise, this story had a happy ending. Phillip successfully did the hard work of the Boot Camp and was able to once again act like the compassionate man Helen had married. I was surprised because I didn't think that he would ever see his presumed superiority as a defense against his pervasive feelings of inadequacy as a husband and provider. Fortunately, he proved me wrong.

Your Voice, Your Value, and Your Boundaries Emerge from *Within*

Once your sense of self has been weakened by walking on eggshells, it is all too easy to be overly influenced by well-meaning friends, therapists, and authors of self-help books. When you're unsure of your own voice, it is likely to be drowned out in the chorus of other people telling you what to think, how to feel, and what to do. A sure sign that this is happening to you is when you find yourself thinking of what your friends or therapist would say about a certain experience with your husband, *while* you're having it. If you hear other people's voices in your head, you are likely to feel inauthentic, no matter what the voices say. If you catch yourself thinking of how you will describe what your husband is doing while he's doing it—or shortly thereafter—stop immediately and go to your Core Value Bank. There you will feel authentic and respond to your husband accordingly.

The most common mistake that therapists and self-help books make is urging women to establish boundaries. On paper this sounds like good advice, since relationships that walk on eggshells certainly violate personal boundaries. The problem is not in the word *boundaries*, but in the word *establish*. Boundaries that are established will always seem artificial, like lines drawn in the sand. For example, my client Alexandra had seen several therapists who "taught her the skills to set boundaries," as she put it. So now she "stood up to him" (her husband), and said things like, "I will not accept this kind of behavior from you." And, "You will not talk to me like that." If he said something critical, she'd reply, "I am *not* someone you can criticize." If he sulked or shut down, she would say, "You will stop abusing me with your silence and talk to me now."

This strategy worked pretty well for Alexandra while she and her husband were in the offices of their various marriage counselors. With therapists there to contain her husband's emotions and coach him into an empathetic response, she felt validated. But how likely was it to work in the routine of daily life with someone addicted to blame? Amazingly, all the therapists thought that her previous failures "to set boundaries that are *heard*," were due to *her* lack of skill (and, presumably, the poor teaching of her previous therapists), and that if she just got it right, she would be successful.

The problem was not in her delivery but in the boundary-establishing strategy itself. Alexandra's boundary statements were lines in the sand, mere reactions to her husband, *not* expressions of her deepest values. Genuine boundaries define who you are as a person. They cannot be drawn on the outside by establishing what you do *not* want or by stating, however clearly, who you are *not*. They emerge from within, from who you are most essentially as a person—from your core value. Once Alexandra was firmly in touch with her core value, she knew who she was and no longer internalized her husband's resentment, anger, and abuse. It became so absurd for him to blame his own inadequacy on her that he *had* to give it up as a tactic. Through her own growth, she modeled for him how to regulate core hurts with core value and compassionately insisted that he do the same. He was able to do it also with the help of the Boot Camp exercises in Part III of this book. But had he been unable or unwilling, she was prepared to leave and allow him to heal on his own.

Your boundaries emerge from knowing who you are. They do not come from what you say. In your core value, you cannot feel as if you are to blame for your husband's inadequacies, so you will not be defensive. When you are not defensive, his mirror will reflect that his pain is telling *him* to improve, appreciate, connect, or protect. You do not have to draw lines in the sand that say who you are not when you know clearly who you are.

Friends, therapists, and authors *can* provide useful feedback about your judgment and behavior. But even here you must always keep in mind that their tastes, values, judgment, and personal agenda always dominate their feedback. What you *cannot* get from others is your core value, your *internal* sense of importance, value, worthiness, equality, and personal power—your ability to act according to your deepest values. These are too personal and too important to rely on the advice or behavior of others. They *must* be *self-regulated*. No matter how wise they are, your girlfriends, therapists, and favorite authors cannot circulate your blood, metabolize the cells of your body, or regulate your core value.

To know your own voice, you must understand your pain and not make the same mistake as your husband. Resentful, angry, and abusive people drastically misinterpret the message of their own pain. We'll go into this more in the Boot Camp section. For now, just know that the bad feelings your husband blames on you are telling *him* to improve, appreciate, connect, or protect, for those are the *only* things that can make him feel better. And *your* pain is giving you the exact same message. Even if your husband changes dramatically and replaces his resentment, anger, or abusive behavior with compassion, *you* still have to heed the message of *your* core hurts to improve, appreciate, connect, or protect. This means that your focus has to be on your own resources, not on your husband and not on outside supports. You can get occasional support from friends, counselors, or advocates, but outside sources cannot help you heal, because they cannot activate your core value. Only your own behavior can do that.

All of this is to say that the answers to the key questions of your life are within you, if you listen to your voice. For instance, *"How do I know that I deserve to be treated with value and respect, if my husband (or anyone else) does not respect and value himself enough to treat me well?"*

The answer is in your core value: *"I am worthy of respect and value because I respect and value others."*

"How do I know that I am worthy of love, when others don't treat me as if I am?" The answer is in your core value: *"I know that I'm worthy of love because I am compassionate."*

Replacing Resentment and Anger with Conviction

Anger and resentment are good motivators, but poor regulators of behavior. In other words, they'll get you to do things, but you won't do them well. And most of the things they get you to do are contrary to your best interests. *Conviction* is just as good a motivator, but it is also a wonderful regulator of behavior. With conviction you make fewer errors and tend to act in your best interests, in accordance with your deepest values. Conviction arises directly from your values, whereas resentment and anger are *de*valuing. Conviction is *for* something, like justice and fair treatment, while anger and resentment are *against* something, like injustice or unfair treatment. Those who hate injustice want retribution and triumph, not fairness; they fantasize about punishment of their unjust opponents, who must submit to humiliation. The fantasies of those who love justice are of equality, harmony, and triumphant good.

Being *for* something generates energy and creates positive feelings and relationships, while being *against* something depletes energy, creates negative feelings, and usually has deleterious effects on relationships—if you're resentful about something at work, you won't be as sweet to your kids when you get home.

- You have stopped walking on eggshells because it is the *right* thing to do and the *best* thing for you, your children, and your husband.
- You are not insisting on change to *spite* him.
- You are compassionately *demanding* value, respect, and compassion from him, because these are in the best interests of

your children, your husband, and yourself, *not* because he *shouldn't* get away with treating you badly.

- You are *for* the health and well-being of your family, not merely *against* your husband's resentful, angry, or abusive behavior.

You are guaranteed to feel more powerful when you move your focus from the behavior you do *not* want and the things you are *against* and focus squarely on the things you are *for* and the behavior you *want*.

Fully Taking Back Your Power: *Forgiving Yourself*

The most insidious aspect of resentment is anger at yourself. Think of how many times you have chastised yourself with thoughts like these:

Why did I trust him?
I should have known he would let me down.
What was I thinking, expecting him to change?
How could I have let it get like this?
I hate being a victim!
How could I have been so stupid?

The Great Lie of Resentment

Resentment *seems* to keep you safe from future hurt by lowering the trust you have for the people you resent. If you get mad enough—and punish yourself enough—you might not be "so stupid as to trust him again." But does your resentment in fact protect you from hurt? When you're resentful, do you get hurt more or less? Remember, resentment and anger toward someone you love is always resolved in guilt, shame, and anxiety, which are likely to make you to trust unwisely and thereby keep you swinging back and forth on a pendulum of pain.

A far more effective defense—and one consistent with your core value—is for you to *forgive yourself.* You're probably thinking, "Why do I have to forgive myself if *he* mistreated me?" Unfair though it may seem, you have to forgive yourself in order to:

- Overcome the unfair harm that being angry at yourself does to you.
- Increase the value you hold for yourself, which will automatically motivate you to act in your long-term best interests.
- Provide a more effective defense against hurt. (You are stronger when you value yourself than when you devalue yourself.)

Beginning Self-Forgiveness

Make a list of everything you resent about your husband. Identify the *deepest* core hurt stimulated by each item on the list.

1. I resent that he _____
_____.
    My deepest core hurt was:_____
2. I resent that he _____
_____.
    My deepest core hurt was:_____
3. I resent that he _____
_____
    My deepest core hurt was:_____
4. I resent that he _____
_____.
    My deepest core hurt was:_____
5. I resent that he _____
_____.
    My deepest core hurt was:_____
6. I resent that he _____
_____.
    My deepest core hurt was:_____

7. I resent that he _____

    _____ .

    My deepest core hurt was: _____

8. I resent that he _____

    _____ .

    My deepest core hurt was: _____

9. I resent that he _____

    _____ .

    My deepest core hurt was: _____

10. I resent that he _____

    _____ .

    My deepest core hurt was: _____

Self-Forgiveness Exercise

Item 1. I forgive myself for losing sight of my core value and feeling (name core hurt): _____ , when he _____ .

Item 2. I forgive myself for losing sight of my core value and feeling (name core hurt): _____ , when he _____ .

Item 3. I forgive myself for losing sight of my core value and feeling (name core hurt): _____ , when he _____ .

Item 4. I forgive myself for losing sight of my core value and feeling (name core hurt): _____ , when he _____ .

Item 5. I forgive myself for losing sight of my core value and feeling (name core hurt): _____ , when he _____ .

Item 6. I forgive myself for losing sight of my core value and feeling (name core hurt): _____ , when he _____ .

Item 7. I forgive myself for losing sight of my core value and
    feeling (name core hurt): _____ ,
    when he _____ .

Item 8. I forgive myself for losing sight of my core value and
    feeling (name core hurt): _____ ,
    when he _____ .

Item 9. I forgive myself for losing sight of my core value and
    feeling (name core hurt): _____ ,
    when he _____ .

Item 10. I forgive myself for losing sight of my core value and
    feeling (name core hurt): _____ ,
    when he _____ .

Now read your self-forgiveness list out loud, and feel the power and value in your voice.

Summary

You have an absolute right to be resentful and angry, but exercising that right will only keep the thorns in your heart. You have a more compelling right to heal the wounds you've suffered. You can heal with compassion for yourself, with sympathy for your own hurt, and with the motivation to heal and improve. Emotional healing is replacing your core hurts to your core value, so that you can realize your fullest potential as the loving, compassionate, competent, creative, person you are meant to be.

Seven

Developing Your Natural Sense of Self, Competence, and Growth

When you have to put so much effort into preventing your husband's blowups or cold shoulders, you're likely to have trouble appreciating your own competence and holding onto a semblance of the self-confidence you once had. Understanding and having compassion for your recurring self-doubt is the first step to gaining certainty, conviction, and confidence. To understand your self-doubt, you only have to consider what it takes to undermine *anyone's* sense of competence and confidence:

- Frequent criticism
- Anxiety
- Repeated rejection (your perspective is blown off, dismissed, trivialized, or ignored)
- Internal messages that you can't do things right or aren't worthy

All of these come from walking on eggshells. To undo their pervasive negative effects, we'll take them one at a time.

Criticism

The Boot Camp section of this book shows your husband how to stop criticizing you. This chapter shows you how to neutralize the negative effects of being criticized, which you can and need to do whether he stops or not.

For the first exercise, think of when you were a young child. You've made a mistake, for which you were criticized or punished. Try to imagine the criticism or punishment in as much detail as you can, and write down what you thought and felt at the time:

Now take a moment to invoke the emotions of your Core Value Bank. Imagine comforting the distressed child in the desert. Think of the most important thing about you as a person and the most important thing about your life in general. Feel the love you have for the people closest to you. Feel your spiritual connection. Think of something beautiful in nature. Think of your favorite art or music. Imagine a community you feel comfortable with, and think of three compassionate things you have done.

While you are in touch with your core value and compassion, write what you would like to tell that criticized or punished child (being sure to tell her what she does right):

(If you're stuck, here's a consensus of what dozens of my clients have written: "You're okay. You love your parents. You're good to people. You're good to your dog. You're smart. You're caring. You have a good heart.")

Rejection by Stonewalling

Most men can make their partners walk on eggshells just by *stonewalling*—a punishing form of emotional withdrawal or shut-down in which they refuse even to consider another perspective. If they listen at all, they do it dismissively or contemptuously. The message is clear: You don't have anything to say that's worth hearing. Such men might refer to their wives as a nag, or garbage mouth, or just choose to ignore them. Or they might say, "Do whatever you want, just leave me alone."

The following can help protect you from the hurtful effects of stonewalling. Think of when you were a young child and you were stonewalled by your parents, siblings, or caregiver. They didn't care about how you felt or what you thought. If you tried to get their attention, you would be ignored, blown-off, or put down. Write down what you felt at the time.

Now take a moment to invoke the emotions of your Core Value Bank. Imagine comforting the distressed child in the desert. Think of the most important thing about you as a person and the most important thing about your life in general. Feel the love you have for the people closest to you, even, for the most part, your critical husband. Feel your spiritual connection. Think of something beautiful in nature. Think of your favorite art or music. Imagine a community you feel comfortable with, and think of the three compassionate things you have done.

From your core value, write what you would like to tell that ignored, blown-off, or put down child (think of what that child needed to hear about how her thoughts and feelings *mattered*):

(If you're stuck, here's a consensus of what some clients have written: "What you have to say matters. When I hear you say what's important to you, *I* feel more important. Your talk contributes so much to my life.")

If this applies to you, think of a time when you were a young child and you felt overwhelmed by the emotional demands of some adult. You felt trapped, like they wouldn't leave you alone. You couldn't be yourself or have your own thoughts and feelings without them trying to dominate you. Write down how you felt:

Take a moment to invoke the emotions of your Core Value Bank. Imagine comforting the distressed child in the desert. Think of the most important thing about you as a person and the most important thing about your life in general. Feel the love you have for the people closest to you, even for the most part, your stonewalling husband. Feel your spiritual connection. Think of something beautiful in nature. Think of your favorite art or music. Imagine a community you feel comfortable with, and think of the three compassionate things you have done.

From your core value, write what you would like to tell that overwhelmed child:

(If you're stuck, here's a consensus of what some clients have written: "I'll protect you and help you find the strength in yourself to cope. We can make each other strong—that's how important you are to me.")

Internal "Failure Messages"

Whenever you are about to do something, your motivational system gives off an *internal impulse* to prepare you for a task that you need to do. Largely unconscious, an action-impulse can start a simple behavior, like picking up a sock from the floor, or a complex one, like making dinner. Internal impulses are almost mechanical in nature and devoid of psychological meaning. *How* we behave when we get the impulse can tell us something about ourselves, but *not* the internal impulse.

Now here's the problem: If you have internalized your husband's (or anyone else's) criticism or stonewalling, you have probably developed a litany of internal "failure messages." These are voices in your head that say things like, "I can't do this," or, "I'll screw it up for sure," or, "It's too hard," or, "I'm an idiot," or, "I'm not worthy." Words like these can stay with you for a lifetime, after they attach to an *internal impulse*. Then every time you have an impulse to do something, you might also think you can't do it right. You might get these defeatist messages hundreds of times in the course of a day.

Husbands don't appreciate the subliminal effect that criticism has on their wives, and parents don't grasp how it affects their children. Even though the number of critical remarks he makes to you or your kids might be small, you and they repeat them in your heads over and over again. Research shows that there must be a ratio of five positive statements for *every one* criticism, just to get back to ground zero. I believe the ratio is more like nine positive statements to one criticism in families that walk on eggshells.

How We Learn

Regardless of where you first heard them, harmful words may have caused you to misinterpret another kind of internal impulse, to learn by making mistakes. We learn good judgment from our own indiscretions, not, alas, from our parents' mistakes. Toddlers cannot learn to walk except by falling. In fact, parents who have too little tolerance of their toddlers falling and try excessively to help them balance their weight can interfere with their skeletal-muscular development.

The human brain is programmed to learn from trials and errors. For example, we learn to judge distances after many mistaken estimates. Think of how you would learn to pitch horseshoes. Unless you have blind luck, your first attempt to pitch a horseshoe either falls too short or goes beyond the mark. The second attempt overcompensates in the opposite direction. The *third* attempt has the best chance of being a ringer. If you see this sequence as three separate attempts with two failures and only one success, your life will be hard. Your brain *naturally* sees it as one successful attempt with two estimate or learning steps.

Think of any defeatist internal signals you might have as *corrective feedback*, telling you to focus, take care, be careful, learn more, and increase your ability to cope.

The True Messages of Anxiety:
Focus, Take Care, Learn More,
Increase Ability to Cope

Next to resentment, anxiety may be the most misunderstood of all emotions. It's a feeling that something bad might happen and that you will not be able or willing to cope. Misinterpreting the true message of your anxiety keeps you walking on eggshells.

Actually, anxiety is an important, useful emotion. Without it, you would be killed crossing the street. It's a response to a real, imagined, or anticipated *change* in the environment. It tells you to *focus*, to figure out how to deal with the change. Mental focus means shutting out all information-processing except that which is immediately useful to solving the problem. For example, a fire in the room stirs anxiety to get you to stop thinking about what you'll wear to the party tonight, so you can focus on how to put out the fire.

Anxiety becomes a problem if it stimulates an underlying feeling of incompetence, caused by core hurts of powerlessness and inadequacy. In other words, you don't *know* what to do, and your brain doesn't know what to focus on. So it begins to *scan*, which means it takes in a lot more surface information a lot more rapidly, with little discernment of what is relevant. Your thoughts race forward like a runaway freight train. The scanning process itself raises anxiety as the problem seems more and more unsolvable in the flurry of possibilities, most of which are unrelated and improbable. That's why, research shows, raising someone's anxiety about making mistakes causes them to make more. You may have noticed this with your children. If you or your husband yells at them for making mistakes, you can bet that they'll keep making the same mistakes over and over. Yelling at children to be careful after they've dropped a glass, for instance, makes them associate anxiety with picking up the glass. Instead of focusing on how to pick it up, they start to *scan* when they get near it and pay less attention to what they're doing and more to what they're thinking. Of course, this increases the likelihood of dropping the glass. (To get them to focus, calmly tell them, "When you pick up the glass, be sure that you can feel it in the palm of your hand.")

Scanning inevitably produces:

- **Conflicting Interpretations:** The anxiety you feel when your husband works late at night gives rise to the interpretation that he may have had an accident or injury and conflicting ones that he is neglecting you, abandoning you, or being unfaithful to you. At the same time that you want to help him, you want to kill him.

- **Uncertainty:** This feels like, "I'm not sure what it means, but it's probably not good."

- **Vacillation:** In one moment the flowers he sent you mean that he loves you and in the next that he's feeling guilty about loving someone else. One moment they mean that he's sweet and thoughtful and in the next that he's setting you up for manipulation, and so on.

Conflicting interpretations, uncertainty, and vacillation only raise self-doubt, lower confidence, and keep you walking on eggshells. The practice of HEALS™, a technique developed to deal with high arousal emotions, will help you regulate the core hurts of powerlessness and inadequacy that aggravate anxiety. (It's presented in the Boot Camp section.) But it takes several weeks of practicing HEALS to make your response automatic. In the meantime, try to see your anxiety for what it is—a signal to focus, learn more about the situation, and increase your ability to cope. The first step in correctly interpreting the signal of your anxiety is to appreciate your competence.

Appreciating Your Competence

Scientific studies of people who have a well-developed sense of competence have taught us a few things about it. Competent people are able to do tasks that are *important* to them *reasonably well*. "Important to them" is the key. People simply do not perform unimportant tasks as well as they perform tasks that are important to them. You make more emotional investment and use more mental resources in performing tasks that you feel are important; for the less important ones, you tend to run on automatic pilot. If your husband says or implies that you are incompetent, he is saying either that something is more important to him than it is to you or that you are not perfect.

And that brings us to the second part of the concept of competence: that one is able to perform important tasks *reasonably well*. Competence does not mean *perfect* performance, it means *good enough* performance. Studies show that perfectionists generally do not feel competent. The measure of *good enough* is always just out of their reach, so nothing ever seems right to them. When your perfectionist husband says or implies that you are incompetent, he

really means that *he* doesn't feel competent, as he can never do anything perfectly. Thus he tries to hold you to a standard of perfec-
tion, which, in his heart, he knows that *he* cannot meet.

Like everything else that is important about you, your sense of
competence is *internal,* and you need to get in touch with it within
yourself—whether or not your husband ever recognizes the folly of
his ways. Always remember, your sense of competence comes from
your core value. Use your Core Value Bank before attempting a
task that's especially important to you.

You are competent because you cope with most day-to-day
tasks and solve most of the problems that are important to you
and within your control. You look for solutions, for ways to make
a situation better; you view mistakes merely as feedback to correct your course of action. In your core value, you know you feel
able, confident, eager, enthusiastic, and realistically optimistic.
Whenever you are thoughtful, solution-oriented, smart, and self-
regulating, you reinforce your sense of competence. The following seven tips can help you appreciate it more:

1. Take responsibility for everything you do, think, and feel.
   Always take responsibility for solutions to your problems.
   Taking responsibility only for solutions (rather than blame for
   causes) gives you power.

2. Focus on what you can control—your ability to improve, appreciate, connect, or protect—rather than what you cannot control,
   such as the opinions and behavior of your husband.

3. *Think* in terms of solutions rather than problems. Be *flexible,*
   think multiple solutions—there's almost always more than one.

4. Realize genuine confidence—if you make a mistake, you can fix
   it. (Research shows that once you give yourself permission to
   make mistakes, you'll make fewer.)

5. Step back and see things in wider contexts, observing the complexity of issues.

6. Stand or sit up straight and take up as much room as possible.

7. Smile as often as you can.

Tips 6 and 7 need explanation: You may have noticed that whenever people feel helpless or dependent, they tend to curl up, arms pressed against the side, bent over slightly, taking up as little room as possible. Their posture takes the form of a hurt child. Very often a simple adjustment in posture makes you feel more competent. Stand or sit up straight; take up as much room as possible, and you are more likely to feel empowered.

Why should you smile more, even when you don't feel like it? Recent discoveries about neuropeptides—the molecules that carry emotional messages throughout the body—suggest that smiling is a two-way street. When you are happy, your brain sends a message to the muscles around the mouth to smile. But surprisingly, whenever you smile the muscles around the mouth send the same message to the brain. It doesn't have to be a whopping, toothy grin; the slightest of smiles will help you appreciate your competence as well as your other wonderful attributes.

If you walk on eggshells, you almost certainly underestimate your personal competence. To get a more realistic view of yourself, take a moment to think of all the things that you do to keep your job and your home running smoothly. Be sure to include everything you do for your family. Fill out the following, then read it out loud and appreciate your outstanding level of competence.

My Competence List:
A Few of the Many Things I Do with *Competence*

_____

_____

_____

_____

_____

_____

_____

_____

_____

_____

_____

_____

_____

_____

_____

_____

_____

_____

Appreciating Your Ability to Grow, Create, and Nurture Yourself

Growth is the ability to learn, appreciate, achieve, expand, and experience. Creativity in a basic psychological sense does not necessarily mean making works of art or craft. It means the ability to take different perspectives when necessary to solve a problem. (If you think about it, we admire artists for helping us see the world from new perspectives.) The most creative people are those who can introduce new perspectives to gain a deeper understanding or more satisfying outcome.

Self-nurturing or self-care means simply meeting your physical and psychological needs. Part of it is simple: eat reasonably well, drink in moderation, exercise, and take mental health days for relaxation and enjoyment. On a deeper level, it includes tending to the garden of your spirit by staying true to your core value.

There are no limits to your ability to appreciate and expand intellectually, emotionally, and spiritually. You can *learn* anything. To reverse the negative effects of walking on eggshells, you will have to constantly ask yourself how you can grow through this, how you can expand your perspectives and become ever stronger and smarter.

Practice *healing imagery*. One of the more exciting areas of research in physical and psychological healing is in the area of imagery. Healing imagery is just what it sounds like—you *imagine* yourself healing. The practice has been shown to boost the immune system significantly and speed recovery from disease and emotional disorders, including bone fractures, anxiety, mild depression, and even some cancers.

Take a moment to think of what it's like when you feel helpless and dependent: "I can't, I don't know how, it's too much for me, I need someone to take care of me, I need someone to feel okay about me."

Now invoke the emotions of your Core Value Bank. Help and comfort a child in the desert, realize the most important things about you, feel your love for certain people, your spiritual and communal connections, the beauty of nature and art, and think of compassionate things you have done. Feel the light of core value. *Imagine yourself enhanced, strengthened, expanded, solidified, through your core value, into your true sense of competence.*

Take a moment to think of a time you felt sad and depressed. Remember how inadequate, defective, or exploited you felt.

Now invoke the emotions of your Core Value Bank. Help and comfort a child in the desert, realize the most important things about you, feel your love for certain people, your spiritual and communal connections, the beauty of nature and art, and think of compassionate things you have done. Feel the light of core value. *Imagine that you are taking care of yourself and healing, as if gentle healing rays of light emanate from your core value and spread throughout your body and spirit, melting away the heavy cloud of depression.*

Power Mode Journals

Rebuilding your sense of competence, growth, creativity, healing, and nurturing is an incremental process. It helps to think of each of these qualities as *power modes*, in which you think, feel, and behave according to your long-term best interests. Use the following journal to add an enhancement to each of your power modes. Fill it out once a week to help you appreciate how valuable and powerful you are.

Power Mode Journal Example

List **3** enhancements of your **Compassionate** mode:

I validate my loved ones' feelings, even when I disagree with their perspectives.

I listen to loved ones without judging them.

I help others without expecting gratitude in return.

List **2** enhancements of your **Heal/Nurture** mode:

I acknowledge all my emotions, even those I want to change.

I take regular periods of relaxation, in which I keep my worries "in a box," until my strength has increased to levels that allow maximal solutions.

List **1** enhancement of your **Growth/Creative** mode:

When waiting in lines, I practice noticing the body language of other people.

List **1** enhancement of your **Competent** mode:

I always know that whatever comes up, even if it's unpleasant, I'll be able to handle it and eventually solve the problem.

Your Power Mode Journal

List **3** enhancements of your **Compassionate** mode:

List **2** enhancements of your **Heal/Nurture** mode:

List **1** enhancement of your **Growth/Creative** mode:

List **1** enhancement of your **Competent** mode:

A Few of the Things I Do to Grow Intellectually, Emotionally, or Spiritually:

_____

_____

_____

_____

_____

_____

_____

_____

_____

_____

_____

_____

_____

_____

_____

_____

_____

_____

Examples of My Creativity (looking at different perspectives):

_____

_____

_____

_____

_____

_____

_____

_____

_____

_____

_____

_____

_____

_____

_____

_____

_____

_____

A Few Examples of My Self-Nurturing (meeting my physical and psychological needs):

_____

_____

_____

_____

_____

_____

_____

_____

_____

_____

_____

_____

_____

_____

_____

_____

Postscript to Part II

Before men realized that there were practical ways that they could learn to change, before they had that hope, only a handful of the more than 3,000 resentful, angry, and abusive men I treated had sought help on their own, without their wives or the courts pressuring them. They haven't volunteered in the past because, in their addiction to blame, they thought they were merely *reacting* to their wives. I'd like you to try to accept that, while there are clearly a lot of problems with your husband's reactivity, there's some good news in it too: When you approach him firmly in your core value, he will most likely change in *reaction* to you. It's awfully hard to be resentful, angry, or abusive to someone who is compassionate to you. This will not be enough to make him as compassionate and loving as you deserve—he has to develop *his* core value to be that. Nevertheless, if you approach him firmly in your core value, you will be able to insist, with compassion, that he read at least the Boot Camp and Resurrection sections, do all its exercises, and master the HEALS technique. Once he's mastered HEALS, he will automatically go to his core value and have compassion for you whenever he feels resentful, angry, or abusive.

Tough Love

The tone of the Boot Camp is healing, not accusatory, compassionate not blaming, valuing not devaluing, and empowering not disempowering. It offers the most promising path for him to realize the loving and compassionate person he has the inner capacity to become. But you may well face a challenge in getting him to do the work. The hard fact is that you may have to leave him to motivate him. If he is violent or threatens violence, call the police or file for a civil protection order. (Most communities have domestic violence hotlines to help you.) These may seem like drastic steps, but they are the most *compassionate* things you can do. Your tough-love demands are likely to be the only way to help him stop behavior that makes him lose his humanity.

The process of change will not be easy for him. For it to succeed, he has to love you and value your relationship enough to put everything he has into it. He must know from the outset that, one way or another, you are prepared to stop walking on eggshells.

Beware of a Quick Fix

He's read the Boot Camp section, done all the exercises, and mastered HEALS. He's behaving differently toward you and your children. You're seeing definite change. You're sure that you are no longer walking on eggshells. But will it last?

No doubt you have experienced honeymoon periods in the past, when he was driven by remorse and seemed to change. He treated you with more value and respect. You felt closer. Everything was fine for a while. But gradually the resentment returned, bringing with it the old irritability, cold shoulders, control, sarcasm, stonewalling, blowups, angry glares, or disgusted looks. Your consistent self-editing and second-guessing returned, and once again, you were walking on eggshells.

What to Look For to Know When Change Is Permanent

You should notice after he does the work of the Boot Camp that he consistently (*everyday*):

- *Values* and *appreciates* you—you are *important* to him.
- *Listens* to you.
- Shows *interest* in you.
- Is *compassionate* when you need him to be.
- *Cares* about how you feel, even when you disagree with him.
- *Respects* you as an equal and doesn't try to control you or dismiss your opinions.
- Shows *affection* without always expecting sex.
- *Regulates* his guilt, shame, anxiety, resentment, and anger, without blaming them on you.
- *Shares* his progress by showing you all his homework from the Boot Camp, including the relapse prevention chapter, which he should review at least once a month.

He doesn't have to be interested in the things you're interested in, but he has to be interested *that you are interested* in them. For example, a friend of mine doesn't like flower shows, but he likes that his wife likes them. He enjoys seeing her enjoy herself.

If you have seen his ongoing desire for positive change in your relationship, the Resurrection section of this book will give you useful things to work on *together* to have the loving and compassionate relationship you deserve.

Note well: If he has not read the Boot Camp but has entered into some kind of counseling or therapy, you still want to look for the changes above to assess whether any gains he might make are likely to last. In the unhappy event that he refuses to do anything to change, you will probably have to skip to Appendix I, which tells you what to do if your relationship doesn't make it.

PART III

The Boot Camp

Introduction to the Boot Camp

Resentment, anger, and abuse are infections of the heart. They attack the very foundation of our humanity, which is our ability to form bonds of compassion and love with the most important persons in our lives. This Boot Camp approach to healing the heart is an intensive "psychosurgery." Like physical surgery, it produces dramatic change in a short time. We *cut out* the infection, instead of treating it with a little bit of salve administered weekly over many months, as in traditional therapy. If you were to treat your problem an hour or two at a time every week or so you would set yourself up for failure. As it is, after each brief intervention session, most men go home to a tense atmosphere to try to use concepts they are not completely clear about and have not had time to master. The next week they go back to therapy or group feeling like failures. The therapist or instructor spends most of the next session trying to undo the damage done between sessions. Progress is painfully slow and tenuous. Even when longer treatments work, which is less than half the time, they take quite a while to show progress. Meanwhile, the suffering at home continues for months on end.

We call our intensive approach Boot Camp, because it is very much like basic training in the military. As a recruit, you undergo rigorous exercises that teach you to regulate your emotions. You build skills for dealing with anger and resentment that will hold under the stress of conflicts with your wife. Our live Boot Camps take eight hours a day for three consecutive days. But you should not have to attend a live Boot Camp, as long as you do the work outlined in these pages. Unless you have complicating conditions, like drinking, taking drugs, a childhood history of violence, or head injuries that caused loss of consciousness (brain lesions can create a hair-trigger response of anger), you should need little or no intervention beyond carefully reading the Boot Camp and Resurrection sections, doing *all* the exercises, and mastering HEALS, which, after a few weeks of practice, eliminates most resentment and virtually all abusive impulses. (If you do need extra help, ample resources are available online at CompassionPower.com.)

Do It for Yourself, Your Wife, and Your Children

This written version of the Boot Camp includes eight chapters, filled with exercises that will help you overcome resentment, anger, and all inclinations to be sarcastic, devaluing, rejecting, verbally aggressive, or emotionally abusive to your wife. The work is not easy—you have to believe that your family's happiness is worth the effort.

What you learn in these pages will help you to heal your considerable wounds, which your resentment or anger has masked—you probably do not know how hurt you really are. You must heal yourself, even if you cannot save your marriage. If it is still possible to save your marriage—and the fact that your wife gave you this book is a promising sign that it is—the Resurrection Section that follows the Boot Camp is three chapters of work that you and your wife can do together, to repair your relationship.

Traditionally, men who are resentful, angry, or abusive enter treatment almost exclusively by court mandate or wife mandate. In other words, they have to be threatened with jail or with their wives leaving before they "submit" to treatment. It is nothing short of revolutionary for resentful and angry men, let alone those who are also verbally and emotionally abusive, to come forward and ask for help—as thousands have done to participate in my Boot Camps . . . and as you are doing by working with this book. I believe that this new phenomenon of thousands of men asking for help has happened becuase they have heard that this Boot Camp works. Previously, men have denied their abuse and struggle with anger because they saw no hope for change. Now, there's hope and a process that works.

How to Use the Boot Camp and Resurrection Sections

First read the next 11 chapters all the way through, then go back and do all the exercises of the Boot Camp section and begin to practice HEALS. After two to three weeks of practicing HEALS, ask your wife if she is ready to do the couples work described in the Resurrection section. Or, you may need a full six weeks of practicing these skills before they become automatic.

Although it will not be easy, thousands of men have been able to heal themselves and save their marriages with these methods. Most of those who were not able to save their marriages became good co-parents with their ex-wives and used the skills they learned to make their next relationship healthier, happier, more loving, and more compassionate.

Good luck and work hard.

Eight

Commitment to Healing

Your wife most likely bought this book because she sometimes feels like she walks on eggshells around you, in the hope that you won't criticize, ignore, yell, complain, reject her, or give her the silent treatment. I'm sure you don't realize how often you do these things. The fact is you don't have to do them very often to get your partner in the habit of walking on eggshells; doing them now and then is just as bad as doing them all the time. The damage is done not so much by the frequency of the negative incidents as by her constant worry that you *might* do them. She feels that she constantly edits her thoughts and behaviors and second-guesses her own judgment, to the point where she sometimes feels like she has lost any real sense of herself.

If you're like the more than 3,000 men I have treated, I'm pretty sure that you don't *want* her to feel like she has to walk on eggshells. But you have to know that, if she does feel that way, she doesn't like the person she's become in your marriage. And if she doesn't like who she's become, it's almost certain that you don't like the person you've become either. That's a strong statement. To test whether it applies to you, ask yourself two questions:

1. Is your relationship the way you thought it would be before you got married?
2. Are you the husband you wanted to be before you got married?

You don't have to agree with your wife's perceptions of *why* she walks on eggshells, but you do have to *care* that she feels bad. You also have to understand and care that *you* feel bad. You have to understand and care that you have isolated yourself from the most important adult in your life. *And above all, you have to understand and care about how deeply your interactions with your wife affect your children.*

Most of what you have tried to do in the past to make things better has made them worse. So don't waste your energy even thinking about how *she* has to change, too—you have no control over that. If you focus on things you cannot control, like your wife's behavior, you will certainly feel powerless and inadequate most of the time. Real personal power comes from *focusing on what you can control, from acting in your best interests.* You feel empowered when you control how *you* behave, in accordance with *your deepest values.* Hence the primary rule of this Boot Camp is that you hold the magnifying glass on *you* and think exclusively of how *you* can do better, regardless of what your wife does. In fact, the only way you can influence your wife to change is by *you* changing for the better.

Grow Beyond "It Takes One to Know One"

You're probably thinking, "She blames, rejects, and criticizes me, too." Well, if you want to feel genuinely powerful and valuable, you have to outgrow the schoolyard mentality of, "It takes one to know one." This childish stance makes you feel utterly powerless because it implies that *you* can't do better until *she* does better. Genuine power is seizing responsibility for making things at least a little better on your own, whether or not your spouse is able to help.

In this Boot Camp, we live by a modified Judgment Day principle: When you die and go to judgment, they won't ask you what your *wife* did. In the Boot Camp, we won't ask what you *did* so much as what you can *do* to make your life better.

Gender Factors in Resentment, Anger, and Abuse

Many guys feel that men are unfairly singled out as "offenders," even though some studies show that women are just as angry as men, and some are more resentful, more verbally aggressive, equally violent, and slightly more emotionally abusive. While these findings are true in terms of the *incidents* of resentful, angry, and abusive behavior, they don't reflect the harsher truth that the *damage* done by men is almost always greater. The reasons are apparent when you consider the results of violent behavior—a slap or punch by a woman is unlikely to do as much damage as a slap or punch by a man. In the case of emotional abuse and verbal aggression, the greater damage done by men is due largely to how we're built. Masculine *physiology* powerfully enhances the negative effects of resentful, angry, or abusive behavior.

The males of all species of social animals have greater muscle mass, quicker reflexes, and deeper, more resonant voices, specifically designed for *roaring*. The voice box actually swells when a man gets angry, which is why he wants to scream in traffic. His voice gets deeper, louder, and more menacing. The angry male voice is designed to envoke fear, whether you want it to or not. Angry women can sound shrill or unpleasant, but rarely will their voices envoke fear in men. In addition, angry or resentful males—of all species of social mammals—experience considerably more blood flow to their muscles with higher levels of central nervous system activity than angry females. The males of all species of social animals, including early humans, developed a defensive strategy of forming perimeters around the threatened tribe or pack, puffing up their muscles and roaring—to warn, threaten, intimidate, and envoke fear in potential opponents.

Female Physiology

To make matters worse, fear-inducing behavior is enhanced by two factors in *female physiology*. The females of most species of social animals have a lower threshold of fear than males. That means they go into involuntary fear reactions at a much lower stimulus and stay in them much longer. What's more, activation of the fear response increases sensitivity to what the brain quickly comes to perceive as a threatening environment. It's relatively easy to control a woman with fear, even when you don't want to. In contrast, men, particularly young men, experience little fear of harm, which is why they engage in so many risky behaviors. This difference between the sexes in their visceral fear of harm, and with the fear-envoking physiology of men combine to make resentful, angry, or abusive behavior more damaging when done by men than by women.

Women perceive facial expressions in more detail than men and they are particularly sensitive to the emotional features of resentment, anger, or aggression—to a woman, it's written all over your face. When you shout, glare, scowl, or grit your teeth around your wife it is likely to make her anxious, even though that is not your intention. You might know in your heart that you are not going to hurt her, but her fear response is *involuntary*—she *cannot* control it. In contrast, I have seen many men who were victims of emotional and physical abuse by their female partners, but I can't remember any who were living in fear of their wives or who felt controlled or oppressed by their fear. The greater physical power of men gives us the greater responsibility to regulate resentment, anger, and any impulse to devalue, criticize, or abuse.

She'll Remember

One other inequality between the sexes makes women more susceptible to walking on eggshells. How many times have you thought to yourself, "She doesn't forget a thing!" Well, you're right. Studies show that women are likely to recall emotional incidents and to reexperience the emotion while they recall it. Men are more likely to forget emotional incidents altogether or to recall them with little of the original emotion This means that your wife's brain, through no fault of her own, will play back fear-inducing incidents over and over and be reminded of them more easily. This means that the negative effects of your behavior are multiplied many times by your wife's tendency to replay it again in her head. But remember, she doesn't want it that way anymore than you do—it is extremely hard to stop involuntary responses.

I am quite certain that you did not realize the full psychological effects of your resentment, anger, or abusive tendencies on your wife and children. But now that you do realize it, you have a better idea of why your marriage is in trouble and why you have to work hard to save it. There are two things you can do immediately to help your wife overcome the negative effects of walking on eggshells. The first and most important is showing compassion.

My Commitment to Be Compassionate to You

My signature on this document obligates me to make a supreme effort to be compassionate with you. I will try hard to understand and sympathize with your perspective. If I disagree with it, I will *respectfully* tell you how I disagree. I will care when you are hurt or uncomfortable. I will not criticize you, or ignore you, talk over you, or try to make you feel bad in any way. I will not try to control, manipulate, coerce, threaten, or intimidate you in any way. I will always treat you with value and respect.

Signature: _____

Building Personal Power and Value *Within*

The second thing you can do to help your wife stop walking on eggshells is to make a firm commitment to *improve*. In the next pages and chapters you will learn many positive—even pleasant— ways to modify your emotions and behavior. Learning and practicing these new skills will enhance your sense of self. Your self-esteem will grow as you experience genuine pride and compassion. However, *it does take an average of about six weeks to practice the skills you will learn in these pages so that they become automatic.* And you want them to become automatic, so they will kick in whenever you are under stress, without your having to stop and think about it. When your automatic stress-related reactions change, your wife will feel secure enough to stop walking on eggshells. In the meantime, she has to know that you are definitely going to do the work necessary to reach that level of emotional regulation. Please sign the following and show it to your wife.

Because I love you and because I want our relationship to be the best it can be, I will:

- Learn something from every paragraph of the Boot Camp.
- Do all the exercises.
- Recognize and sympathize with my hurt.
- Recognize and sympathize with your hurt.
- Appreciate my value.
- Appreciate your value.
- Master HEALS so that I can act according to my deepest values under the stress of resentment, anger, and the impulse to criticize and devalue.

Signature: _____

Love *before* Resentment

Take a moment to think about when you were falling in love. Think of how you felt when you were around her and how you felt when you were not around her. Rate each of the following, according to how you felt *at that time*.

5—Highest level possible   4—A lot   3—Some   2—A little   1—None

1. My excitement about seeing her _____
2. My interest in what she had to say _____
3. My desire to protect her from harm, distress, or worry

   _____
4. My interest in her happiness _____
5. How much I missed her when I wasn't with her _____
6. My hope for our future together _____
7. List any pet names you had for each other (for example, "Sweetheart, Love Face, Honey"):

   _____

When people are falling in love, they talk to their friends about special qualities of their loved ones. Write what you said to your friends about your significant other:

Nine

Finding Your Real Power

Under sufficient stress, most people in love relationships fall into the trap of substituting power for value. We really want to feel loved and valued, but instead, we try to feel powerful. For example, say your wife complains—yet again—that you never listen to her. The sheer repetition of the statement, along with her tone of voice, makes you feel accused and devalued. So you respond with some kind of power assertion—you contradict her or accuse back or blow her off, or say something sarcastic. (Any of these, by the way, will prove that she's right, because you're *not* listening to her when she tells you that she doesn't feel *heard* in the relationship.) Even this false feeling of power can feel better than feeling devalued and powerless, because it involves an amphetamine-like arousal. You get a surge of energy, which temporarily increases your confidence—you *know* that you're right, as long as you're resentful and angry. Sound familiar? Now ask yourself this: *Why does the substitution of power for value* never *work?* When you feel the power of being right, why do things *always* get worse? I'll give you a hint; it has nothing to do with your wife being *wrong,* and nothing to do with how she reacts to you. It has to do with your own deeper values, the same ones that probably made you get married in the first place.

Did you get married thinking, Man, now I'm really going to feel *powerful*? I'm always going to be right and win every argument. I'm always going to have the last word. If she doesn't agree with me, I'll just shout over her or refuse to speak to her or reply to her with one-word answers. I'll be able to criticize her and get her do anything I want her do. Did you fantasize like that when you got married? Or did you imagine giving love, care, and compassion?

Somewhere along the line you learned to substitute power for value. But as you must be aware by now, it's a lousy substitution. Power tactics sometimes get you compliance, occasionally fear, sometimes hostility, *always* resentment, but *never* love and *never* value.

The sad irony here is this: In close relationships, love and *genuine* power are not all that different. The key word is genuine. Genuine power is not merely the ability to do something or to get somebody else to do something. For instance, you have the power to leave your house and crash your car into the side of it. (You might even be able to coerce your wife into doing it.) Would you be *powerful* if you did that? You'd be crazy, stupid, or a maniac maybe, but not powerful.

Real power is acting in your best interests, and your long-term emotional best interests depend entirely on acting according to your deepest values. If you do that, you will feel valuable and powerful at the *same* time. So if you were in your core value when your wife complained about you not listening to her, you would probably respond with something like, "I want you to feel heard. So I do need to listen to you more and appreciate how important you are to me."

To understand the power of your deepest values, consider this question: "What is the *most* important thing about you as a person?" There are a lot of important things about you, but I want you to identify the *most* important. This quality is so essentially you that you would be a completely different person without it.

Some men write things like, "honesty," or, "being a hard worker," or, "fairness." While these are important values, they are not the *most* important. To sort out what is *most* important, think of what you would rather have your grown children say about you: "He was always honest, but I'm not sure he always loved us." Or, "He was human and made some mistakes, but I always knew that he loved us." For most human beings, the ability to love, protect, and support their loved ones is the most important thing to them and about them.

The Most Important Questions

What is the *most* important thing about you as a person?

What are the *most* important qualities of a husband?

What are the *most* important qualities of a father?

What is the *most* important thing about *you* as a husband and father?

If you were always true to what you wrote in answer to the most important questions, you would have little problem with resentment or anger and utterly no chance of being abusive. The vast majority of our negative emotions comes from violating the most important things to us and about us. Whenever we violate our deepest values, we automatically experience guilt, shame, and anxiety—even though we are not always conscious of them. You don't notice how often you have these unconscious emotions because they usually surface as resentment, anger, irritability, or criticism of others. You can bet that if you feel resentful, angry, or critical, you're also experiencing some form of unconscious guilt, shame, or anxiety.

The Powerlessness of Blame

The road to psychological ruin begins with blame.

If you feel bad and you blame it on your wife, what can you do to make yourself feel better? Not a thing. The act of blame renders you powerless. It also strips your painful emotions of their primary function, which is to motivate corrective behavior. Human pain—both physical and psychological—is part of a sophisticated *alarm* network. The purpose of your guilt, shame, and anxiety is not to *punish* you. Its primary function is to motivate behavior that heals, corrects, or improves. For instance, the purpose of a pain in my foot is to get my attention so that I will do something to make it better. My conscious mind decides *what* to do, choosing a behavior with a specific goal: I take the rock off my foot, or get better fitting shoes, or use medicine to treat an infection. If you doubt that this is the purpose of the pain, consider what would happen if you were pinned down and could not take the rock off your foot. It would hurt like hell for a while and then, once your brain figured out that there's nothing you could do about it, it would go numb. You probably know married couples who, after years of being unable to relieve their distress, have gone numb.

The crucial point is that *your* pain always motivates *you*—not your wife or anyone else—to make it better. The discomfort in your bladder doesn't tell you that she needs to go to the bathroom or that she drank too much water. Neither does your guilt or shame tell you that she has to do something. Your wife can disappoint or sadden you, but your guilt and shame—and the resentment and anger they cause—are ultimately about you being true to your deepest values.

Like physical pain, negative emotions are internal alarms meant to attract attention to perceived injury or threat, for the *sole* purpose of motivating *corrective* behavior. (Once again, this unconscious motivation doesn't tell us what to do; that's up to the conscious mind, it merely gets our attention to make us improve, correct, or heal.) The difference is that the injury or threat is not primarily to the body, but to your personal values, including how you value yourself. *Unlike* physical pain, emotional distress does not motivate mere relief of pain, which is why alcohol and drugs make you feel worse in the long run. A few beers might seem to numb your resentment of your wife, but you won't really feel better until you find something to appreciate about her. Emotional pain moves you to do something that will make you feel more *alive*, not numb. The primary purpose of emotional pain is to make us take action to increase the *value* of our lives. The purpose of guilt, shame, and anxiety is to get you to be more *loving* and *protective*. They hurt us until we act with love and compassion.

To appreciate how emotional pain works to keep you closer to loved ones, try this experiment with your wife. (Be sure to explain to her before you start that it's an experiment!) Ask her to do or say something that typically irritates you and pay attention to your own internal and external reactions very carefully. When she does, you will have a conditioned reaction to criticize or avoid her.

Whichever you do—avoid or attack—exaggerate it for the purpose of the experiment. If you criticize, say it louder and more forcefully, and if you turn away from her, get up and walk out of the room. But all the while that you're doing this exercise, monitor your emotional response, particularly what it feels like in your body. You will notice that, as you exaggerate your response, your negative emotion gets worse—you get more resentful, angry, or disgusted. As soon as you notice the rise in your negative emotion, stop in your tracks, do a 180-degree shift, and force yourself to reconnect to your wife. See her as the person you love, who gives meaning to your life. Hug her and tell her how important she is. Even if you have to force yourself at first, you should notice that your negative emotion subsides. In fact, compassion for your wife is the *only* thing that will make you feel better, once the adrenaline rush of the negativity wears off. You will relieve the bad physical and emotional feelings only when you reconnect to her in some way.

Even a destructive emotion like jealousy has this natural self-correcting effect. A toddler who sees his parents hugging and kissing is likely to feel a stab of jealousy, which makes him feel left out and abandoned, and that makes him feel unlovable. His first instinct is to wedge himself between his mother and father and be as cute and loving as he possibly can be, to reattach to them and strengthen their bond. If his parents respond to his loving efforts with acceptance and affection, his feeling of safety and of being loved and lovable is reinforced. He will grow more secure in his basic worthiness of love and become more tolerant of his parents' expressions of affection for one another.

But if his embracing parents get annoyed with his intrusion or regard him as spoiled, they might push him away or chastise him as selfish. In that case he learns to interpret his pain as a sign of failure, inadequacy, and unworthiness. Stripped of the natural way to relieve his vulnerability, he feels powerless. Instead of becoming more loving, he becomes angry.

I can't emphasize too much that your emotions are part of a motivational system; they exist to get you to do things, not to punish you. Your negative emotions do not indicate that you are bad, only that you need to do better. If you feel that your emotions are punishment, you will feel unfairly treated by other people, particularly loved ones. You'll *blame* the very guilt, shame, and anxiety designed to make you more loving *on* the people you love. Once blame becomes a habit, it poisons your relationship and your very sense of self.

Reactaholism

As blame becomes chronic, so does powerlessness. Most men expend enormous amounts of emotional energy trying to avoid feeling powerless. Some try so hard that they become *reactaholics—* forever reacting to other people who push their buttons. Reactaholics never achieve their fullest potential. They've had so many plans go wrong (because someone else made them screw up), they stop planning and eventually stop thinking about the future altogether. Reactaholics are addicted to blame.

Reactaholic Test

Are you concerned about getting your buttons pushed? _____
Do you ever worry about how you're going to react at
    home? _____
Do you brace yourself before you walk in the house? _____
Do you *not* bring up certain things because you don't want to
    overreact? _____
Do you make plans for the future? _____

Blame versus Solving Problems

Blame makes it almost impossible to find good solutions to problems, in part because it puts you in the wrong place in your brain and in the wrong dimension of time. Here's what I mean by that:

The impulse to blame comes from the limbic system, the emotional part of the brain, which is fully developed in a three-year-old child. (If you have kids, you know that the toddler's primary defense is blame: "She did it!") Solutions must come from the neocortex, the thinking part of the brain, which is not fully developed until age 25. The impulse to blame comes from the child brain, while solutions have to come from the adult brain; which brain would you rather use in your home?

Blame is always about the *past*. Solutions must occur in the *present* and *future*. Blame obscures solutions by *locking you into the problem*—you think more about how bad it is and whose fault it is rather than about solutions. You focus on damage, injury, defects, and weakness, on what is *wrong*, rather than on your intelligence and creativity, which you need to use to make a problem better. Finally, blame puts you in a *punishment* mode rather than in an *improving* mode. Is your punishment mode more likely to make your wife defensive or cooperative? Even if you use blame to get her to do what you want, she'll do it grudgingly, with hidden (and not-so-hidden) resentment.

The bottom line is *you must choose between blaming someone else and solving problems; you cannot do both.*

Blame and the Natural Purpose of Anger

Blame perverts the primary function of anger which is not self-protection in humans. When will you get angrier, if I attack you or your wife and children?

The survival purpose of anger is to *protect* loved ones. In fact, that's the natural function of anger in most social mammals—but humans are the only species that consistently uses aggression against attachment figures. We do it because we've developed a specialized, defensive form of anger unique among Earth's inhabitants. It's called *resentment*. Whereas the primary purpose of anger is protection of loved ones, the purpose of resentment is protection of the ego, through a process of chronic blame.

How to Be *Wrong* Even When You're *Right*

Blame-driven resentment or anger makes you wrong, even if you're right. You can start out factually correct, but if you fail to appreciate your wife's perspective, you'll soon get resentful and angry, and so will she. Resentment and anger *simplify, amplify,* and *magnify* a negative stimulus. They make you reduce the object of your resentment or anger to one or two negative aspects. That's fine if you're dealing with a saber tooth tiger, because then you don't need to know about its kittenhood or the number of cubs it has back at the nest that it has to feed or whether it's on the endangered species list. The anger *makes* you reduce it to one negative aspect—the threat it poses—and you either attack or retreat. But in marriage, amplification, magnification, and oversimplification *distort* issues by blowing them out of proportion and taking them out of context. It's easier to see how this works when you are the recipient of your wife's resentment or anger. Think of a time when she was resentful or angry at you, and she was factually right, you *did* do something wrong. Even though she was right, you probably felt that she was making too much of it or overlooking crucial details or *reducing* you to that one mistake, as if all the good things you've ever done in your life didn't count. Well, your wife and kids react to your resentment and anger in the same way. Most human beings subjected to the amplification, magnification, and oversimplification of resentment or anger get resentful, contentious, or sulky in return, just like you do.

Resentment and anger also cause you to focus only on your own perspective, to the *exclusion* of everyone else's. Did you ever go out to lunch with someone resentful about something that happened that morning at work and try to talk about anything other that what he's upset about? You could probably say, "I was thinking about killing myself last night," and you'd get a reply of, "Oh, really? But did you hear what she said to me this morning?" Of course this narrow and rigid focus makes it impossible to see another person's perspective. You can't see your wife's perspective, and she can't see yours.

It should be clear by now that anger and resentment are for dominating, not for negotiating. If you're resentful or angry when discussing family finances, for instance, you don't just want your wife to agree with you, you want her to feel stupid for not agreeing with you. Resentment and anger exist exclusively to devalue, reject, warn, threaten, intimidate, or attack, in your head or in reality, behind her back or in her face. You may feel as if you're doing these things defensively, but you are nevertheless rejecting, warning, threatening, intimidating, or attacking.

Approach, Avoid, Attack

If you're having trouble figuring out when you're resentful, angry, or abusive, think in terms of what is *motivating your feeling*, rather than the feelings themselves. All behavior that is not habit has one of these three, usually unconscious, motivations: Approach, avoid, or attack. In love relationships:

- *Approach* is showing interest, enjoyment, compassion, or care.
- *Avoid* makes you want to get away from her, blow off her perspective or have her shut up. It devalues her by implying, accidentally or on purpose, that she's not worth your attention. (By the way, "not noticing her" is nothing more than a conditioned avoidance response. You noticed her well enough before you started resenting her.)
- *Attack* is an attempt to undermine her confidence, to get her to agree with you or do what you want.

Motivation +/– Inhibition = Behavior

Most unconscious motivations do not get acted out or rise to the level of overt behavior—they just stay in your head. Motivation *starts* behavior, but most of the time some other emotion *inhibits* it and keeps you from acting it out. For instance, your motivations to avoid or attack your wife are usually stopped by the most common of all inhibitions: *fear of consequences*—you don't want to make bad things worse. A far more important inhibition is, unfortunately, less common, and that is compassion—you don't want her to be hurt. Fear of consequences stops you from avoiding and attacking all right, but it doesn't exactly inspire you to approach your wife with compassion. It might keep you from making things worse, but it won't make them better. And eventually it erodes your self-esteem. If the only reason you don't avoid or attack your wife is that you're afraid of her response, you'll start to feel weak and cowardly.

On the other hand, compassion not only keeps you from avoiding and attacking, it also motivates behavior to improve, appreciate, connect, or protect, all of which are likely to make things better with your wife. They will also improve your self-esteem. You can probably recall some incident from years ago in which you devalued your wife. If you think about it right now, you'll feel bad about it. You can also think of compassion you had for her about something that happened many years ago. If you think about it right now, you'll feel good about yourself because of it, at least before you start to feel guilty for not having more of it. Compassion directly activates your core value—the *most* important things about you. In your deepest values, you act with conviction and strength. *Compassion is power.*

Avoid and *attack* motivations damage love relationships even if they are only in your head and never become overt behavior. They betray the implicit promise you made to your wife when you fell in love: that you would care about how she feels, especially when she feels bad. Even in your head, an impulse to avoid or attack represents a failure of compassion, which probably violates your deepest values.

Motivations versus Intentions

Don't make the mistake of confusing the unconscious motivation of your behavior with your conscious *intention*—what you think you're trying to do. For instance, your attack motivation may be to devalue your wife because she disagrees with you. It is probably not your conscious *intention* to make her feel stupid, incompetent, lazy, or unlovable; you just want her to see your perspective or at least care about how you feel. But human beings, like most other mammals, are programmed to react to aggressive and devaluing motivations, not to intentions. (Try soothing an animal when you're angry.) Unless you're married to Mother Teresa, you will scarcely achieve any of your positive intentions by acting on avoid-or-attack motivations. *The only way to get her to see your perspective is for you to see hers, and the only way to get her to care how you really feel is to care about how she really feels.* That means you must be in an approach motivation most of the time.

The good news is that motivations are much easier to regulate than overt behavior. Think of the difference in effort between changing your *urge* to devalue your wife and stopping yourself once you've begun to do it.

Identifying Your Motivations

Describe a complaint your wife has about your behavior:

Was your motivation in the behavior she complains about *approach* (showing interest, enjoyment, compassion, or care)? _____

Was it *avoid* (get away from her, blow off her perspective, or have her shut up)? _____

Was it *attack* (undermine her confidence, to get her to agree with you or to do what you want)? _____

Describe a dispute or argument you had with your wife:

Was your motivation in this dispute or argument *approach* (showing interest, enjoyment, compassion, or care)? _____

Was it *avoid* (get away from her, blow off her perspective, or have her shut up)? _____

Was it *attack* (undermine her confidence, to get her to agree with you or to do what you want)? _____

The First Law of Attachment:
Your Emotional Well-Being Is Tied Up with Hers

This is both the pleasant and the painful truth about love: When she feels good, you will feel better, if you let yourself. But if she feels bad, you will be utterly unable to keep from feeling bad, although it may not be the same bad feeling. You and she and your emotions are attached. The following exercise demonstrates the *most* painful truth about love.

The Painful Truth

Write down the most hurtful thing that you ever said or did to your wife:

Write down how you would feel and what you would do if a stranger said or did that same hurtful thing to her.

I'm pretty sure that I know more or less what you wrote. When social mammals, including humans, are attached, they have an unconscious, automatic instinct to protect. If you were to see your loved one harmed verbally, emotionally, or physically, you would feel anger, an aggressive impulse, and loathing. For that moment at least, you would hate the person who harmed your wife; you'd want to hurt him in return.

So what happens to that anger, aggression, and loathing when *you* are the one hurting her? Part of your brain is still committed to protecting her, so where do the anger, aggression and loathing go?

When you hurt someone you love, the ultimate object of your anger, aggression, and hatred is *you*. The unavoidable legacy of spiteful, angry, or abusive behavior directed at loved ones is self-loathing. *Every harsh word you say to her and every cold shoulder you turn toward her makes you hate yourself a little more, makes her hate herself a little more, and makes your children hate themselves a little more.*

No One in the Family Escapes the Effects of Walking on Eggshells

The bottom line is *a slap to the heart hurts more than a punch to the face.* (The next couple of pages are a reprise of the effects of anger, resentment, verbal aggression, and emotional abuse on you and your family, which I wrote about for your wife in Chapter 2, but which you now need to understand, too.)

Families do not communicate primarily by language. That

might sound surprising, until you consider that humans were bonded in families for millennia before we even had language, and that the most sensitive communications, with the most far-reaching consequences of our lives, occur between parents and infants without the use of language skills.

Though less obvious than interactions with young children, most of your communications with your older children and with your wife also occur through an unconscious process of emotional *attunement*. You tune in your emotions to those of the people you love. That's how you can come home in one mood, find your wife or children in a different mood and—bam!—all of a sudden, out of nowhere, you're in that mood. Quite unconsciously, you automatically react to one another.

Emotional attunement, not verbal skills, determines how we communicate, from our choice of words to our tone of voice. If you're tuned in to a positive mood, you are likely to communicate pleasantly. If you're in a negative mood, your words will be unpleasant.

Now here's the really bad news. Due to this unconscious, automatic process of emotional attunement, your children are painfully reactive to your wife's walking on eggshells and to the tense atmosphere of the house, even if they never hear you say a harsh word to one another.

Everyone in a walking-on-eggshells family loses some degree of dignity and autonomy—the ability to decide your own thoughts, feelings, and behavior. You yourself lose autonomy when you live in a defensive-reactive pattern that runs largely on automatic pilot. No fewer than half the members of these unfortunate families, including the children, suffer from clinical anxiety and/or depression. (Clinical doesn't mean feeling down or blue or worried, it means that the adult's or child's mental and physical symptoms interfere with his or her normal functioning. Adults can't sleep, can't concentrate, can't work as efficiently, and can't enjoy themselves without drinking.) Most adults walking on eggshells lack genuine self-esteem (based on realistic self-appraisals and not wishful thinking or sheer fantasy). The children rarely feel as good as other kids and are ten times more likely to grow up to be resentful, angry, or abusive adults. If the family is violent, children are ten times more likely to become abusers or victims of violence as adults. They are also at increased risk of becoming alcoholics, drug addicts, or criminals and to be anxious, depressed, or poor.

The most common symptom of children in families that walk on eggshells is depression. But the signs can fool you; childhood depression looks different from the weepy, withdrawn adult version. In children the disorder resembles chronic boredom. Children normally have high levels of interest, enjoyment, and excitement. If your child is not interested in the things that children are normally interested in, lacks enthusiasm, and is seldom excited, he or she is probably depressed. Another common symptom of these children is anxiety, particularly worry about things that children do not normally worry about, like how their parents are going to get through the evening with each other. Many kids have school problems, show aggressive tendencies, hyperactivity, and either over-emotionality—anger, excitability, or frequent crying that seem to come out of nowhere—or the polar opposite: no emotions at all. In the latter condition, they can look like little stone children; you could slice up a puppy in front of them and they wouldn't care. They have turned off all emotion to avoid the pain of walking on eggshells.

One piece of research on children in abusive families might startle you: Witnessing a parent victimized is usually more psychologically damaging to children than injuries from direct child abuse. In my own family, that was certainly true. I have only the faintest memories of child abuse—a small hole in my skull and a knocked-out front tooth—but I have vivid nightmares of seeing my mother ignored and dismissed as well as demeaned and terrified. Seeing a parent abused is the more profound form of child abuse. And emotional abuse is usually *more* psychologically harmful than physical abuse.

There are a couple of reasons for this. Even in the most violent of families, the incidents tend to be cyclical. Early in the abuse cycle, a violent outburst is followed by a honeymoon period of remorse, attention, affection, and generosity, but not genuine compassion focused on her healing. (The honeymoon stage eventually falls away, as the victim begins to say, "Never mind the damn flowers, just stop hitting me!") Emotional abuse, on the other hand, tends to happen every day. So the effects are more harmful because they're so frequent.

The other factor that makes emotional abuse so devastating is the greater likelihood that victims will blame themselves. If you hit her, it's easier to see that you have the problem, but if the abuse is *subtle*—saying or implying that she's ugly, a bad parent, stupid, incompetent, not worth attention, or that no one could love her—she's more likely to think it's her problem.

Clearly, the conditions that make someone have to walk on eggshells create gifts of pain that keep on giving throughout the generations. The rest of the Boot Camp will show you have to reverse these corrosive effects on you, your partner, and your children.

Ten

Connecting with Your Core Value

The impulse to be aggressive can be mental (in your imagination), verbal (using nasty or demeaning language), emotional (trying to make the other person feel bad or inferior), or physical (using force). Aggressive urges are always accompanied by one of the more than 20 forms of anger that seem to hijack your brain and make you do things against your best interests. Anger and aggression are powerful, pervasive emotional states. Thankfully, they are not deep; they go away abruptly when you feel a deeper emotion such as compassion, love, sorrow, or grief.

When You're Angry or Aggressive, You're Hurt

Anger and aggression are reactions to hurt; that's why when you bang your thumb hanging a picture, you don't pray. They also protect you against the possibility of hurt, which is why you get resentful when someone stumbles near your sore foot. To feel resentment, anger, or an aggressive impulse, you have to be hurt or fear that you will be hurt.

The connection of anger, resentment, and aggression to vulnerability—actual hurt or the possibility of hurt—is easier to see in the case of physical vulnerability. Suppose I were giving you directions and pointing out where to go. I would probably touch your shoulder. This is so common a behavior when giving directions that you probably wouldn't even notice it—*unless* you had a broken collar bone, in which case you'd have an impulse to push me (or worse) when my hand came near your shoulder. It's the same thing when your foot is sore and someone comes stumbling around it—you have an impulse to kick him with your good foot. You resent someone for just getting near your injured areas, even if he doesn't come close enough to touch. Just as your brain puts out hair-trigger resentment, anger, and abusive impulses to protect vulnerable areas of your body, it does the exact same thing with vulnerable areas of your sense of self or your ego—which is why you've developed resentment and anger at your wife. Who gets closer to your vulnerabilities than she does?

I call these vulnerabilities of the sense of self *core hurts*. If *anyone* gets near them, he or she gets zapped with anger or resentment.

Core Hurts

Core hurts are vulnerabilities to the sense of self. They are the difference between feeling bad—sad, disappointed, lonely, anxious—and feeling bad about *yourself.* The core hurt list was compiled by a consensus of the first 100 men in our treatment groups. You do not have to use the same words to describe your particular vulnerabilities, as long as you understand that all vulnerabilities are *hierarchical*—some things hurt more than others. So the hurt gets worse as you go down the core hurt list.

In general, the deeper core hurts, especially the last pair, are stimulated only in interactions with someone you love.

> Feeling or suspecting that you might feel:
> Disregarded, unimportant
> Accused
> Guilty

> Devalued
> Rejected
> Powerless
> Inadequate, unlovable

Because of their great influence in building the sense of self, the deeper core hurts control the top ones. Say that your wife is still upset about an argument you had the night before. You might feel disregarded or unimportant in response to her withdrawn or sulky behavior, but you are also likely to feel some sort of *inadequacy* as a husband and you may feel *unworthy* of her love. You will feel adequate as a husband and more worthy of love if you do something like sympathize with her perspective, try to comfort her, let her know how much you value her. If she feels that you devalued her in the course of your disagreement, sincerely apologize for that. You will also no longer feel disregarded or unimportant. However, if you do something that only makes you feel regarded and important, like demand her attention or try to control her behavior, then you will feel less adequate (as a protective and caring husband) and more unlovable.

Your Innate Value

Although they can reside deep in the structure of self, core hurts do not comprise the deepest or most important part of you. You were not born with core hurts. Did you ever see a newborn who felt unlovable? "Who am *I* to cry, they're *busy*." Newborns feel valuable enough to express their needs, and expect that parents will drop whatever they're doing and meet those needs. But meeting physical needs alone does not maintain the health of the child. If you just shove a bottle into a crying baby's mouth, she most likely will not stop crying. Once her distress system (crying, reddened face, writhing body) gets going, you need to comfort her by connecting to her emotionally. This drive to value and connect gives comfort, security, and confidence to human beings. I call it *core value*. If you go deeply enough into yourself, you must arrive at your core value. And that is what you must do to save your marriage.

Before expanding on the all important concept of core value, let's take a look at the structure of your emotional self. The top layer is what the world sees. These are emotions you have and actions you take to numb or avoid the pain of core hurts.

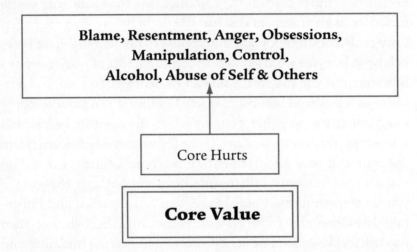

No matter how disappointing, inconvenient, unfair, unfortunate, or expensive the behavior of other people might be, it can cause a top-layer reaction—resentment, anger, and so on—*only* if it stimulates a core hurt. Otherwise, it is *merely* disappointing, inconvenient, unfortunate, unfair, or expensive. For example, you might be inconvenienced, disappointed, and saddened by your wife refusing to make dinner for you. But if you can activate your core value, you won't feel inadequate or unlovable and you won't get resentful or angry. Just as important, in your core value you will be able to see that your wife feels inadequate or unlovable (unappreciated or taken advantage of) for *having* to make your dinner. Your negotiations with each other can now be about the division of labor, deciding who needs to do what, when, and where, not about how lovable either of you is. *Core value is never negotiable and never at stake in ordinary interactions.*

The Formula for Resentment = Core Hurts + Blame

Connecting your core hurts to resentment and anger is all too easy for your brain to do. Core hurts hurt. They drain energy. Anger and resentment are built-in pain relievers and energizers. As derivatives of the fight-or-flight instinct, they prepare us to fight or flee despite injuries. They temporarily and superficially numb pain and replenish energy. No core hurt, no resentment.

Core Hurts Are Almost Always *Inadequate* or *Unlovable* with Your Wife

When it's someone you love, the core hurts causing your resentment and anger are almost always vulnerability to feeling *inadequate* or *unlovable*. We do this *unconscious* distortion all the time with loved ones: "If she loved me, she would pick up the towel. If my own wife doesn't love me, I must be unlovable." Your resentment punishes her for reminding you that you sometimes feel unlovable. But the trouble with this particular distortion is that even if she picks up the towel, you're not going to feel more lovable because the towel has nothing to do with how lovable you felt in the first place. As long as you felt unlovable, your resentment would merely shift to something like, "Why did I have to tell her, why can't she just do what she's supposed to do?" Of course she has no idea that you feel unlovable. From her perspective, you're forcing her to pick up the towel just to gratify your own power trip. If she *submitted* to your order, *she* would feel inadequate and unlovable.

Most of your resentment, anger, criticism, and rejection of your wife occur because, at that instant, you are vulnerable to feeling inadequate or unlovable. To appreciate how *self-destructive* these behaviors are, ask yourself this: In the history of humankind has anyone ever felt more lovable by hurting someone he loves? Is that even possible? As we've seen, whatever you think your wife did to make you resentful, angry, or abusive she probably did because *she* was vulnerable to feeling inadequate or unlovable at that instant. To appreciate how destructive these behaviors are to your relationship, ask yourself: In the history of humankind has anyone ever felt more lovable when hurt by someone she loves?

The great tragedy of walking on eggshells is that you *both* feel inadequate and unlovable. Instead of helping one another, you let your resentment and anger lead you to do things that can only make you both feel worse.

The figure below illustrates that trying to work out problems and disagreements on the top layer of the emotional self—through blame, resentment, criticism, or verbal and emotional abuse—can only cause more problems. You must learn to recognize your core hurts, as well as your wife's and to appreciate her core value as much as your own.

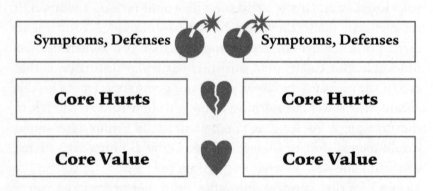

Your only hope of a better marriage lies in seeking solutions from your core value and in fully appreciating your wife's. Always ask yourself:

> *What level am I on?*
> *What level is she on?*
> *How can I get to my core value and appreciate hers?*

The only way to heal yourself and save your relationship is to connect your core hurts to your core value, the way you used to do as a young child.

Core Value

Core value is present in all of us at birth. It is the *drive* to value—to experience a sense of safety, security, and emotional connection to others. The *first* value that newborns create is love for their caregivers. The experience of that emotional connection makes them feel valuable and worthy of having their needs and desires met. Thus core value becomes the source of personal security, well-being, self-esteem, competence, creativity, and personal power (the ability to act in your best interests). All that you value in life grows out of your core value.

Your core value is your deepest experience of the self, your very sense of *humanity*. In appreciation of your humanity, you automatically feel equal to everyone on earth. On the most profound level possible, you feel *worthy* of love. You have an emotional awareness that no problem, behavior, or event can reduce your value as a person. It's a deep feeling that you are valuable enough to change any behavior that is harmful to you or to someone you love.

Your core value is *invincible*. It cannot be damaged by the outside world. The world can cause you expense and inconvenience, it can hurt your feelings and body, but it can *never* diminish your core value. Only *your* behavior can affect it. But while you can never lose core value, you can lose touch with it. *The impulse to criticize, devalue, control, or harm your wife tells you that your current state of core value is too low.* These negative impulses do *not* tell you that you need more power; they tell you that you need more of a sense of core value. They're like a sensitive gas gauge showing that your core value is running on empty—you need to fill it up!

Statement of Core Value

(Read aloud)

I am worthy of respect, value, and compassion, whether or not I get them from others. If I don't get them from others, I must make myself feel more worthy, not less. I must behave in a way that affirms my own deep value as a unique person (a child of God). I respect and value myself. I have compassion for my hurt. I have compassion for the hurt of others. I trust myself to act in my best interests and in the best interests of loved ones.

Improve, Appreciate, Connect, Protect

Sometimes people experience their core value as a sense of humanity, intimacy, community, or spirituality, but it occurs most frequently as an unconscious motivation to *improve, appreciate, protect,* or *connect*. Now here's the really good news: Not only do these four motivations flow unconsciously from core value, you can consciously activate your own core value by *trying* to improve, appreciate, connect, or protect.

Improve means make it a *little* better. *Appreciate* means allow yourself to feel enriched by the qualities of another person or something in nature or something human-made, like music or art. *Connect* means emotionally fitting together with another person or with something larger than the self, like God, nature, social causes, or a community. *Protect* means safeguarding the physical and emotional well-being of another person.

In addition to their direct connection to your core value, these motivations also change your negative emotions into positive ones. No matter how bad you feel, if you do one of these—improve, appreciate, protect, or connect—you will feel better. If you do two, you'll feel much better, and if you do all, you'll feel euphoria or joy. If you do none, you'll feel numb. If you violate one, you feel bad. If you violate two, you feel worse, and if you violate all, you're guaranteed to feel resentful, depressed, angry, or anxious.

I have framed and mounted the four core value motivations on my bedroom wall. This is the first thing I see in the morning:

Core Value Exercise

Here's an exercise to invoke core value and keep it in reserve for whenever you need it. Imagine that you're driving by yourself, and just ahead you see a car lose control and crash into a tree. Two people are in the car, a mother and a four-year-old child. The mother is unhurt, but she's trapped in the front seat and cannot help her little girl, who climbs out the back window. Though unhurt, she feels helpless and panicky. You are the only car close to the victims. What will you do?

Of course, most people would call 911, reassure the mother that help is on the way, and comfort the child.

Imagine that you've done the first two, and now you're comforting the child. You tell her it will be okay, her mother is fine. You very much want to make her feel better. It's become so important to you to comfort her that you don't notice right away how it's working.

- The child is calming down and starting to feel okay.
- She holds tightly onto you, arms around your neck, her head on your chest.
- She now feels peaceful and good, because of you.

As you imagine helping the mother and comforting the child, you experience your core value. This image—along with many others you will learn—will overcome any impatience, resentment, or anger you experience. They will help you to act always in your best interest.

Your core value is a powerful light within you. You will learn to activate it *anytime* you feel impatient, resentful, or angry. *From your core value you protect the safety and well-being of everyone you love.*

Power Statement

Read the following aloud, and feel the *power* in your words as you renounce reactaholism and reclaim control of your emotions and your deepest values:

> *I will work hard to heal my hurt. This means understanding my own deepest emotions and those of all my loved ones. I will not hurt their feelings or try to control them, even if they hurt mine or try to control me.*

Your Core Value Bank

The *Core Value Bank* is designed as a repository of your core value, a kind of bank account of the most important things. You can think of each of the eight segments as a safe deposit box containing images of the most important things to and about you. The Core Value Bank is itself an image of your *internal* value. Its contents correspond to persons and things in the world, but it resides entirely *within* you. It's *always* there, ready to give you strength whenever you need it. Each time you see, hear, smell, touch, or taste something in the world similar to the contents of your Core Value Bank, it will remind you of your core value and thereby activate it within you. In other words, you will be motivated to improve, appreciate, connect, or protect. The next time you see a sunset, for example, it will not only seem beautiful, it will remind you of your core value. Put as much content as you can in your safe deposit boxes—you'll be amazed at how many reminders you'll start to find in your environment.

The best thing about the Core Value Bank is that you make deposits at the same time you make withdrawals. You will *never* run out of core value.

After you fill in the boxes, we'll put your bank to use as a tool of emotional reconditioning. Get ready for magic.

Box 1 is already filled in. This is the emotion you felt when you imagined helping and comforting the desperate child after an auto accident.

Box 2: Fill in:

The *most* important thing about you as a person.

The *most* important thing about your life in general. (Fast-forward 60 years and think of what you would want your eulogy to be.)

Box 3: Fill in the names of your loved ones. You're writing their names, but the emotional content of this box will be the actual love you feel for them.

Box 4: Fill in a symbol (a drawing, mark, or word will do) of some-

Core Value Bank

Box 1	Box 2
The emotions I felt as I imagined rescuing and comforting the child after an auto accident:	The most important thing about me as a person: The most important thing about my life in general:

Box 5	Box 6
Something beautiful in nature:	Something beautiful human made (art, music, architecture, furniture, etc.):

Core Value Bank

Box 3	Box 4
The people I love:	My spiritual connection:

Box 7	Box 8
My community connection:	Compassionate things I have done: 1. 2. 3.

thing that has spiritual importance to you. It can be religious, natural, cosmic, or social—anything that connects you to something larger than the self, which, while you are connected to it, seems more important than your everyday, mundane, or selfish concerns.

Box 5: Name, draw, or describe a nature scene that you value—something that you feel is beautiful.

Box 6: Identify a piece of art, music, or other human creation that makes you feel value.

Box 7: Identify a sense of community connection, for example, a church, school, work, or neighborhood.

Box 8: List three compassionate things you have done. These do not have to be a Mother Teresa kind of compassion. They can be relatively small gestures, when you helped or comforted someone else, with no material gain to you.

Emotional Reconditioning

You can use your Core Value Bank to recondition all your emotions. You can work step-by-step, associating core value with distress, the way that well-nurtured children learn to do early in life (Chapter 2). To get started, try using your Core Value Bank to convert relatively minor resentments involving situations that occur in traffic into a motivation to improve, appreciate, connect, or protect.

1. You're running late, and the car ahead of you won't speed up or get out of your way. Imagine for a moment how irritating this would be when you have to get somewhere—feel the frustration of how *unfair* or *wrong* it is.

   Now experience your core value—helping and comforting the child after the auto accident, the most important things about you, the people you love, your spiritual and communal connections, something beautiful in nature and art—the items in your Core Value Bank. Feel the warm light of your core value.

2. Someone cuts you off—you have to hit the brakes hard. Imagine for a moment how irritating this would be—try to feel the frustration of how *unfair* or *wrong* it is.

   Experience your core value—helping and comforting the child after the auto accident, the most important things about you, the people you love, your spiritual and communal connections, something beautiful in nature and art—the items in your Core Value Bank. Feel the warm light of your core value.

3. The traffic totally jams up—nothing but gridlock for miles and miles. Imagine how irritating this would be—try to feel the frustration of how *unfair* it is when you have to get somewhere.

   Experience your core value—helping and comforting the child after an auto accident, the most important things about you, the people you love, your spiritual and communal connections, something beautiful in nature and art—the items in your Core Value Bank. Feel the warm light of your core value.

4. A guy in another car flips you the finger and yells at you. Imagine for a moment how irritating this would be—try to feel the frustration of how *unfair* or *wrong* it is.

   Experience your core value—helping and comforting the child after an auto accident, the most important things about you, the people you love, your spiritual and communal connections, something beautiful in nature and art—the items in your Core Value Bank. Feel the warm light of your core value.

5. Somebody is tailgating you. Imagine for a moment how irritating this would be—try to feel the frustration of how *unfair* or *wrong* it is.

   Experience your core value—helping and comforting the child after an auto accident, the most important things about you, the people you love, your spiritual and communal connections, something beautiful in nature and art—the items in your Core Value Bank. Feel the warm light of your core value.

6. A jerk leans on the horn and *won't* stop! Imagine for a moment how irritating this would be—try to feel the frustration of how *unfair* or *wrong* it is.

   Experience your core value—helping and comforting the child after an auto accident, the most important things about you, the people you love, your spiritual and communal connections, something beautiful in nature and art—the items in your Core Value Bank. Feel the warm light of your core value.

7. A van speeds by too close to you. Imagine for a moment how irritating this would be—try to feel the frustration of how *unfair* or *wrong* it is.

   Experience your core value—helping and comforting the child after an auto accident, the most important things about you, the people you love, your spiritual and communal connections, something beautiful in nature and art—the items in your Core Value Bank. Feel the warm light of your core value.

Core Value Bankers

We'll use our composite client, Carl, to demonstrate the ways that we teach our clients to use their Core Value Banks to cope with the situations above. Sherry walked on eggshells every afternoon, waiting for Carl to come home from his stressful commute. Every day he experienced at least one of the traffic conditions described above and would go home to take his irritability out on Sherry and their kids.

One night the traffic wasn't moving at all, and Carl had to prepare for a meeting. By reducing his anger and resentment at the traffic with his Core Value Bank, he automatically shifted into a motivation to *improve*. He began thinking of who he could call to start the meeting and preside over it until he got there. He thought of the specific instructions that he would give his substitute-leader. He then called the man on his cell phone and ran through the major points on the meeting agenda. The Core Value Bank shifted his focus automatically from what he could not control—the traffic—to what he could control—how he could compensate for the problems the traffic presented. He kissed Sherry and hugged the kids when he got home that night.

On the night that a speeding van passed by his car much too closely, Carl invoked his Core Value Bank, which automatically put him in a motivation to *appreciate*. He thought of how hard Sherry had been working to get the house ready for his relatives who were coming for Thanksgiving, and how sweet it was of her to go out of her way to make the visit go smoothly. How do you think their evening went?

On the night that the guy flipped him the finger and cursed at him, Carl invoked his Core Value Bank, which automatically put him in a motivation to *protect*. He thought of how he needed to drive more carefully to protect the safety of all the children that were in the cars around him. It was especially important for him to drive carefully, with so many jerks on the road. He felt powerful and protective on the road and was especially glad to see his kids when he got home.

On the night that another driver cut him off, Carl invoked his Core Value Bank, which automatically put him in a motivation to *connect*. He thought of his son, who was having trouble in school, and how he had been too hard on him. He decided to take him for ice cream when he got home and talk about only fun things with him.

Notice that in each one of these instances, Carl's use of his Core Value Bank readjusted his values. He automatically focused on things that were more important than the irritation of the traffic. The problem with resentment is that it seems to make less important things more important than the *most* important things.

Anger, resentment, and distress work like a sensitive gas gauge, warning that your core value is running on empty and that you need to fill it up. You can fill it up to the high level you deserve in just one week. Every day, for the next seven days:

- Appreciate at least one thing about each person you love.
- Make at least one spiritual connection.
- Appreciate a new thing of beauty in nature, in art or music, and in your community.
- Do at least one compassionate thing for another person.
- Do at least one compassionate thing for yourself.

Soon you will be in the habit of looking for aspects of value in everyone and in everything you see.

The next chapter teaches you a skill that, with practice, will help you *automatically* reconnect to your core value whenever you get resentful, angry, or feel the urge to be verbally or emotionally abusive.

Eleven

HEALS:
Automatically *Regulating Resentment, Anger, and the Impulse to Criticize, Reject, or Abuse*

HEALS™ is a technique designed to replace your habitual response of anger, resentment, or an impulse to be mentally, verbally, emotionally, or physically aggressive with automatic activation of your core value. This is not a *new* emotional pattern. Your brain *used* to connect core hurts to core value when you were a young child. Remember, the natural impulse of the jealous child is to be more loving. The natural instinct of the hurt, embarrassed, or rejected child is to seek love from parents.

We *are* creatures of habit. Most of the emotions we experience in our lifetimes are *conditioned*. We have a conditioned response when an emotion has been associated with a certain stimulus. For example, the Russian researcher Ivan Pavlov conditioned dogs to get excited whenever they heard a bell ring. He simply rang the bell before feeding them. After a few repetitions of getting fed immediately after the ringing of the bell, the dogs got the idea and started salivating at the sound of any bell, even if they didn't get food afterward. Of course they didn't think, "Oh, the bell has rung, we are going to be fed!" They reacted *automatically*, on a visceral level, to the sound of the bell, which their central nervous systems had associated with getting fed. Pavlov called this phenomenon *classical conditioning*, which is the primary way that people (and animals) form habits—that set of emotions and behaviors that we feel and do without thinking.

The vast majority of our emotional experience is a series of conditioned responses. These habits are prominent in human and animal behavior because they are metabolically cheap; that is, they consume little energy. The difference in mental exertion between habituated behavior and a consciously decided action is hundreds of millions of multifiring neurons.

Conditioned responses, or habits, allow us to behave with little thought and virtually no conscious attention about the behavior. That's how, without thinking about it, you know where to turn in the newspaper for something of interest. It's also how you know what not to bring up in conversation if you want a peaceful evening. You drive home without thinking about it and sit on the sofa in the living room without looking. You can also fall on your butt if the sofa has been moved. When your emotions become overly habitual, they can be *knee-jerk* reactions, like the way some men react when their wives smile at a waiter.

HEALS Basic Training

The goal of practicing HEALS is to train your brain to reach your core value *automatically*, in a *fraction* of a second, at the *very beginning* of an impulse to avoid or attack. The skill is not connected to any particular *thing* your wife does or says (or doesn't do or say); it's connected to the arousal that *precedes* the impulse to avoid or attack. It takes an average of *six weeks of 12 repetitions per day* for this skill to become *automatic*.

Think prevention, *not reduction*. The purpose of HEALS is to *pre-*

vent avoid-and-attack behaviors that violate your core value. Do not *wait* until you're resentful or angry to practice. Military basic training prepares you *before* the battle by teaching you to keep your head under fire. So does HEALS.

Because it will serve primarily as a prevention reflex, you want HEALS to kick in at a *low level* of arousal to avoid or attack. In your practice, choose the point at which you *first noticed* any impulse to avoid or attack. If you can control a low-level impulse, it will never rise to a level where it can hurt anyone's feelings.

Like all skill acquisition, mastering HEALS is hard at first but gets much easier with practice. It took you a while to learn how to ride a bike and even longer to learn how to drive a car, but now you do these things without thinking. The same is true of learning HEALS. You will feel better and have higher self-value, with increasingly less effort, as the figure below indicates.

The Effort and Reward of Learning HEALS

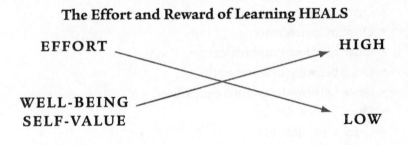

EFFORT ⟶ HIGH

WELL-BEING
SELF-VALUE ⟶ LOW

Practice Time: Beginning   2 weeks   4 weeks   6 weeks

Vaccination with One Second of a Core Hurt

When we are vaccinated against a disease, we get an injection of a small or weakened dose of the virus. This stimulates the immune system to create antibodies that neutralize any toxic effects. For example, when a child gets a measles, mumps, and rubella shot, he is injected with live measles, mumps, and rubella viruses. His immune system is prompted to fight the invaders and build resistance. Working in the exact same way as a vaccination, HEALS exposes you to a very small dose of a core hurt—for *one second* each time you practice. With repetition, the technique builds immunity to the negative effects of core hurts. When that happens, *no one* will be able to push your buttons, for no one will be able to make you feel vulnerable to a core hurt.

Practicing HEALS

It's best to establish a *routine* of practicing HEALS for the next six weeks. Something like:

- Once before you get out of bed—this is the most important repetition, as it will start a positive flow of unconscious emotions
- Once before you leave the house
- Once before you go to work
- Once at morning break time
- Once at lunch time
- Once at afternoon break time
- Once before you leave work
- Once before you go into the house
- Once before dinner
- Once after dinner
- Once while preparing for bed
- Once in bed.

There are *no bad times or places* to practice HEALS. However, for maximum positive effect, do not practice it twice in a row. Your emotional system needs a little time to recalibrate so allow at least five minutes between repetitions.

Practice HEALS about *12 times* per *day*.* Start each practice rep-

---

*If you have suffered a head injury in which you lost consciousness, it may be necessary to practice 20 times per day. HEALS works following head injuries, but requires more practice to build the regulatory reflex.

etition by recalling a relatively *mild provocation*. As with any skill, you start small—you learn to swim in shallow water, not in the ocean during a storm. For the first three weeks, stay away from the more complex forms of anger like jealousy and disputes about raising your children. HEALS can help you work on those issues, too, if you give yourself time to build up the skill before tackling them.

The Steps of HEALS

H*EALS*, **H***EALS*, **H***EALS* flashes in your imagination (it should
    start flashing *abruptly*, to cut-off the arousal)
Experience the *deepest* core hurt
Access core value
Love yourself
Solve the problem

Begin a practice session by recalling a time when you felt disregarded, ignored, accused, devalued, disrespected, made fun of, lied to, or betrayed.

- Imagine the incident in as much detail as you can.
- Pretend it's happening *now*.
- Feel the tightness in your neck, eyes, jaw, shoulders, chest, stomach, and hands.
- Do your typical self-talk: "It's not fair, they shouldn't be doing this, it isn't right! I'll show them!"
- And, "Here we go again! It'll never stop! They always do this!"

As soon as you start to feel the arousal, see **HEALS** abruptly flash in your imagination—see the word flashing and hear the sound of it: **HEALS ... HEALS ... HEALS.** *Feel* yourself move downward to your core value. *Experience* the *deepest* core hurt *causing* the arousal. Say, *"I am inadequate, I am unlovable."*

Have the courage to feel deeply, for just *one second*, what it's like to *be* that core hurt. Feel what it's like to be completely powerless, inadequate, and unworthy, something like, "I'm a puppet on a string. They control everything I think, feel, and do." Or, "No one could ever pay attention to my opinions or feelings. No one could love the *real* me."

Access the glow of *core value,* the most important part of you. Invoke the emotions of your Core Value Bank. Imagine comforting the distressed child in the car crash. Think of the most important thing about you as a person and the most important thing about your life in general. Feel the love you have for the people closest to you. Feel your spiritual connection. Think of something beautiful in nature. Think of your favorite art or music. Imagine a community you feel comfortable with, and think of three compassionate things you have done. You have the *power* to act in your best interest, regardless of what anyone else does. Feel your core value grow.

Love yourself. Prove, beyond a doubt, how powerful and worthy you are; recognize the core value of the person who offended you. She has a Core Value Bank like yours and would rescue the child as surely as you would. Feel compassion for the core hurt that has disconnected her from her core value. If it's someone you love, it's almost always the same one you felt. If you felt unlovable, you can bet the farm that she did, too. Appreciate her core value and yours will soar.

Solve the problem in your best interest, according to your deepest values.

After each practice repetition, ask yourself these three questions:

- Will you solve it better from your core value and compassion or with resentment, anger, criticism, rejection, or controlling behavior?
- Which do you prefer to experience, core value and compassion or resentment and anger?
- In which do you feel more *powerful,* more able to act according to your deepest values?

Each time you practice HEALS, you reclaim a little more of your inner self. You become wiser, more powerful, and better able to understand yourself and the people you love.

It's important to note that HEALS is a highly personal, *inner* skill, not a relationship activity. You do HEALS on your own, without your wife's help or advice, and you certainly don't help or advise her to do it. HEALS is not the solution or the negotiation. But it removes the emotional barriers to solutions and negotiations—it allows you to act in your best interests, according to your deepest values.

The figure below shows the proper path of HEALS.

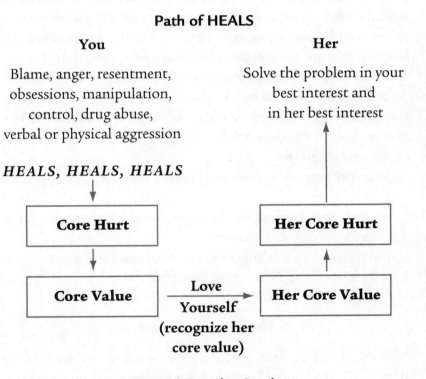

Path of HEALS

You	Her
Blame, anger, resentment, obsessions, manipulation, control, drug abuse, verbal or physical aggression	Solve the problem in your best interest and in her best interest

HEALS, HEALS, HEALS

Core Hurt	Her Core Hurt
Core Value	**Her Core Value**

Love Yourself (recognize her core value)

A HEALS Practice Session

Joe begins his first practice session before he gets out of bed in the morning. He thinks of the unpleasant words he exchanged the day before with his wife. She had reminded him twice to mow the lawn, as he had agreed to do. When she heard him mumble "nag" under his breath, she went into one of her sulks. He imagines that this unpleasant event has just happened. He feels the tension in his neck, around his eyes, jaw, in his chest, shoulders, arms, hands, and stomach. "I can't believe she's starting again," he thought. "After all I've done for her. It's not fair! If I'd said it to her out loud, it would be different!" Abruptly, he imagines the flashing letters, **"HEALS, HEALS, HEALS!"** over his wife's face as he hears the word in his head. He *experiences* his deepest core hurt for one second. (He felt unlovable.) He *accesses* his Core Value Bank—rescuing the child, the most important thing about him and about his life, his love for his wife and son, the spiritual connection he sometimes feels, the beauty he can see in nature and in music, his connection to his neighborhood, and compassionate things he has done. He *loves himself* by recognizing her core value and appreciating that she felt unlovable too. The problem he has to *solve* is that he doesn't want his wife to remind him of things he forgets to do. He knows that he can make her understand this if he's compassionate to her. Although she is still asleep, he kisses her on the cheek and gets out of bed to start his day.

After each practice repetition of HEALS, ask these three questions:

- Can I solve this problem better with anger and resentment or core value and compassion?
- Which do I prefer, anger or core value and compassion?
- Which makes me feel more powerful?

The Emotional Wave

After about four weeks of practice, your conscious awareness of the steps of HEALS should begin to fall away. By then you should experience a purely emotional wave, going from resentment, anger, or anxiety, quickly through core hurts, to core value, to solving the problem by reconnecting with your self-worth and valuing others. The emotional wave will be *without thought* but might be labeled:

HEALS flashing
Core hurt
Core value (a warm glow)
Love (compassion)
Solve the problem

By the end of your six weeks of work with HEALS, you will have little or no awareness of the transition from anger or resentment to core value, because you will be focused on how to make the situation better.*

Directions for the Experience Step of HEALS

Always go to the *deepest* core hurt. HEALS will not work if you do not go deeply enough. If the core hurt is "rejection" and you identify "unimportant," you have not validated your true emotional experience. That unregulated core hurt will cause more resentment and anger.

However, HEALS *will* work if you do go too deep. If you feel unimportant, and you identify the feeling as being unlovable, you'll still get it. Always err on the side of going too deep.

If you're feeling:

Disregarded: Feel what it's like to feel unworthy of regard, not to count enough for anyone to pay attention to your opinions, desires, and emotions.

Unimportant: Feel what it's like to be totally unimportant, not to matter at all, to be so unimportant that no one should consider having a passing positive thought about you.

Accused/Guilty: Feel what it is like to have done something wrong, to have hurt someone, to have done terrible damage, to have betrayed someone, to have been immoral.

---

*The major problem most people encounter when they first start practicing HEALS is trying to experience the emotion while remembering the steps *and* the incident that provoked resentment, anger, or anxiety. A CD-ROM is available to help you learn the steps (www.compassionpower.com).

Devalued: Feel what it's like to be totally without value as a person. You are *worthless*.

Rejected: Feel what it's like to be completely unacceptable, banished, put down, thrown out, abandoned.

Powerless: Feel what it's like to be completely without power over your internal experience, to be out of control in your thoughts, your emotions, and your behavior. You're like a puppet on a string or a robot whose buttons anyone can push. Anybody can make you think, feel, and do anything they want.

Inadequate/Unlovable: Feel what it's like to be so bad at relationships and love that you are unworthy of either. No one could love you. No one could love the real you. No one ever will. Don't be afraid to feel it so that it can be associated with—and healed—by your Core Value Bank.

Directions for the Love Yourself Step

We hear the term *love yourself* so often that we seem to know what it means. But if you think about it, what *does* it mean? Does it mean sending yourself flowers, taking yourself to dinner, kissing yourself? "Love yourself" has no literal meaning because love is a *transactional* verb, and you can't transact with yourself. It's like shaking your own hand—you can sort of do it but it's not really *shaking hands*. Yet "love yourself" does have an intuitive meaning. I think it means making yourself feel *worthy* of love. Take a moment to think of people you know who are especially worthy of love. I'll bet you're not thinking of people who care only about themselves and make no investments in the well-being of others. You're not thinking of resentful, angry, or abusive people. The lovable quality you're most likely thinking of is some form of compassion, which is the ability to make emotional investments in others, especially when they're in need. If you want to love yourself, you must feel something like compassion. The quickest way to feel lovable is to feel compassion for the person who offended you, but *not* for problematic behavior, which you handle in the "Solve the problem" step of HEALS. You feel compassion for the core hurt causing the bad behavior.

The core hurt of someone who intentionally offends you will most of the time be the same one that you felt in the Experience step of HEALS. For example, when my friend was a child, she sent a Valentine to a little boy on whom she had a crush. To her surprise and horror, he got irritated with her and told her never to send him another card. She was well aware of her own core hurts—feeling inadequate and unlovable—but it took the maturity of adulthood to see that the boy's core hurts were the same. He felt inadequate to return her feeling and therefore unworthy of it. He blamed his sinking value on her, and substituted power for value by attacking her. Once she understood that the boy felt inadequate, she understood that his behavior was about his own inadequacy, not hers. (People's behavior reflects the current state of *their* core value, no one else's. We devalue others *only* when we are in devalued states.) Compassion for his core hurt made my friend feel lovable, which made the false empowerment of resentment unnecessary.

Here's another example of the subtle symmetry of core hurts. My client Fran was angry at her husband for not calling her when he got to the hotel on a business trip. (They had been dealing with jealousy issues in their relationship for some time.) She said she could understand her core hurts but could not completely heal them until she could see his. Having to call her "to report in" as he put it, made him feel untrustworthy and unlovable. Her anger and jealousy, of course, could only make him feel more untrustworthy and unlovable. To regulate her anger, she had to sympathize with his core hurts. Otherwise, he would be defensive and unable to see hers. As a result, calling her would feel like submission to him, rather than cooperation or an act of caring.

This is a crucial point about relationships. It is not sufficient for Fran and her husband to control their anger; they must do it with compassion for themselves and for one another. Failure of compassion is the primary cause of anger, resentment, contempt, disgust, and abuse in relationships. The core hurt beneath your anger will almost always be the same as your loved one's, because both are reactions to the other's failure of compassion.

Problems with HEALS

If you have problems with HEALS, try the following:

1. Go deeper on the core hurt list. Don't be afraid to feel inadequate or unlovable, even if it seems worse than the core hurt you actually felt. Try to get as close as you can to feeling the *deepest* core hurt for *one second.*

2. If you have trouble making the transition to core value, try rapid eye movement. Focus your eyes on your finger and move it rapidly back and forth a few seconds.

3. In the Access core value step, deeply appreciate that, no matter what the trigger-incident, you do not deserve to continue feeling core hurts. Continuing to feel core hurts *impedes* your ability to make things better.

4. In the Love yourself step, recognize the core value of the person who offended you. He/she is far more complicated, complex, and humane than whatever he or she did to you. Appreciating the complexity of other people reinforces your own value.

5. In the Love yourself step, sympathize with the other person's core hurt that caused the behavior you don't like. (It will almost always be the same one you felt.) Feel compassion, not for the behavior, but for the hurt.

Practicing and mastering HEALS is essential to reverse the conditioned habits that have caused your relationship with your wife to suffer. I understand that it takes discipline and a high level of motivation to practice 12 times a day for six weeks. You have to decide that saving your family is worth the effort.

Twelve

The Power of Compassion

How do you know that you are worthy of love?

In a way, it's a trick question. So I'll give you a hint. It's not be-cause your wife loves you. The best she can do is make you feel *loved*. But if you don't feel *worthy* of love, it really doesn't feel good to be loved. It makes you feel like you're getting something you don't deserve and makes you feel guilty for not giving back as much as you get. It's very hard to love well if you don't feel lovable.

Here's the hot and hard truth: Only your own loving behavior can make you feel *worthy* of love. It's not rocket science. The only way to feel lovable is to be loving and compassionate.

Compassion is the most important emotion for forging inti-mate relationships. It contributes far more to happiness than love does. Relationships can be happy with low levels of love and high levels of compassion, but not the other way around. Why is com-passion so necessary for love relationships? For one thing, it sensi-tizes you to the individuality and vulnerability of your loved ones. It makes you see that your wife is a different person from you, with a separate set of experiences, a different temperament, different vulnerabilities, and, in some respects, different values. In contrast, if you feel the intensity of love without compassion, you can't see who she really is. She becomes merely a source of emotion for you, rather than a separate person in her own right. When she makes you feel good, she's on a pedestal. When she makes you feel bad, she becomes a demon. Love without compassion is possessive, controlling, rejecting, and dangerous.

Compassion, on the other hand, makes you protective, rather than controlling. The difference is crucial. When you're protective, you want to help her achieve what is best for her. Most of all, you want her to feel okay about herself. When you're controlling, you want her to feel bad for not doing what you want her to do.

Compassion versus Defensiveness

Practice and mastery of HEALS will automatically make you less defensive and better able to view your wife's worries, requests, and complaints with compassion for the core hurts that cause them. I'm talking about a basic, gut-level sensitivity to her hurt, even when she is not *showing* the hurt. This is especially important if she seems to be accusing you of something. It's natural to feel defensive when you're accused. But the implication when you defend yourself is that you don't care about her hurt, you care only about defending your own ego. The trick is to respond automatically to the hurt under the complaint, and then disagree with the accusation. But most of the time, when you are sympathetic to the hurt, she'll withdraw or at least attenuate her accusation. Consider the following examples of defensiveness versus compassion. First, we'll hear the common defensive response—I'd be rich if I had a dime each time I heard some variation on this one in my office.

"You're *never* home," Ruth said when Terrell came in late from work. "If you think I'm going to warm up your dinner, forget it. I'm not your maid."

"I came home on time two days this week," he countered. "You *know* how much work we have."

"Oh, two days out of five. I guess I should consider myself lucky.

I really wanted to get married to have a husband 20 percent of the time."

"Why should I bother to come home when I have to put up with *this*!"

You get the picture. They could go on like that all night, and sometimes they have done just that. They'd go back and forth at each other trying to decide who was right. Should he work less and spend more time with the family or should she be more understanding that he's working *for* the family?

Of course, they're *both* right. But it's not the either-or proposition they make it out to be. She *would* be more understanding of his hard work, if she felt connected to him when he *was* home. The problem is he feels guilty for not being home and blames it on her, which makes him insensitive to the fact that she misses him. Think about it, she's complaining because she misses him and wants to be with him.

Now here's how it looks when compassion overrides defensiveness.

"You're never home," Ruth accuses.

Terrell puts his brief case down and hugs her warmly. "I miss you when I have to work so much. You deserve more attention. I wish we didn't have so much work."

"Do you want me to warm up your dinner?"

Not only does compassion sensitize you to the core hurts under her resentment and anger, but it *calms* both of you with the soothing connection of attachment. This is what they *both* wanted in the countless defensive dialogues they had previously—to feel calm and connected. Substitute compassion for defensiveness, and you'll find that you won't have to be defensive at all.

Failures of Compassion: Definitions of Abuse

Abuse is hurting the feelings or body of someone else. All abuse begins with a *failure of compassion*. It actually begins with a failure of compassion for yourself. You fail to recognize your own core hurt and fail to heal it by activating your core value. When you fail at self-compassion, failure of compassion for your loved ones is inevitable.

Physical abuse is hitting, pinching, punching, slapping, pushing, grabbing, kicking, and any unwanted touching, sexual or nonsexual, as well as threatening, coercing, or intimidating.

Emotional abuse includes attacks on autonomy (the ability to decide one's own thoughts, feelings, and behavior), identity, privacy, sense of self, or self-esteem. You try to disempower her, to make her think poorly of herself and feel bad about herself. You may attempt to control, isolate, or force behavior against her will. You criticize who she *is*, rather than what she *does*.

Probably the most common kind of abuse is negative labeling. Besides the fact that it's about unchangeable characteristics of personality rather than negotiable behavior, negative labels virtually guarantee that you'll get more of the behavior you're describing. After all, what do lazy people do? Well, they don't help around the house, for one thing. What do bad kids do?"

Abusive	Nonabusive
"You're lazy."	"I feel you can do a little more to help keep the house clean."
"You're stupid."	"I disagree with your opinion."
"You're a slut."	"I felt jealous when I saw you talk to him. I need to regulate my jealousy."
"You're a bitch."	"I feel bad when you shout."
"You're a bad kid."	"I don't like it when you talk disrespectfully to me."

Criticism

Research shows that two negative characteristics of relationships predict divorce with more than 90 percent accuracy. The first of these is criticism. Even when criticism is about behavior, it will be destructive if it is filled with blame; if it devalues—you are "less than" because of this behavior; if it focuses on what the person has done wrong rather than how to do it right; or if it implies that there is only one right way to do things.

Criticism inevitably causes two other conditions that contribute mightily to divorce: defensiveness and contempt. It's hard *not* to be defensive when you are criticized. If the criticism is chronic, you develop a defensive-resentment that all but eliminates intimacy. You begin to see the person you love as an opponent first, then as an enemy. Contempt soon follows, unless you have evolved enough to love your enemies.

Critical people tend to be highly *self-critical*. As hard as they might be on others, they are usually harder on themselves. They were almost always criticized as children, at least implicitly—the message was clear that, in important ways, they weren't quite good enough. Self-critical patterns tend to form in early childhood, and by early adulthood they mutate into chronic criticism of others. The following exercises can help you sort through this kind of criticism.

Identify the core hurts your wife or children are likely to experience when you criticize them overtly or by implication:

1.

2.

3.

Dialogue with the Roots of Criticism

Think of when you were a young child and you made a mistake for which you were criticized or punished. Try to imagine the criticism or punishment in as much detail as you can, and describe what you thought and felt (be sure to identify your deepest core hurts):

Invoke the emotions of your Core Value Bank. Imagine comforting the distressed child. Think of the most important thing about you as a person and the most important thing about your life in general. Feel the love you have for the people closest to you. Feel your spiritual connection. Think of something beautiful in nature. Think of your favorite art or music. Imagine a community you feel comfortable with, and think of three compassionate things you have done.

From your core value, write what you would like to tell that criticized or punished child:

(If you're stuck, here's a consensus of what dozens of my clients have written: "You're okay. You love your parents. You're good to people. You're good to your dog. You're smart. You're caring. You have a good heart.")

From your core value, write what you would like to tell your criticized or punished wife or significant other:

Stonewalling

While men and women can be equally critical, the second relationship characteristic that predicts divorce with greater than 90 percent accuracy is almost exclusively male. *Stonewalling* is refusal even to consider your wife's perspective. If you listen to her at all, you do it dismissively or contemptuously—as if she doesn't have anything to say that's worth hearing. You might refer to her as a nag, or garbage mouth, or just choose to ignore her. Or you might say, "Do whatever you want, just leave me alone." If you continue to stonewall, you can expect to be divorced within five years.

Identify the core hurts she is likely to experience when you stonewall:

1.

2.

3.

Dialogue with the Roots of Stonewalling

Think of when you were a young child and you were stonewalled. Someone didn't care about how you felt or what you thought. If you tried to get that person's attention, you would be ignored, blown-off, or put down. Describe what it was like for you and which core hurts you felt.

Take a moment to invoke the emotions of your Core Value Bank. Imagine comforting the distressed child. Think of the most important thing about you as a person and the most important thing about your life in general. Feel the love you have for the people closest to you. Feel your spiritual connection. Think of something beautiful in nature. Think of your favorite art or music. Imagine a community you feel comfortable with, and think of three compassionate things you have done.

From your core value, write what you would like to tell that ignored, blown-off, or put-down child? Include what that child needed to hear about whether his thoughts and feelings matter.

(If you're stuck, here's a consensus of what some clients have written: "What you have to say matters. When I hear you say what's important to you, *I* feel more important. You contribute so much to my life.")

From your core value, write what you would like to tell your ignored, blown-off, or put-down wife. Do her thoughts and feelings matter?

(If you're stuck, here's a consensus of what some clients have written: "I'll protect you and help you find the strength in yourself to cope. We can make each other strong—that's how important you are to me.")

If this applies to you, think of when you were a young child and you felt overwhelmed by the emotional demands of some adults. You felt trapped, like they wouldn't leave you alone. Write down what that was like.

Take a moment to invoke the emotions of your Core Value Bank. Imagine comforting the distressed child. Think of the most important thing about you as a person and the most important thing about your life in general. Feel the love you have for the people closest to you. Feel your spiritual connection. Think of something beautiful in nature. Think of your favorite art or music. Imagine a community you feel comfortable with, and think of three compassionate things you have done.

From your core value, write what you would like to tell that overwhelmed child.

In your core value, realize that you are no longer a child who needs to shut down to protect himself. Now you're a man who can be protective of your wife or significant other. Write how you can be protective of your partner's anxiety, fear, vulnerability, guilt, and shame.

Compulsion to Control

Resentful, angry, or abusive behavior—attempts to substitute power for value—often come from blaming your anxious *temperament* on your wife. In other words, you were *born* with a higher-than-average level of anxiety. If that is the case, from the time you were a young child you've probably had a pretty consistent sense of dread that things might go wrong and that you'll *fail* to cope in some way. As a result, you expend enormous amounts of emotional energy trying to *avoid* terrible feelings of failure and inadequacy. Unfortunately, instead of investing your emotional energy in becoming successful and feeling adequate, you waste most of it trying to control other people. This is a common strategy to numb the pain of anxiety. Most people who employ it experienced one of two extremes as children: They were either over-controlled by their parents, which implied that they were incompetent, or they were not guided or disciplined enough, which made them feel uncertain and confused, as it does most children. The following exercise will help both of these anxiety conditions.

Dialogue with the Roots of Controlling Behavior

Think of when you were a young child and you felt that you were constantly being told what to do. Your own judgment, ideas, thoughts, or feelings didn't matter. Describe what that felt like (be sure to identify your deepest core hurts):

Invoke the emotions of your Core Value Bank. Imagine comforting the distressed child. Think of the most important thing about you as a person and the most important thing about your life in general. Feel the love you have for the people closest to you. Feel your spiritual connection. Think of something beautiful in nature. Think of your favorite art or music. Imagine a community you feel comfortable with, and think of three compassionate things you have done.

From your core value, write what you would like to tell that controlled and disregarded child:

From your core value, write what you would like to tell your
controlled or disregarded wife or significant other:

Dialogue with the Roots of Controlling Behavior II

Think of when you were a young child and you felt that you
had to raise yourself—you had to make all the important
decisions about your day-to-day activities and your life in
general on your own—without reliable guidance or support.
Try to feel what it was like to face uncertainty by yourself.
Describe what it felt like (be sure to identify your deepest core
hurts):

Invoke the emotions of your Core Value Bank. Imagine
comforting the distressed child. Think of the most important
thing about you as a person and the most important thing
about your life in general. Feel the love you have for the people

closest to you. Feel your spiritual connection. Think of something beautiful in nature. Think of your favorite art or music. Imagine a community you feel comfortable with, and think of three compassionate things you have done.

From your core value, write what you would like to tell that alone and unsure child:

From your core value, write what you would like to tell your controlled or disregarded wife or significant other:

Resentment

Chances are, you don't have a good sex life. It's either not frequent enough or not completely satisfying when it does happen. How do I know that? Resentment is the number one intimacy barrier. Intimacy requires letting down defenses, and resentment will not allow you to do that. *If you want to have any hope of enjoying a decent sex life, you have to resolve resentment.*

Resentment actually destroys *all* levels of intimacy; it's just that in the bedroom the lack of intimacy is most noticeable. You are likely not touching as much, not sharing experiences, and not talking to one another, although you probably talk *at* one another quite a bit. If you want to have any hope of enjoying a better relationship, you have to resolve resentment, which is the heart disease of relationships. Unhealed, resentment leads inevitably to contempt and contempt leads more than 90 percent of the time to divorce.

Of the three demons that threaten so many relationships—resentment, anger, and abuse—resentment is the most insidious. It's the hardest to notice, so it can build up while still under the radar and then lead quickly to the other two. In fact, most anger and abuse rise out of deep wells of resentment. This is how it works. If you're at baseline, with no resentment at all, and something happens that you don't like, it will typically get you about 30 percent aroused, which is no big deal. You might think something sarcastic but you probably won't say anything and it will go away in a few minutes.

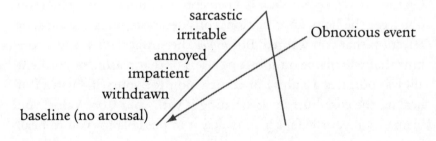

Dissipates in minutes

sarcastic
irritable   Obnoxious event
annoyed
impatient
withdrawn
baseline (no arousal)

But if you start out resentful, you're already 30 percent aroused. So that same event that would hardly cause any trouble at baseline, gets you about 60 percent aroused, which is where you start getting angry, controlling, and aggressive.

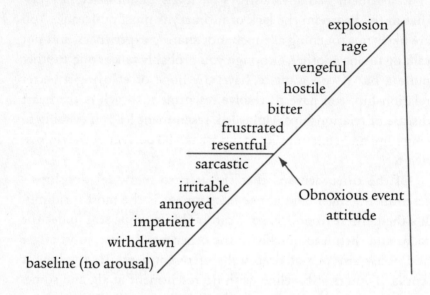

Add caffeine, nicotine, anxiety, or a startle response to the mix, and the adrenaline can easily go through the roof.

Replacing Resentment with Compassion

On the surface, resentment is a perception of unfairness, when you don't get the help, appreciation, consideration, praise, reward, or affection that you wanted. But *under* the surface, it's really a core hurt that you blame on someone else. For that reason, resentment always indicates a failure of compassion for yourself—instead of healing the core hurt by associating it with your Core Value, you blame it on your wife, which makes it impossible for you to heal. Restoring compassion for yourself heals you and automatically increases compassion for loved ones.

Use the following list of resentments to identify your core hurt and indicate what you can do to improve it. For example, if the core hurt is feeling *unlovable*, indicate what you can do that will make you feel more lovable. Then identify your partner's core hurt, and what you can do to help.

Resentment List

List the things you resent about your wife or significant other. Be as thorough and honest as you can. This means that some of the items on your list will be petty. *Nothing* is too petty to resent. When you have finished, read your list *slowly* and *out loud.*

1. I resent:

   a. This is the core hurt driving my resentment:

   b. This is what I can do to make my core hurt better:

   c. This is my significant other's core hurt:

   d. This is how I can help:

2. I resent:

   a. This is the core hurt driving my resentment:

   b. This is what I can do to make my core hurt better:

   c. This is my significant other's core hurt:

   d. This is how I can help:

3. I resent:

   a. This is the core hurt driving my resentment:

   b. This is what I can do to make my core hurt better:

   c. This is my significant other's core hurt:

   d. This is how I can help:

4. I resent:

   a. This is the core hurt driving my resentment:

   b. This is what I can do to make my core hurt better:

   c. This is my significant other's core hurt:

   d. This is how I can help:

5. I resent:

    a. This is the core hurt driving my resentment:

    b. This is what I can do to make my core hurt better:

    c. This is my significant other's core hurt:

    d. This is how I can help:

6. I resent:

    a. This is the core hurt driving my resentment:

    b. This is what I can do to make my core hurt better:

    c. This is my significant other's core hurt:

    d. This is how I can help:

7. I resent:

    a. This is the core hurt driving my resentment:

b. This is what I can do to make my core hurt better:

c. This is my significant other's core hurt:

d. This is how I can help:

8. I resent:

a. This is the core hurt driving my resentment:

b. This is what I can do to make my core hurt better:

c. This is my significant other's core hurt:

d. This is how I can help:

9. I resent:

a. This is the core hurt driving my resentment:

b. This is what I can do to make my core hurt better:

c. This is my significant other's core hurt:

d. This is how I can help:

10. I resent:

    a. This is the core hurt driving my resentment:

    b. This is what I can do to make my core hurt better:

    c. This is my significant other's core hurt:

    d. This is how I can help:

Power

Write what you can do to improve (not necessarily fix) each item on your resentment list. *Note:* Ignoring it improves nothing.

This is what *I* can do to improve *my experience* of item 1 on my resentment list.

This is what *I* can do to improve *my experience* of item 2 on my resentment list.

This is what *I* can do to improve *my experience* of item 3 on my resentment list.

This is what *I* can do to improve *my experience* of item 4 on my resentment list.

This is what *I* can do to improve *my experience* of item 5 on my resentment list.

This is what *I* can do to improve *my experience* of item 6 on my resentment list.

This is what *I* can do to improve *my experience* of item 7 on my resentment list.

This is what *I* can do to improve *my experience* of item 8 on my resentment list.

This is what *I* can do to improve *my experience* of item 9 on my resentment list.

This is what I can do to improve *my experience* of item 10 on my resentment list.

Jealousy

Jealousy is a dramatic example of an ordinary emotion that becomes a problem when it sets off a cycle of core hurts and blame. When that happens, jealousy becomes an obsession—you can't stop thinking about it. The more we obsess about something, the more imagination takes over, distorting reality and rational thinking even further. Jealousy is the only natural emotion that can make you psychotic.

The hidden meaning of pathological jealousy is, "I'm not lovable, so she must want someone else." If deep in our hearts we feel that we're not worthy of love (because we can't sustain compassion for others), we won't believe those who say they love us. They either love the false self—the show that we all put up to some extent in dating—or they want something else—like my money, my house, my car, my socks, or *someone* else.

The more you try to manage jealousy by swallowing it or by attempting to control your wife's behavior, the more powerless you get because you become totally dependent on her to feel okay about yourself. Jealousy, like all negative emotion, must be regulated *within*.

Once jealousy stimulates a core hurt, it becomes a signal that you need to access core value. You can't do this through accusations or demands that your wife tell you her schedule and account for her every minute away from you. The *only* thing that can turn the pain of jealousy into core value is for you to be more compassionate and loving. Remember the natural instinct of the toddler who first experiences jealousy and tries to squeeze between the embracing parents and be more *loving*.

You can think of jealousy as a distance sensor in your relationship. You're most likely to experience jealousy when you are disconnected—there's too much psychological distance between you and your wife. Learn to interpret your feelings of jealousy as a signal to close the distance between you. That means that you *must* be more loving and compassionate at the very first sign of jealousy.

If you are not, the distance between you will widen. You will get more and more jealous and do greater damage to yourself and to your relationship.

Jealousy Eradicator:

1. Restore core value.
2. Be more compassionate and loving.

Jealousy List

List three instances when you became jealous. Identify your core hurt in each one. Identify your partner's core hurt. Indicate what you could have done to make your core hurt better. What could you have done to make your relationship stronger and more loving?

1. My jealous incident:

   a. My core hurt:

   b. Her core hurt:

   c. What I could have done to heal my core hurt:

   d. What I could have done to make my relationship stronger and more loving:

2. My jealous incident:

---

    a. My core hurt:

    b. Her core hurt:

    c. What I could have done to heal my core hurt:

    d. What I could have done to make my relationship stronger and more loving:

3. My jealous incident:

    a. My core hurt:

    b. Her core hurt:

    c. What I could have done to heal my core hurt:

    d. What I could have done to make my relationship stronger and more loving:

Perspective-Taking

When you are compassionate, you can see things from someone else's perspective. A study of marriage and divorce shows why this is so important: More than 70 percent of all divorces are initiated by women who say they feel isolated and unheard by their husbands. Your marriage cannot be successful unless you strive to see your partner's perspective. You must learn to understand it and to value it, *especially* when you disagree with it. That's the key point: you don't have to agree, but you have to value.

Perspective-Taking Exercise

Take each item on your resentment and jealousy lists and give *her* perspective of it. Write how you think she would describe it, not what you think of it.

Her perspective of my resentment item 1:

Her perspective of my resentment item 2:

Her perspective of my resentment item 3:

Her perspective of my resentment item 4:

Her perspective of my resentment item 5:

Her perspective of my resentment item 6:

Her perspective of my resentment item 7:

Her perspective of my resentment item 8:

Her perspective of my resentment item 9:

Her perspective of my resentment item 10:

Her perspective of my jealousy item 1:

Her perspective of my jealousy item 2:

Her perspective of my jealousy item 3:

Describe your perspective in a recent dispute with your wife.

Which symptom or defense (anger, resentment, anxiety, obsessions, depression, manipulation, controlling behavior, etc.) did you act on?

What was your deepest core hurt during the dispute?

What was *her* perspective or point of view—not as you would judge but *as she would relate it?*

Which was her deepest core hurt?

Did she feel that you understood her?

How would she describe you at that moment?

Did you feel understood by her?

From your core value, what solution to this problem would you suggest now? (Keep in mind that anything worsening core hurts will fail).

Increasing Interest in Your Wife

For this exercise, ask your wife how her day was. After she answers, briefly describe her:

Body language:

Facial expression:

Tone of voice:

Speech inflections:

Mood:

Emotions:

General thoughts:

Now share your observations with her and check their accuracy.

List the reasons to feel compassion (understand, sympathize, support, and empower) for your wife.

1.

2.

3.

4.

5.

Supporting Your Attachment Bond

List *five* things you can do to enhance and support your attachment bond with your wife.

1.

2.

3.

4.

5.

Cooperation: Behavior Requests and Tolerance of Differences

You do not want *obedience* in your home, you want *cooperation*. When people feel valued, they cooperate. When they don't feel valued, they naturally resist—it feels to them like they're being asked to *submit*.

The two keys to resentment-free cooperation are to make behavior requests and tolerate differences.

Many of the things that make you want to criticize, control, or

reject your partner involve little more than differences in temperament, tastes, experience, family of origin history, and to some
extent, culture and values. In other words, one way is not *superior* to
the other, each is just *different*.

Jason used to get so resentful about his wife putting her purse
on the dining room table. He considered her behavior to be
thoughtless and inconsiderate. One of his favorite sayings was that
"*decent* people don't clutter up their houses like this!" So in this
dispute, who is *right*, Jason or his wife?

Actually *both* are right. He has the right to keep his home free of
clutter and she has an equal right to relax in her own home and put
her purse wherever she wants. There are no neatness police or eti-
quette courts. They are *both* right.

Once you realize that you are equally right in most of your disputes, you can no longer make demands for *compliance* or *obedience*.
You have to make behavior *requests* for *cooperation*. Requests for cooperation differ from criticism and attempts to control in one simple
way. In a request, you recognize that the other person doesn't *have*
to do what you ask. Accordingly, you pose no threat of reprisal if
she doesn't carry out the request.

"Would you please do this, but I'll understand if you don't want
to do it or can't get to it."

About 70 percent of the time, requests like the one above get a
positive response. (It will be an even higher percentage once you resolve the resentment in your relationship.) If you're thinking that
70 percent is not good enough, compare it with the alternative.
How often do you think controlling behavior, including demands
and directives, will get a negative response? Virtually 100 percent
of the time. (Even when you get what you want at the moment,
you'll pay for it down the line with resentment and hostility.)
When one person in a family wins, *everybody* loses—the winner
wins only resentment and hostility. Either everyone wins and feels
okay about the resolution, or everyone loses.

Remember, requests for cooperation are not demands, so you

cannot mete out any consequences, such as complaining, bitching, withdrawing affection, pouting, or sulking if your request is not met.

Requests for cooperation work on the principle of equality *despite* differences. If you want to have a good relationship, you *must* respect personal differences. Very often, the differences you bicker about are the very things you used to love about that person. Jason, the man who complained about his wife putting her purse on the table, first fell in love with her because she was "mellow and laid back." He bragged to all his friends how this wonderful woman "helped me relax." And she first fell in love with him because he was "so organized and paid attention to detail." She bragged to all her friends too, "Nothing gets by him—I feel so safe and secure with him." Their dispute about household appearance was entirely predictable from what they loved about each other. That's almost always the case with couples, simply because we are not attracted to our own temperaments. We want someone to energize us if our temperamental energy is low and someone to relax us if it is high. If you're the type of person who pays a lot of attention to detail or to tasks with deadlines, you want a partner who can see the big picture and process things more deliberately. In other words, you look for someone with whom you can make a good team.

A successful basketball team needs a point guard *and* a center. No matter how good the individual players might be a team of all point guards or all centers will lose. You can make a good team in a relationship only if you don't try to make the other person be just like you. Have you ever noticed that in your arguments you're actually saying to your wife, "Why can't you be more like me?" Of course, the irony is you wouldn't have been attracted to her if she were more like you. We want *differences* in relationships (so we can make *harmony*); we don't want clones of ourselves that keep playing the same note over and over.

Try this experiment. Review your resentment list and pick out the items that represent qualities you first came to love in your partner. You will be surprised to realize that you used to admire the very characteristics that produce the behaviors you now find so irritating. The difference is that your core value was high when you were falling in love, and that made you more tolerant.

We'll return to this subject in Chapter 17. There you will learn how most power struggles between husbands and wives occur when they resent each other for the very qualities they used to love about one another. There you will learn a proven technique to resolve such power struggles with mutual compassion and caring.

Thirteen

Your Wife Needs Time and Lots of Compassion to Recover

Earlier in this Boot Camp section we talked about how resentful, angry, and abusive behavior affects men and women differently. The greater fear response that women have also means that their recovery from walking on eggshells is especially difficult. It's hard for men to understand this, because the male experience of fear is so different from that of women. Men are less likely to perceive a situation as dangerous and when they do, they are less likely to carry residual effects of their fear—once whatever made a man afraid is over, his fear is over. What's more, when men are injured, they are less likely to connect fear with the injury, which is why they continue to do things that have injured them in the past. When women are injured, the pain becomes etched with any fear they may have experienced around the injury. Repeated experiences of fear condition women to think that something harmful *could* happen at any time and that they are never really safe. Consequently, it takes a very long period of sustained safety and security for their central nervous systems to accept that a threat to their safety or well-being is unlikely to recur.

This slow recovery period has nothing to do with your wife's personality. It has to do with the survival implications of pain. The brain processes pain (and fear-invoking memories of pain) on a dedicated neural network that gives pain priority attention. This creates an overly sensitive, *involuntary*, almost reflexive response to avoid the recurrence of pain that invoked fear. The recently burned hand *flinches* near the heat of a stove because the pain has been associated with the heat, which then triggers the automatic alarm. This involuntary flinch persists until new experience shows that pain caused by the stove is unlikely to recur, as long as behavior around the heat is careful.

Sensitivity Threshold Pre-Burn　　　　　　**Sensitivity Post-Burn**

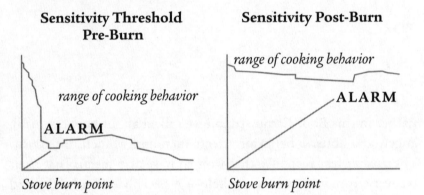

Stove burn point　　　　　　*Stove burn point*

Just as feeling heat triggers the flinch in burn victims, the reinstatement of intimacy, which requires that she let her defenses down, can trigger the same kind of involuntary "flinch." The alarm can sound in her head at the most inopportune time, like during a warm embrace or a moment of enjoyment: "Wait a minute! The last time we trusted him. . . ." She'll push away from you or just freeze. You'll feel rejected and she'll feel guilty. Both painful emotions will likely surface as anger or resentment.

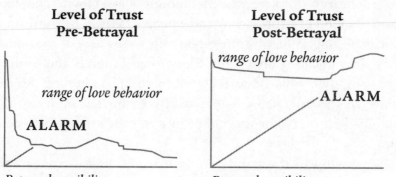

**Level of Trust
Pre-Betrayal**

range of love behavior

ALARM

Betrayal possibility

**Level of Trust
Post-Betrayal**

range of love behavior

ALARM

Betrayal possibility

You must absolutely understand that your wife isn't flinching to hurt you. Believe me, she doesn't like feeling that way. Here are just a few of the symptoms she may be experiencing:

- Flashbacks from the past (sometimes from past relationships or from childhood).
- Anxiety or anger that comes out of nowhere.
- Confusion.
- Impaired decision-making.
- Depression.
- Aggressive impulses.

It's important enough to repeat that these symptoms are not part of her *personality*. They are merely a delayed *physiological* response to a history of walking on eggshells. For many people they are a perfectly natural stage of recovery from a prolonged period of stress.

The Steps of Healing

Healing *always* occurs in discreet stages. Take a cut on the hand for example. The first stage in the healing process is an elevation of heart rate, to bleed out any bacteria that might have entered the body through the open wound. The second stage is a precipitous drop in heart rate, to decrease the amount of lost blood. (The steep drop in blood pressure is why some people faint.) The third stage is massive migration of white blood cells to the area of the injury, to destroy invading organisms. Blood then congeals and forms a soft scab, then a hard one, followed by complete healing. All the while, the body remains hypersensitive to further injury of the wounded area—if someone bumps into it, your instinct is to deck him.

What happens if you interfere with any of these discrete stages of healing? If you pick at the scab you're back to square one, and the process begins all over again.

The psychological effects of walking on eggshells take quite a bit longer to heal than a cut on the hand. But like a cut on the hand, any interference with the discreet stages of healing, such as you urging that she, "Get over it," or, "Let it go already," or, "Stop living in the past," is the emotional equivalent of picking at the scab. It will not only retard the healing process but also run the risk of returning you both to square one. *Only an uninterrupted flow of compassion will renew a bond capable of enduring over the long run.*

Time Dimensions of Recovery

There are three dimensions to recovery from abuse, and each is characterized by its own set of behaviors and challenges. It's important to know which reactions are from the past and *label* them as leftovers of the past. *Blaming* and threats to safety and well-being will certainly bring back the past. You must replace them with responsibility, respect, value, support, and mutual growth. Only when the following *present behaviors* are firmly established can you expect to move into the future with intimacy and trust reinstated.

THE PAST	THE PRESENT	THE FUTURE
blame	**responsibility**	**responsibility**
danger	**safety**	**safety**
insulting	respect	trust

injured feelings	value	intimacy
emotional battering	support	support
physical harm	mutual growth	mutual growth
police, court, jail		

Once betrayed, trust is slow to be restored. Any attempt to renew full trust too soon sets up both of you for almost certain failure. There most likely have been many intervals in your relationship when your wife did not have to walk on eggshells. There's no way her overstressed central nervous system can know whether the improvements you make after mastering the skills described in these pages are just another pause in the tension that causes her to walk on eggshells. No matter how much she wants to trust you, her brain will not let her drop defenses completely for *at least* six to nine months of uninterrupted compassion and understanding from you. And you're going to have to maintain this compassion and understanding even when—*especially* when—she cannot reciprocate. For quite a while there will be little reward besides that inherent in compassion.

Caution

When recovery fails after the Boot Camp, and the relationship dissolves, it is almost always for one of two reasons: alcohol/drug abuse or the man's failure to maintain compassion and understanding of his wife's long recovery process. One abuser I worked with did very well in his Boot Camp and went home to his wife full of compassion and love, with a strong desire to start a new life with her. But he could not appreciate how hurt she had been and how long a recovery process was required. When she could not return his compassion and exuberance within a few weeks, he gave up. He never returned to the yelling and flagrant abuse shown on the hidden cameras, but he withdrew from her and devalued her in a quieter but just as hurtful way.

The Secret of Recovery

You and your wife need to understand that her current trouble with diminished trust and intimacy is actually a rejection of the *past* abusive relationship, and not of the *present* healing relationship. This knowledge will limit flashbacks and shorten the time you need to replenish trust, love, and uninhibited intimacy.

Your Statement of Compassion

Perhaps the most crucial step in your healing is the next exercise, your Statement of Compassion. It will not only help you to heal, it can also help your wife heal. You can accomplish this dual goal by keeping your focus on helping her feel better now and in the future, rather than on how bad you feel about the past. Accordingly, do not ask for forgiveness in your statement. True compassion respects that forgiveness has to do entirely with her personal healing process. She may never be able to completely forgive you. But whether she can or not, her forgiveness is unnecessary to your healing and to your compassionate identity.

Don't attempt to *justify* whatever hurt you did, for that will serve to *keep open your wounds*. Don't say, "I only hurt you because you hurt me." Healing requires acceptance of the fact that you *don't have to hurt back*, indeed that hurting back only hurts you more. Your statement of compassion is an exercise in *pride*, clearly showing the difference between what you were in the past and what you're becoming with the development of your new skills.

Statement of Compassion

1. State *how* you hurt your wife. List all instances of *verbal*, *emotional*, and *physical abuse*.

2. What effects has your behavior had on her, *especially* her capacity to sustain the attachment emotions: *interest, compassion, trust, intensity of affection, intimacy,* and *commitment*?

3. What effects has your behavior had on you, *especially* on your capacity to sustain the attachment emotions: *interest, compassion, trust, intensity of affection, intimacy, and commitment*?

4. Did your behavior make the situation better or worse?

5. State how you intend in the future to negotiate and cooperate rather than engage in power struggles (include the difference between negotiation/cooperation and power struggles).

6. State *specifically* what you need to do to keep the fangs retracted in the future so that you will never intentionally hurt her.

The *Great* Achievement of Earning Back Trust

Earning back trust is a slow, difficult process. Fortunately, it is also an opportunity to strengthen your relationship, to make it stronger than it was before you began walking on eggshells. It gives you an opportunity to right the wrongs of the past and sets the stage for the most stirring of all human experiences: redemption.

You deserve compassion unconditionally. But you have to *earn* trust, especially once it has been betrayed.

The Earning Back Trust Formula

Increased compassion + Increased value + Respect for her recovery timing
÷ Impulse to punish (to get back at her for rejection)

To earn back trust, you *cannot* stay on the top layer of emotional interactions depicted in the following figure. You must be sensitive to your core hurts *and* to hers. You must be true to your core value and appreciate hers.

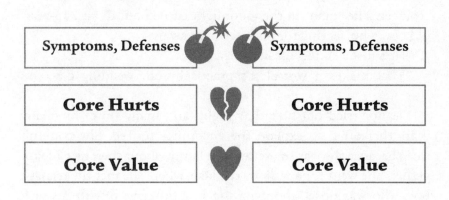

Most of your interactions and all of your disagreements, for the next six to nine months *at least*, must occur in recognition of your core hurts and of hers. They must occur in appreciation of her core value as well as your own. The following is a partially fictionalized composite of several different clients and circumstances to illustrate crucial points about recovery from walking on eggshells.

Ted and Eleanor had only one fight in their marriage. It started shortly after their honeymoon and ended many years later, following his work in the Boot Camp.

In the middle of the first night in their new marital home, Ted startled awake—a fairly common occurrence when you're going through a lot of changes in your life. His startled reaction turned to anxiety when he saw the empty place beside him where Eleanor had been sleeping. He got really worried when she didn't answer his calls and when he couldn't find her anywhere in their new lakeside town house. By the time he ran outside to look for her, he was panicked. He walked in one direction and saw nothing, then he started running the opposite way, when he noticed a lantern-flashlight about 500 yards in the distance, where the lake meandered around an old rock formation. As he ran toward the light, he saw that Eleanor, in her pajamas, was talking to the man holding the lantern. His fear instantly turned to fury. He ran toward them as fast as he could and as soon as he was within earshot, accused his new bride of having planned a midnight rendezvous with the stranger. The "man" in the moonlight turned out to be a 15-year-old boy, who, fearing for his safety, ran away.

"He's just a child," Eleanor pleaded.

"That makes it worse! It's practically our wedding day, you slut!"

Eleanor tried her best that night, and many times for many years thereafter, to explain the encounter to Ted. She couldn't sleep because she was so excited and happy about their new life together. She went for a walk by the lake, where she met the teenage boy, who was upset about having just broken up with his girlfriend.

Most of the time, Ted was rational enough to accept this obvious explanation. But for reasons he couldn't entirely understand, he never trusted Eleanor after that night. For the rest of their marriage, she walked on eggshells, never sure when his jealousy would flare up again. She had to account for almost every minute of her time and had to take care not to be too courteous to waiters and service men in his presence. She felt like an ex-con, constantly under suspicion by the police. Ted was just as tormented by his own vacillation between logical reality and the totally irrational jealousy that would come out nowhere, with awful regularity.

Like most men, Ted made a dramatic recovery in his Boot Camp. He realized that jealousy is about feeling unlovable and if he just tried to be compassionate and loving when he *first started* to feel jealous, he would train his brain to greatly reduce the frequency and intensity of this most uncomfortable feeling. But Ted's problem with jealousy had an added feature, which I had seen several times before; it would give him a deeper sympathy for Eleanor's dilemma: He had *startled* when he woke up and saw that she was gone on that unfortunate night. Then he *panicked* while he was looking for her. His exaggerated fear response elevated his core hurt to priority processing in his brain, making it an involuntary, visceral reaction, similar to what we experience if we suddenly see a snake coiled by our feet. Ted was so irrational in his jealousy because his involuntary, visceral response never got to the higher, logical processing of his brain, just as the initial response to what seems to be a snake near your feet is not to calculate the statistical probability of a reptile being in that region of the country at that moment. Frequent practice of HEALS *reconditioned* his unconscious response. Just as important, it also made him realize how difficult it would be for Eleanor to recover, as her reactions to him over the years had been laced with fear.

How They Rebuilt Trust

About 10 days after his Boot Camp, Ted was, without warning, fired from his job as an electrical engineer. Actually, the company said that it was downsizing, but Ted felt like a loser and could hear no other explanation for being let go. He tried at first to find another job, but the downsizing in his field seemed to be industry-wide. After a few weeks, he gave up and sank into a deep depression. Eleanor, who had been a stay-at-home mom for their two boys, got a job as a secretary in the very company that had let her husband go.

Unemployment is a major predictor of emotional abuse and domestic violence. Ironically, when men feel like they have failed to protect their families financially, they tend to turn against them emotionally. This is a tragic misinterpretation of their instinct to protect, which goes beyond money to include *all* areas of your family's well-being. *If you lose your job, you must be* more *emotionally protective of your wife and children.*

Many times during his unemployment, Ted was tempted to drink, but he knew that the power of HEALS would be diminished if he did, so he had promised Eleanor that he would not to touch a drop. (Actually, the effects of HEALS will hold for one drink but not reliably past that.) He stayed true to his word about drinking, yet, to his deep disappointment, the old jealous feelings started to return. They came to a head on the night that Eleanor called from her car to say that she got a flat tire but that a nice man was stopping to help her. All Ted could imagine was a handsome stranger kissing and fondling his attractive wife in the backseat of her car. When she got home later that night, he said nothing about his suspicions or destructive fantasies. He didn't have to. She knew the way that he was avoiding her that something was wrong.

Once again, Eleanor started second-guessing herself—not as bad as when she had been walking on eggshells every day—nevertheless, she told herself that she shouldn't have accepted help from anyone, that she should have waited for Ted to come and help her. She blamed herself for the resentment she saw in his face and worried that he would soon relapse. She was right about Ted's resentment, but it wasn't directed at her. He was angry at himself for allowing his jealousy to flare up again. He, too, was thinking how he *should* have responded. He thought that he should have done HEALS before she got home. He didn't realize that, with tension mounting, this was a perfect time to practice. Had he done HEALS at that moment, he could have reconnected with Eleanor and made them both feel better.

The next day, Ted tried to explain to me, he let the wind blow the front door shut behind him as he walked in the house from the backyard, and it made a loud noise. Anger at himself was the more likely explanation of how the door got slammed, but that's not the one that occurred to Eleanor. The door-slamming startled her, and the adrenaline rush that followed turned her anxiety into anger.

"I am so sick of this crap!" she screamed. "Why did I ever think you would change? How *stupid* could I be?"

Ted pretended not to know what she meant—a flashback to their walking-on-eggshells days. "*What* are you talking about, woman?" he grumbled.

"I am so sick of you!" she screamed back at him. "All you ever think about is yourself. You're supposed to be compassionate now? Compassion my ass! You haven't changed one single bit."

"You know how hard I've worked," he protested, hardly able to get out the words.

"I know how hard you *say* you've worked, but you're just as much of a Neanderthal as ever. I was just so stupid to think you could be different."

"You don't think I've changed at all?" He was astonished and defensive—a serious lapse of compassion for his own core hurt and for Eleanor's.

"This whole compassion thing is all just another one of your *manipulations*," she shouted. "You didn't take that damn Boot Camp to change; you took it to make me feel guilty. Well, the only thing I feel guilty about is putting up with you for all those years. It disgusts me just to look at you. Who wouldn't want to be with another man, after living with you? A real man would never put his wife through what I've been through with *you*."

Ted had never seen this much rage and disgust from his petite, usually demure wife. He turned away from her and practiced HEALS to himself.

"Go ahead, turn away," she shouted. "Act like a goddamn wimp!" She knew she was taunting him but couldn't help herself. It was as if years of frustration from walking on eggshells were pouring out of her at that moment. She hurt her foot when she kicked the sofa then got even angrier when she realized that he was sitting at the dining room table doing HEALS. It reminded her of all the years she had to suffer when he didn't know about HEALS— a very common reaction in recovery from walking on eggshells.

I don't tell men what to say to their wives when they are trying to recover from a lapse like Ted's. (If you try say something by rote, it will sound phony and rehearsed.) The important thing is to show a sincere desire to make an emotional connection, which means caring about how she feels. Don't worry about the words you use, it's typically a nonverbal connection at first anyway. But to drama-tize what the connection *might* sound like, we'll give it words below.

Eleanor finally got tired of shouting and sat down hard on the sofa. She couldn't stand to look at Ted when he came over and sat next to her. He respected that she didn't want him to touch her at that moment. He could have said something like the following.

"I know that I've hurt you so much in the past and that it will take a long, long time for you to heal yourself enough where you can trust me again. I want you to know that I will do all I can to help you heal and won't expect you to trust me *at all*, until you feel ready. And if you *never* do, I will still love you and be the best husband I can be."

She probably would have replied with something like, "You were feeling it again—that crap again."

"I did feel some of the old jealousy. But that's my problem to deal with, not yours. Don't you even think about trying to protect me from it—I have to learn to handle it. I can't promise that I won't feel it again, but I *do* promise that I'll never take it out on you again."

This kind of temporary setback will almost certainly happen to you—the walking-on-eggshells feelings are so automatic and the behaviors so entrenched in both your heads. If you show compassion each time, you can heal a little more of the hurt with each occurrence.

What do you think would have happened if Ted had tried to blame Eleanor for her reactions that were, strictly speaking, *exaggerated* responses based on residual effects of her past hurt? What if he'd told her, "You're making too much of it," or "Stop living in the past," or "Get over it, already," or if he'd gotten defensive or aggressive in *any* way? That was certainly his initial response to Eleanor's anger and disgust that night and on the several other times she reacted similarly over the next few months. Had he yielded to those defensive and angry impulses, he would have proven to Eleanor that she couldn't trust him to be compassionate. Just as important, he could not have trusted himself to maintain compassion for her during her long, complicated healing process, in which she would be revisited many times by powerful memories of past hurt, just as we he would be revisited by his recurring feelings of jealousy.

It helps to think of the level your impulse to respond to your angry or resentful wife falls on—is it defensive-aggressive, or is it sympathetic to your core hurts and to hers? If you can feel compassion for yourself and for her, you will be *in* your core value and will clearly recognize hers.

Your wife will wonder if she'll ever be able to trust you again. That depends a lot more on you than on her. If you are consistently compassionate, eventually she'll feel the difference between the aggressive and demeaning behavior of the past and this new, compassionate side of you. But it will take a long time of you meeting each one of your lapses and each one of her angry reactions and memories of pain with compassion and understanding.

That the process of recovery is long and difficult is, no doubt, a sad thing for you to read. Feel the sadness for a while, and then it will be easier to look toward the future. Just remember that your consistent compassion and patience will bring healing and the ability to trust yourself. And that will make it much easier for your wife to heal and to regain her ability to trust you.

Fourteen

Reestablishing Connection

In a relationship that has suffered chronic resentment, anger, or abuse, reestablishing connection is not a fifty-fifty proposition. For a few months at least, it is more like a ninety-ten proposition, with you—the man—doing 90 percent of the work. There are a couple of important reasons for this seemingly unfair division of recovery labor.

The first is that it is much easier to do the hard work of relationship healing if you have been resentful, angry, or abusive than if you have been *reacting* to a resentful, angry, or abusive partner. Remember, even if your wife has been *as* resentful, angry, or abusive as you, the effects are more damaging to women, and men can recover much more quickly than women.

The other reason is perhaps more important. In general, men have a much lower tolerance of feeling inadequate than women. "Death before dishonor" is not a phrase associated with women's groups. No matter how you feel about that slogan in general, it simply doesn't apply to love. In our love relationships, we need to feel inadequate occasionally to learn how to do the right thing. The sense of not knowing what to do to make a bad situation better is what motivates us to *learn* what to do, that is, to become adequate. The first time a newborn cries, no new parent really knows what to do to make the child feel better. You learn by acting on a gut-level, compassionate instinct to relieve the child's distress. That same instinct works in adult relationships. But if we cannot tolerate the momentary inadequacy that precedes the compassionate motivation, we will not act on it.

This crucial dynamic—tolerating feelings of inadequacy to learn how to be adequate—is made even more difficult for men by the fact that we're not routinely taught relationship skills in childhood. To paraphrase psychiatrist Alvin Poussaint, "Mothers love their sons, but teach their daughters." In other words, relationship skills are imparted to girls, who seem more interested than their action-oriented brothers in learning them. This pretty much leaves us men on our own to learn how to respond to our wives' needs. That means we have a greater sense of inadequacy to tolerate in order to become adequate. We have to build the skills to convert feelings of inadequacy into the motivation to improve, appreciate, connect, or protect. It's a process much like lifting weights to build strength and stamina. If you do 90 percent of the recovery work for the next few months, instead of relying on your wife to do the work, you will become emotionally fit and buff enough to handle the more tender challenges of the most important relationship of your life.

Building Deep Connection

Deep emotional connection is a mental state and a choice. You *choose* to feel deeply connected to your wife or significant other, just as you *choose* to feel disconnected from her. In general, you like yourself more when you choose to feel connected and you feel bad (resentful, depressed, anxious, bored, numb, or angry) when you choose to feel disconnected.

Now here's the really good news. You can choose to feel deeply connected *on your own*, even if she doesn't cooperate or doesn't know about it. What she *will* know about is the positive change in your emotional demeanor. Your mental choice to be deeply connected to her will *guarantee* this change.

Deep connection is not based on shared preferences of what you like and enjoy. Rather, it's based on shared *values*; that is, what is *most* important to both of you. Couples almost always share:

- Love of some of the same people
- A capacity for some kind of spiritual connection (to something larger than the self; for example, God, nature, cosmos, sea of humanity, political or social causes)
- A capacity to appreciate (though not necessarily the same things or in the same way):
  - Nature
  - Human efforts to creates beauty (art, music, architecture, crafts, etc.)
  - A value-connection with certain groups of people (neighborhood, social. political, religious, school groups)
  - A capacity to do compassionate things

Lifelines

Like the lines that tether astronauts to a space capsule, emotional lifelines provide maximum movement, while providing lifesaving connection. They keep us anchored to what matters most to us. Imagine a long, flexible lifeline connecting you and your wife. No matter what you are doing or feeling, you remain connected. Even when you are angry at her, you are connected.

My *Lifeline* to You

ME_____YOU

These are the ways I am deeply connected to you:

1.

2.

3.

4.

5.

If you imagine yourself constantly connected by an invisible lifeline, your whole emotional demeanor around your wife will change for the better. Give her time (six to nine months) to see that your new interest in her is not a passing fancy, and she will most likely respond with appreciation and fondness.

Think positively about her when you're not with her. One of the most powerful ways to enhance your connection is to think positively about your wife as often as you can in the course of your workday. This primes your brain to feel closer to her when you are with her.

The Power Love Formula

The key to big change in relationships lies in small, everyday emotions. The Power Love Formula fosters connection and it takes less than five minutes a day of brief thoughts and behaviors. If they become part of your daily routine, they will certainly strengthen your marriage. The 4¾ minutes include:

- Some brief *acknowledgment* of your wife's importance to you at four crucial times in the day:
  - waking up
  - leaving the house

- coming home
- going to sleep
- Six hugs per day, holding each for six seconds
- Implementing your contract once a day.

Acknowledgment of How Important She Is to You

Come up with something that you can easily do four times a day. It can be a phrase like, "You are so important to me," or a thought like, "You give value to my life," or a gesture, like a brief touch, gentle eye contact, or just reaching out to take her hand. Whatever you come up with should, of course, come from your heart.

My Brief Acknowledgment of How Important You Are to Me

At four crucial times during each day—waking up, leaving the house, coming back home, and going to bed—I will do the following as a code for you to know how important you are to me:

Make your acknowledgment, be it a phrase, thought, or gesture, the *second* thing you do when you wake up in the morning. (The first, for the next six weeks, should be a practice session of HEALS.) For your overall emotional well-being, this is the most important time to do it. Research shows that emotions flow one into another more or less continuously, something like a stream that starts in the morning and extends throughout the day. If your first emotion of the day is positive, it is more likely that your next one will be positive. And then it becomes more likely that the one after that will be positive and still more likely that the next one after that will be positive, and so on. In other words, emotional experience is not like flipping a coin, where the chances of heads or tails is always 50 percent, regardless of how many flips you've made. Preceding emotions greatly influence subsequent emotions, forming positive or negative streams that continue to gain momentum, until something good or bad in the environment changes them. If you think about some of your best days, you'll likely see that most of them started early in the morning with a positive thought or gesture that subtly increased the value of your experience at that moment. You will see within a few weeks that affirming your wife's value first thing in the morning is one of the best behaviors you can do for your overall health and well-being.

Hugging 6 x 6

Hugs are usually the first thing to go when a chain of resentment takes over a relationship. The disaster formula is simple: The less you touch, the more resentful you get, and the more resentful you get, the less you touch. The following regimen, which takes 36 seconds per day, is designed to reverse this negative momentum.

Hug your wife, in a full body embrace, six times a day, holding each hug for at least six seconds. The 6 × 6 formula is not arbitrary. You probably do not hug more than once a day now. Increasing that to six times a day will bring a new level of closeness. The six-second minimum for each hug recognizes the fact that in the beginning some of those hugs may seem artificial. It's all right if you have to force yourself to start a hug, as long as it becomes more genuine at about the fourth or fifth second. That is likely to happen if you are still attached and have not yet entered into the contempt stage of *de*tachment. (If you are, reconnection may not be possible.)

The 6 × 6 hugging formula will do more than strengthen your

relationship. The added touch will boost your serotonin levels to make you feel better in general and less edgy, irritable, and sad in particular.

The Contract

Your contract is to declare: *"This is how I will show my love for you every day."* Keep it brief and simple, write it out like a formal contract, and do it at an agreed upon time *every* day. Think of it as the equivalent of your love song; it must come from deep within your heart. To structure your thinking, complete this sentence: If I loved her, I would:

AGREEMENT

For value received (the privilege of loving you), I, _____,
of _____ [street address], _____ [city],
_____ County, ___ [state], assign to _____,
of _____ [street address], _____[city],
_____ County, ___ [state], to receive the following
from me everyday. I warrant that I will:

In witness, I have executed this assignment at _____
[designate place of execution], on _____ [date].

_____

_____

[Signatures]

The simple, daily behaviors of your Power Love Formula will re-sensitize you to your wife's emotional world. That by itself can restore your relationship to the level it was before the chain of resentment *de*sensitized you to what you value most about her. This 4¾-minute daily routine can also help you concentrate and perform better at work and create more value in your life in general.

When You Occasionally Blow It: The Four R's

Because emotions operate mostly out of habit, you will make mistakes inevitably. No matter how strong your marriage becomes, you will certainly do and say the wrong things on occasion, and so will she. Research shows that people in happy marriages make mistakes all the time but are able to recover from them and repair any hurt feelings. They hardly ever go to bed angry or resentful. Instead, they do what I call the Four R's: recover, repair, receive, and reconnect

Recover means regulating anger and resentment. Even if you get so upset that you have to leave the room or the house, recovery is always your goal. If you do have to take a time out and leave the room, you still have your *lifeline* connecting you. The key to recovery is reminding yourself of your connection and keeping ever in mind the most important things about you as a person and as a husband and father.

In the long run, *repair* works best with the intention to make things *just a little* better, rather than fixing them. Once you make it a *little bit better,* you can improve a little more, which in turn makes it easier to improve yet a little more. If your wife rejects your attempt to repair the problem, try again—always respecting her boundaries—once she's had a chance to recover. If she rejects you again, wait for recovery, then try again. Keep trying until you are successful. The *power* lies in trying. Resentment, regrets, and despair inevitably appear once you stop trying.

Receive her repair attempts. This means forgoing the right to pout. *Your license to pout and sulk is hereby suspended.* Even if she causes the disconnection—and it is usually mutual—you have the responsibility to repair and to receive her repair attempts. (Don't even think about an adolescent sense of fairness. Think *success*.) Because the level of upset is rarely equal, it will usually be harder for one person to repair than it is for the other. Even on those few occasions when you absolutely *cannot* repair, you must be open and appreciative of her attempts to do so.

Reconnect means feeling the value you hold for one another.

Under stress, always ask yourself, *"What would a compassionate husband do?* Is it possible for me to do that? What would happen if I did that? Can I feel okay that doing what a compassionate husband would do reflects my core value, *regardless* of how she receives it?"

More on Repair

Research consistently shows that chronic distress results not from conflict, which is inevitable in close relationships, but from an inability to repair hurt feelings. "Repair" *does not mean undoing, minimizing, or justifying hurt.* Repair means that you restore a sense of connection. A sincere repair attempt recognizes that:

- Hurt needs time to heal.
- Healing progresses more rapidly with a sense of connection.
- Feelings of disconnection and isolation impair healing.

Your attempt to repair is also an attempt to heal. If you ignore or deny the injury, it will recur whenever anything remotely associated with it happens. For example, Francesca was hurt when her husband, Shakur, purposely ignored her birthday when they were in the depths of their walking-on-eggshells relationship. From then on, she would feel hurt whenever a friend or relative had a birthday. But after Shakur's Boot Camp, he worked hard to make her birthdays special for her. He dedicated every detail of his planning to repairing the painful memory he had caused. His efforts and the sincerity of his intentions conveyed to Francesca far more care than merely apologizing could have done. By the time her second special day had passed, the birthdays of her friends and relatives—and even the ones she saw on TV—made her feel a stronger sense of connection to Shakur. Birthdays had changed from a symbol of hurt to one of caring and enjoyment. Of course, Francesca could have healed the hurt of the birthday memory on her own, with greater investment of value in other areas of her life. But it fell on Shakur to repair the injury he had done to their relationship.

Fill in the Repair Excercises with repairs that you can perform to help your wife associate care and compassion with hurtful memories. Always ask her what you can do to help her healing.

Repair Exercises

Hurtful thing I said or did: (Example: Tore up pictures of her as a child.)

Repair: (Example: Have the pictures restored professionally. If that's not possible, draw representations of the pictures as carefully as you can. The point is not artistic verisimilitude, but the desire to associate caring repair with the painful memory.)

Hurtful thing I said or did: (Example: Cursed her family)

Repair: (Example: Write a description of how your words hurt her and how much you want to repair her hurtful memories with love and compassion.)

Hurtful thing I said or did:

Repair:

Hurtful thing I said or did:

Repair:

Remember to ask her what you can do to help repair.

Fifteen

Preventing Relapse: Weekly and Monthly Checklists

Most couples experience a honeymoon period after they do the Boot Camp exercises and master HEALS. Honeymoons are nice and can be launchpads for new, more compassionate and loving relationships. But you most likely have experienced them in the past. Everything was fine for a while. But gradually your resentment returned, along with the old irritability, cold shoulders, control, sarcasm, stonewalling, blowups, angry glares, or disgusted looks. Once again, your wife had to walk on eggshells.

The great task before you now is holding onto the gains you've made from the Boot Camp. Resentment, anger, and abusive tendencies are highly prone to relapse. Remember, emotional responses are mostly habit; it takes many weeks for new habits to supplant old ones. In the meantime, your default command—what you'll do when you're not paying conscious attention to your actions—will still be to devalue your wife when your connection to your own Core Value is weak.

The emotional pain of walking on eggshells works like the *bite of the vampire*. Once we acquire the fangs, we *always* have them and will always be visited by the impulse to make others become like ourselves. *Relapse* is forgetting that we have the fangs or forgetting that we can and must keep them retracted.

Here's what to do at the earliest sign of relapse:

- Rehearse **HEALS** (After six weeks of practice, you should have to do HEALS only occasionally, when the early warning signs of relapse appear.)
- Complete the following:
  - This is the *most* important thing about me as a person:
  - This is the *most* important thing about me as a husband:
- Add at least one new item to each safe deposit box of your Core Value Bank.
- Communicate with your partner about the early warning signs of relapse.
- Exercise (improves mood).
- Eat well—avoid substances that stimulate anxiety or depression, such as caffeine, nicotine, drugs and alcohol, excessive salt, sugar, and preservatives.
- Take vitamin supplements, particularly vitamins B and C.
- Do something nice for yourself.
- Do something nice for your wife.

What She Will Look for to Know That Change Is Permanent

Over the next few weeks, she should feel that you consistently (*every day*):

- *Value* and *appreciate* her—she is *important* to you.
- *Listen* to her.
- Show *interest* in her.
- Are *compassionate* when she needs you to be.
- *Care* about how she feels, even when you disagree with her.
- *Respect* her as an equal and don't try to control her or dismiss her opinions.

- Show *affection* without always expecting sex.
- *Handle* your core hurts, anxiety, resentment, and anger, without blaming them on her.
- *Share* your Boot Camp progress by showing her all your homework, including the following weekly and monthly checklists.

You don't have to be interested in the things that she's interested in, but you do have to be interested *that she is interested* in them. For example, a friend of mine doesn't like flower shows, but he likes that his wife likes them. He enjoys seeing her enjoy herself. You must learn to enjoy your wife's interest and enjoyment.

Use the following checklists once a week for the first six weeks and once a month thereafter. *Share them with your wife.*

Early Warning Signs That the Fangs Are Inching Forward

- Resentment
- Jealousy/Envy
- Getting angry in traffic
- Irritability
- Restlessness
- Moodiness
- Trouble sleeping (sleep too little or too much)
- Isolation (don't want to go out or see friends)
- Don't want your family to go out or socialize
- Emotional chill, closed off from loved ones
- Sadness, loneliness
- An *urge* to control or spy on family members
  - discouraging them from friendships
  - wanting them to tell you their every move
  - listening to their phone calls
  - reading their mail

The following must be an utterly honest attempt to monitor your behavior and attitudes toward loved ones. (Put a check for each thing you have done during the month.)

Self-Compassion

1. I validated my core hurts and accessed my core value on a regular basis.

2. I recognized the core value of others on a regular basis.

Compassion for Wife

3. I validated her core hurts whenever they occurred.

4. I empowered her to seek solutions from her core value.

Communication Skills

5. I accurately reflected her meaning and intentions to communicate, regardless of how she put it.

6. I maintained an attitude of respect.

7. I tried to find some truth in what she said, even when I disagreed with most of it.

8. I responded to the underlying positive wishes beneath her complaints. (For instance, a complaint about you not calling has her underlying positive wish to feel more connected.)

9. I expressed my *true* feelings, not symptoms and defenses, that is, core hurts, not the anger or resentment they cause.

Communication Blocks

10. I moralized, preached, or lectured.

11. I ordered, directed, or demanded.

12. I told her what she should do, when she didn't ask for my advice.

13. I interpreted or psychoanalyzed what she said.

14. I interrogated her.

Fighting Dirty

15. I failed to use compassion or be open to her perspective.

16. I blamed, accused, or showed disrespect.

17. I threatened to leave her.

18. I predicted a bleak future for her. (For example, "You'll fail, you won't make it, no one will love you.")

19. I ignored her or otherwise withdrew attention or affection.

20. I distracted or diverted attention from things important to her.

21. My unregulated resentment or anger created a hostile atmosphere.

22. I denied personal responsibility. ("I'm the victim!")

23. I wanted to win.

24. I expressed martyrdom.

25. I manipulated her (hidden agenda).

Abuse

26. I tried to hurt her feelings.

27. I called her names, insulted, or ridiculed her.

28. I criticized her personality rather than her behavior. (For example, "You're lazy, selfish, ignorant.")

29. I attacked her self-esteem—tried to make her feel bad about herself.

30. I threatened her.

31. I tried to humiliate her (knock her down a peg).

In the following spaces, list how many times in the past month you failed to act like a compassionate husband. For each item you list, state what you could have done differently.

Have I Acted Like a Compassionate Husband?

1. How I failed at compassion:

What I could have done to be more compassionate:

2. How I failed at compassion:

What I could have done to be more compassionate:

3. How I failed at compassion:

What I could have done to be more compassionate:

4. How I failed at compassion:

What I could have done to be more compassionate:

5. How I failed at compassion:

What I could have done to be more compassionate:

WARNING!!!

Emotional regulation skills deteriorate during alcohol and drug use! Intoxicant drugs put the regulatory part of the brain to sleep. After the *second* drink, your skills won't be available to you.

Weekly Logs

To monitor your progress toward full recovery, fill out a HEALS Log and the Power Log on the following pages once a week for the next six weeks.

HEALS LOG

I have rehearsed **HEALS** _____ times this week (minimum 72 times). **HEALS requires *practice* to make it automatic and to get its full healing benefit.**

The steps of **HEALS** are:

    H-
    E-
    A-
    L-
    S-

Times this week I successfully avoided hurting my wife's feelings _____.

Times I was unsuccessful (I hurt her feelings) _____.

POWER LOG

This week I felt:

Irritable	A lot	Some	Hardly	None
Grouchy	A lot	Some	Hardly	None
Annoyed	A lot	Some	Hardly	None
Impatient	A lot	Some	Hardly	None
Angry in traffic	A lot	Some	Hardly	None
Like blaming someone	A lot	Some	Hardly	None
Like making other people do things	A lot	Some	Hardly	None
Like getting revenge	A lot	Some	Hardly	None
Like hurting someone	A lot	Some	Hardly	None

What are my anger, attitude, anxiety, irritability, grouchiness, impatience, restlessness, impulse to blame, hurt, or get revenge always a reaction to?

       Her behavior   My core hurt   The situation

What can I do to make it *better*?

    Get back at them
    Do HEALS
    Hope it will pass

This week I felt the power to:

Regulate anger, anxiety, attitudes, resentment	A lot	Some	Hardly	None
Choose behaviors in my best interest	A lot	Some	Hardly	None

Be flexible	*A lot*	*Some*	*Hardly*	*None*
Feel self-compassion	*A lot*	*Some*	*Hardly*	*None*
Feel compassion for my family	*A lot*	*Some*	*Hardly*	*None*

***When my wife ignores, offends, or disrespects me,
it is becoming easy for me to:***

Acknowledge my deepest core hurt and reconnect to my core value.	*Very true*	*True*	*?*	*Can't do it*
Sympathize with her core hurt.	*Very true*	*True*	*?*	*Can't do it*
Try to negotiate in everyone's best interest.	*Very true*	*True*	*?*	*Can't do it*

PART IV

Resurrection for Your Marriage

Sixteen

How to Know That Change Is Permanent

This chapter will help you both tell whether the changes in your relationship resulting from the Boot Camp are just another honeymoon period, like those you've had in the past, or a process of *permanent* change.

Look for *Compassion*, Not *Remorse*

Most resentful, angry, or abusive people can show guilt and remorse about their behavior. What they don't realize is that if these painful emotions do not lead them to improve, appreciate, connect, and protect, they are likely to produce resentment, anger, or abuse. This happens when the discomfort of the emotions keeps you focused on how bad *you* feel, rather than helping your partner's process of recovery. As a result, you are likely to rush him or her into fully trusting and forgiving you, to get over it, so *you* can feel better.

Unregulated guilt virtually guarantees tension and irritability at the very least. Think of the most common kind of guilt people feel in America—not spending enough time with their kids. (Parents now spend an average of just 13 minutes a day interacting with their children.) Does the guilt that most parents feel motivate them to be sweeter and more loving to their children, or does it make them more tense and irritable? Do they spend what little time they have striving for quality interactions with their kids or trying to control them? Or, feeling overwhelmed by their guilt, do they shut down emotionally and let their children do whatever they want?

The ability to regulate guilt and remorse, without blaming them on anyone else, is a key indicator of relationship recovery.

Look for *Support,* Not *Control*

It's easy to confuse control with support when you feel protective of loved ones. You would probably try to keep your partner or kids from going outside in the dead of winter without a coat. While that might seem controlling to them, you would do it out of *concern* and *protectiveness*. The following pointers can help you discern the sometimes fine line between support and control.

Control is:

- Telling people what to do and then criticizing or withdrawing affection if they don't do it.
- Implying that they're not smart, creative, or resourceful enough to decide things on their own.
- Making it clear that their perspectives and opinions aren't valid, relevant, or important.

Support is:

- Giving encouragement to find the best course of action and then standing by them if what they decide doesn't work out.
- Respecting their competence, intelligence, creativity, and resourcefulness.
- Valuing their opinions, even when you disagree with them.

If You Want to Love Big, You Have to Think Small, *Every Day*

Recovery from a walking-on-eggshells relationship is not about big waves of emotion. Interventions such as highly-charged marriage retreats and cathartic therapy sessions may have some temporary benefits, but they are unlikely to help you *sustain* a close connection while healing your wounds. Think of your recovery in terms of a small current moving steadily beneath the surface of a greater stream. Waves attract attention and make a lot of noise, but it's the small, steady current that determines where the stream flows. For change to be permanent, it has to be small enough to fit into a *daily routine*. For reasons enumerated in the Boot Camp section, these small gestures of connection should be initiated by the man for the first six to nine months of recovery. Specifically, he should:

- Initiate at least six hugs per day, holding each for at least six seconds.*
- Stop what he's doing and greet you whenever you come into the house.
- Tell you how he's trying to feel connected to you when you're apart.
- Keep his contractual agreement to make a daily gesture (something small and brief) to let you know that you are important to him.

If he stops doing any of these, positive change is not likely to last.

---

*If this is uncomfortable for you, you're probably associating the touch with the hurt of the past. Try to associate it with the future, with how you would like your relationship to develop.

Tolerance

The following *Tolerance Scales* can help you determine the extent of your progress in becoming more tolerant as a couple. The first one assesses the man's tolerance of his wife, and the second one measures the woman's tolerance of her man.

Tolerance Scale

Indicate the current level of tolerance as well as what you would like to reach in the future.
2 = absolute tolerance   1 = giving some slack   0 = no tolerance

His tolerance of me when:	Now	Goal
I am hyper and he is calm or vice versa	____	____
I am serious and he is joking or vice versa	____	____
I am neat and he is messy or vice versa	____	____
I want to plan and he wants to be spontaneous or vice versa	____	____
I am punctual and he is laid back or vice versa	____	____
I am worried and he is evasive or vice versa	____	____
I want to hug and he wants to be left alone or vice versa	____	____
I want to express emotions and he wants to shut down or vice versa	____	____
I am talky and he is quiet or vice versa	____	____
I am romantic and he is not or vice versa	____	____

I am interested in something and he is
bored or vice versa   _____ _____

Her tolerance of me when:	Now	Goal
I am hyper and she is calm or vice versa	_____	_____
I am serious and she is joking or vice versa	_____	_____
I am neat and she is messy or vice versa	_____	_____
I want to plan and she wants to be spontaneous or vice versa	_____	_____
I am punctual and she is laid back or vice versa	_____	_____
I am worried and she is evasive or vice versa	_____	_____
I want to hug and she wants to be left alone or vice versa	_____	_____
I want to express emotions and she wants to shut down or vice versa	_____	_____
I am talky and she is quiet or vice versa	_____	_____
I am romantic and she is not or vice versa	_____	_____
I am interested in something and she is bored or vice versa	_____	_____

Minimizing the Risk of Renewed Trust

What is lonelier than distrust? Human beings very much need to
feel trust and to be trusted by others. The most ordinary of inter-

personal behaviors become perilous without some presumption of trust. On a basic gut level, trust allays anxiety and lends predictability and reliability to behavior. Attachment with little trust can become an utter hell of suspicion and dread. In a context of love relationships, trust:

- Assures your acceptability as an attachment figure: "You will always think that I am worthy of love."
- Eases the fear of rejection stirred by the high risk of intimate self-disclosure: "Once you know everything about me, you will still love me."
- Mediates the survival-based terror of abandonment and engulfment: "You won't leave me and you won't hurt or overwhelm me."

I wish I could tell you otherwise, but the hard fact is that your recovering relationship will have to function on low trust for quite some time. You have to reciprocate the emotions of interest, compassion, and love—these are unconditional. But trust, once betrayed, has to be earned back. The good news is that you can go a long way on low trust, provided that compassion remains high on both sides.

Compassionate Trust

Once you are hurt, it's perfectly normal for your warning alarms to remain overly sensitive for a long time. The important thing to know is that they signal *caution*, not *catastrophe*—they're *yellow* lights, not *red* lights. Like a smoke detector that goes off every time you cook something, overly sensitive internal alarms respond to the *possibility* of hurt. To begin the process of healing, you need to assess the *probability* of risk.

Our brains are quite capable of figuring out probabilities, but our emotions preceded this kind of reasoning by many thousands of years. Hence they focus on possibilities with little regard for how likely they are to happen. Left to its internal alarm signals, your brain tends to be a better-safe-than-sorry system. It would prefer to be wrong 999 times in thinking that the moving shadow of your husband is a saber-toothed tiger rather than risk being wrong once thinking a saber-toothed tiger is your husband. *Compassionate trust* combines your brain's computations with the wisdom of the heart. Compassionate trust uses probabilities based on compassion, whereas distrust is about possibilities based on anxiety.

The first step in building compassionate trust is to convert anxiety into thought and language, which activate the computational parts of the brain. Here's a helpful formula to follow. When you are worried about something, ask yourself out loud:

"How likely is this to occur? What are the odds?

"Is it *necessary* to assume the worst?"

Increasing your capacity to trust your partner ultimately means increasing your ability to trust yourself to handle whatever happens, even if it should be the worst. Your ability to manage the risk of trust comes from your knowledge that any failure of *your partner's* cannot reduce *your* core value. From your core value, you can trust yourself enough to assess the probability of betrayal and to balance the risk against the rewards of your relationship. As always, the wisdom must come from deep within your heart.

The Probability of Betrayed Trust

Use the following scale to assess the probability that another betrayal of trust will occur in your relationship. In the last column, write what you can do to reduce the likelihood of betrayal and what you can do to improve the situation if it should occur.

5—Very Likely   4—Somewhat likely   3—Even chance   2—Unlikely   1—Very unlikely

Possible Transgression	Probable Cause (Core Hurts)	Probability	How I Can Prevent This or Make It Better If It Happens
Failure of support			
Failure of interest, compassion, love			

Possible Transgression	Probable Cause (Core Hurts)	Probability	How I Can Prevent This or Make It Better If It Happens
Rejection of my true-self (he demands role-playing)			
Criticizing, stonewalling, ignoring, cold shoulder,			
Shouting, demeaning, intentionally inflicting hurt			

Seventeen

Replacing Power Struggles with Mutual Empowerment

Power struggles happen when people contend with one another to avoid feeling core hurts. When they fail to regulate vulnerable feelings, they try to control or force each other to *submit*, even though triumph over the other provides only *temporary* relief of core hurts. Because human beings hate to submit, power struggles *always* result in more *resentment* and *hostility*.

SHE: If you do this, I will feel (okay, loved, appreciated, grateful, or entitled). If you *don't* do it, I will feel (sad, unloved, exploited, betrayed, angry, or resentful).

HE: But if I do what you want, *I* will feel (sad, unloved, exploited, betrayed, angry, or resentful).

SHE: Even if you *do* it and feel *those* things, I will feel (sad, unloved, exploited, betrayed, angry, or resentful).

HE: You have no right to feel that way.

SHE: You have no right to say I have no right to feel *that* way. If you loved me you would do it.

HE: If you loved *me* you wouldn't ask me to do it.

SHE: You don't care about me. All you care about is yourself.

HE: Nothing's good enough for you. No matter what I do, I can't win!

SHE: You just throw me a few crumbs now and then.

HE: Nobody could meet your needs! You're insatiable!

The way this is going, someone will have to give in. The problem with giving in is that it virtually guarantees more resentment. You might be thinking, "Well, they could both give in—they could *compromise.*"

Why Compromise Usually Fails

Of course they've tried to compromise on issues like this in the past, just as you have tried to do in your marriage and with just as little success. Although it works well in most human transactions, compromise is less effective in relationships recovering from high levels of resentment. Here's an example. Say that she wants to go to New York for vacation, and he wants to go to Los Angeles. They *compromise* and go to Iowa. So there they are sitting on the front porch of their rented farmhouse, watching the corn trucks go by. She's not happy, but damn it, neither is he.

The figure on the next page shows why compromise is not a viable way out of power struggles in a walking-on-eggshells relationship. It tends to be confined to the facts they *seem* to be fighting about—when the problem is on the deeper levels of core hurts and core value. Their disconnection from one another is what they really fight about.

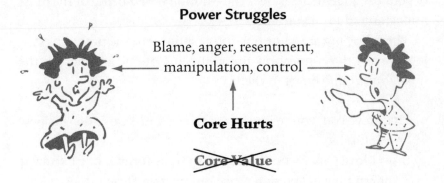

Power Struggles

Blame, anger, resentment,
manipulation, control

Core Hurts

~~Core Value~~

The couple depicted in the figure feel devalued and unlovable. She thinks he doesn't care about how she feels and he's convinced that she doesn't care anything about his feelings. Both suffer a double whammy of core hurts: "*I'm* not important to you and neither is our *relationship*." Seeking compromise—as opposed to connection—has the effect of putting limits on how much they *can* care about one another. The tacit implication is, "I'll care about you up to a point, but not beyond that." Worse, compromise *devalues* their connection by making it less important than getting the other to "meet me halfway." This is less an attempt at resolution than at saving face. The implication is, "Our connection is not worth my losing face." Just as nothing can be more important to you as an individual than remaining true to your core value, nothing can be more important to you as a couple than your emotional connection to one another.

Think Connection *before* Solution

You cannot resolve disputes with someone you love while being emotionally *disconnected* from that person. The disconnection hurts too much and feels too much like betrayal. To have any chance of finding your way out of a power struggle, you must try hard to make connection *before* you even attempt to solve the problem. Your relationship has to be more important than the content of your disagreement, as does the emotional well-being of the most important adult in your life.

The following are some possible responses to the preceding dialogue when the connection and well-being of one another are the most important things to them:

HE: I love you, you're important to me, I just can't do this now because. . . .

SHE: I love you. I would like you to do it for me, but I know it doesn't mean you don't care for me if you don't do it.

Or it could go like this:

HE: I don't want to do it, but I *will*; I can see that it's more important to you that I do it than it is for me *not* to do it.

SHE: I appreciate that. Is there any way I can make it easier for you?

Now they are making it clear both that the feelings of the other and their connection to one another are more important than the content of their disagreement. Once they know that much—once they're *connected*—they can begin to *negotiate* for cooperation.

Negotiation and Cooperation in a Family Context

Because people tend to cooperate when they feel valued and resist when they feel devalued, the task of negotiation is to bring about cooperative behavior through an attitude of value and respect. The rest of this chapter gives strategies for achieving this important goal through compassionate awareness of one another.

1. Cooperative behavior is willing (not necessarily preferred) participation in work, enjoyment, communal goal-pursuit, problem solving, or task-accomplishment.

2. With cooperative behavior, everyone enjoys freedom of choice, *so long as the choice violates no agreements and encroaches on no one's personal boundaries or autonomy.*

3. Negotiation is the attempt to bring about cooperative behavior in others, and must, therefore, be respectful of the inherent importance, value, and equal rights of others. It requires far more intelligence, skill, and responsibility than dominance or submission.

4. Negotiation affords everyone equal respect, regardless of unequal gifts, talents, or division of resources.

5. Negotiation is never threatening, coercive, punishing, or shaming.

6. Negotiation requires *flexibility* and *tolerance*.
   - Flexibility allows you to respectfully consider behavior requests by loved ones, while staying true to your core value.
   - Tolerance is the ability to accept opinions and behavior of others with which you disagree.

7. The most effective form of negotiation is *empowerment*. Empowerment involves fostering the competence, creativity, skill, and compassion in all parties of the negotiation.

Empowerment Formula

- Listen
- Reflect
- Validate feeling
- Respectfully state disagreement with idea *or* problem with behavior
- Ask for input on solutions

> ## Shortened Version of Empowerment Formula
>
> ### Validate
> ### Disagree

The order of the empowerment formula is so important that I use the world's worst joke to help you remember it. The absent-minded cowboy held his gun in front of his mouth to blow away the smoke after each shot. He went, "*Bang*! Blow. *Bang*! Blow. *Bang*! Blow. Blow. *Bang*!" Like the absentminded cowboy, you shoot yourself in the head if you disagree before you validate.

Family Empowerment Agreement

We hereby agree that our connection as a family is important and valuable to us. We care about each other and want the best for one another. We acknowledge that each individual in the family:

- is a separate person, important, valuable, and lovable in his/her own right;
- has the right to grow and develop fully and to realize his/her fullest potential;
- has needs, desires, and preferences that will sometimes conflict with those of other members of the family;
- has the right to come up with solutions to problems that consider the rights, needs, desires, and preferences of other family members and that fall within safety, health, and growth guidelines set by parents and the law;
- agrees to negotiate respectfully with other members of the family, without resorting to the use of power, control, and violence.

Accordingly, we agree to take the following actions:

Solution-Finding:

- state our problems clearly and specifically, *without blame*;
- try to think of more than one solution for each problem, considering the point of view of everyone involved;
- discuss the possible effects of solutions;
- have the goal of finding solutions that make everyone feel as good about themselves as possible;
- implement agreements with sincere effort to make them work;
- stay cool if agreements don't always work at first;
- give ourselves and each other permission to make mistakes with occasional feedback, but without shame-inducing criticism;
- regularly reevaluate solutions to see how they're working.

Communication:

- think before we accuse;
- criticize only behavior, never the person or personality;
- make "I-statements," not "you-statements" about how we feel. Example: "I'm disappointed to hear this," not: "You make me furious;"
- listen to each other *respectfully*, especially when we disagree;
- do not insult, call names, or make sarcastic remarks;
- stick to the topic;
- stay in the present and future—don't dredge up the past;
- hold dialogues, not lectures;
- try to answer each other, not withdraw or say, "I don't know," or, "Do whatever you want";
- think realistically:
  - don't think the worst right away, consider evidence
  - avoid "all or nothing" or "black and white" thinking
  - don't overgeneralize
  - don't make everything a catastrophe
- avoid the words, *never* and *always*.

Signatures:*

Resolving Disputes

The primary goal of resolving disputes among loved ones must be that each person feels important, regarded, respected, and valuable, and no one feels put upon, taken advantage of, exploited, or used. With this as your overriding principle, the following steps can be of great help in maintaining connections while you resolve disputes.

Step One: *Define the problem* with an explanation, *and ask for solutions.*

State the problem and why it's a problem for you. Ask your partner what he or she thinks is a good solution.

Example: "I have a problem with the stereo being so loud, because I'm trying to concentrate on my work (or relax or watch TV). How can we work this problem out?"

If you disagree with the solution, don't *attack* or *put down* the other person.

- Validate the suggestion as a *possible* solution.
- State your reasons for disagreeing.
- Solicit another solution.

Example of a solution with which you'll disagree: "You could concentrate on your work later."

---

*Everyone in the family should sign, even if toddlers have to make an "X" with a crayon.

Response: "Okay, that's one solution, but I need (want) to concentrate *now*. What's another solution?"

Step Two: Reach a **mutual** *agreement about which solution to* *implement.*

Step Three: Implement the solution with a **commitment** **to make it** **work** *(Don't set it up to fail.)*

Step Four: Evaluate the solution after it's had a chance to work.

Examples: "Our solution has been great; we just don't have that problem anymore."

"We need to review our solution to the trash problem; it's building up again in the kitchen."

This approach unites the family in *solution-finding* (rather than struggling for power and advantage). It opens the door for creative solutions and enriches the experience for everyone. It works especially well with children. To make it successful in a couple, both parties must *make a sincere attempt to understand the partner's personal goals and preferences.*

Example: Family members rarely share the same tolerance for mess (or compulsion for neatness). This often results in no-win power struggles, with everybody feeling put upon and resentful. A sincere attempt to understand both points of view is necessary:

"I know it's a problem to carry your glass into the kitchen, because you like to feel like you can relax in your own home. (And I appreciate when you do carry in your glass.) I'm not trying to put a power trip on you, but it's important to me that the house looks neat. What do you think is a fair solution?"

"I don't really mind carrying in my glass, you just hassle me about it if I forget. I don't *try* to forget."

"If you make a sincere effort to remember to carry in your glass, I'll make a sincere effort not to hassle you if you really do forget. Is that fair?"

Reaching Out More Deeply

The spacing of children is a common disagreement between married partners. Take, for example, a couple that disagrees about when to have their second child. Their baby is 10 months old, and they very much want to have another. The problem is she wants to have it right away, and he wants to wait five years. Since they cannot compromise and have half a child now and half later, they see no way out of their dilemma except that the other one has to give in.

"I want to have a child now," she says.

"I want to wait till we can afford one," he counters.

"You're so selfish! It's always just what *you* want."

"You're so irresponsible! You never listen to reason!" he shouts.

"All you think about is money!"

"You're just like your mother!"

"You're a cold, inconsiderate person!"

"You're stupid, self-centered, and emotional!"

To have any chance whatsoever of resolving such a difficult matter, both parties need to make a *sincere* effort to understand the importance of the other's beliefs, goals, and desires *and* to sympathize with any disappointment, if the other's desire cannot be met.

Here is how this couple solved the problem, working within a new, *compassionate* framework.

Step One: If either is angry, do HEALS.

Step Two: State and validate the other's perspective.

"I appreciate that it's important for you to be able to provide for our child and not have our standard of living decline," she says.

"I know it's important for you to have a child now, because you're a caring and nurturing person," he replies.

You might wonder how they came up with this information about one another, since it hardly shows in their previous destructive exchanges. They know it because these are the very qualities that caused them to fall in love in the first place. If you heard her talking to friends while they were falling in love, you would have heard her say the following:

"I feel so secure and alive with him. He thinks all the time about our financial future. He's already planning our retirement! And he's so energetic! He's up at dawn on Saturday morning and has all his errands and chores done by 10. That's when I'd just be crawling out of bed before I met him. But he really energizes me. If his steak isn't cooked just right, he sends it back without a blink of the eye. *I'm* too timid to stand up for myself, so I just take it any way they bring it. Maybe he'll make me more assertive."

And this is what he said to his friends about her: "I wish I could be more intuitive and emotional like her. She's so mellow and laid back. If they bring her steak a little overdone, she just makes do and doesn't let it bother her. But *me*, I'm so inflexible, I have to have it done precisely the way I want it, or it has to go back. But *not* when I'm with her. With her I can relax. I'm so uptight when it comes to emotions, but she's really in touch with hers. She knows who she is as a loving person. And the way she loves kids! I don't have to worry about my kids having a mother like mine."

Their disagreement about the timing of a second child is entirely predictable from what they knew and *loved* about each other from the very beginning of their relationship. As a nurturing person, of course she would want to have that cuddly baby as soon as possible, while she still had time to enjoy it before going back to work. And as a fiscal planner he would naturally want to rebuild capital before incurring the financial deficits of another child. They knew this about each other. But the gradual accumulation of resentment had desensitized them to the inner worlds of one another. They hurt each other the most by attacking the very qualities they used to love. They both felt deceived and betrayed.

Step Three: Express the true reason for disagreement.

"I feel that, if we wait, it will be that much harder for me to find work when the child's in school and I'm that much older," she said.

He responded, "I know, but I worry a lot about not being able to meet expenses. I don't feel I make enough money to support a family the way I want to."

Notice how they no longer blame one another for the disagreement? It's not about what the other is doing; it's about their core hurts.

Step Four: Express the deeper emotions.

"I guess I feel insecure about finding a job when I'm older," she said.

"I guess I'm insecure about whether I'll ever be successful."

Step three is the hardest. Just look at how they abused intimate information about each other at the beginning of the session. Risky though it is, I believe this step is necessary to establish lasting emotional connection. Once your partner has betrayed you, it's extremely difficult to reconnect on the same emotional level; scar tissue forms to keep you from taking that person into your heart again. However, you can go *under* the scars and form a deeper connection than you had before the betrayal, provided that the deeper sense and knowledge of one another stirs a more profound compassion. It's tricky to pull off, but the rewards are worth the try.

Step Five: Validate his or her deeper emotion.

"I'll love you no matter how much money you make."

"I'll love you even if you can't find a job when you're older."

This couple chose to validate one another with the assurance that, even if the worse case scenario happened, they would be there for each other.

Step Six: Try reconciliation. (If agreement does not occur, start the process over.)

"I don't mind waiting to have a child, because it's important to you."

"We don't have to wait. It's important to you to have a child now."

Most couples working through this process switch sides. Having forged a connection deeper than the scars of resentment and betrayal, they can return to one of the greatest joys of relationships: pleasing the person you love. Remember how much pleasure it gave you to do something nice for your lover, before the chains of resentment separated you?

By using the following grid, you'll be able to solve all of your disputes with compassion and respect.

Disagreement in the Compassionate Mode		
State and Validate	**You**	**Him**
Express True Reason for Disagreement (usually a core hurt)		
Express Your Deeper Emotion		
Validate His/Her Deeper Emotion		

Try Reconciliation (If
agreement does not occur,
start the process over.)

Eighteen

Rituals of Repair and Reconnection

The behaviors described in the Boot Camp and in the previous chapter are designed to help you maintain connection routinely. Although they go a long way to establishing positive change that lasts, they need to be invigorated occasionally by certain *rituals* of connection. A ritual is a formal set of behaviors performed in a special way for a special purpose. Weddings, church rites, graduations, and inaugurations are examples. This chapter offers a series of personal rituals designed to deepen and invigorate your connection to one another. Do them at the beginning of your recovery and at least once a year thereafter.

Commitment to Protection and Safety

The husband should make his declarations out loud, preferably in front of a witness. They should have equivalent emotional significance to a renewal of marriage vows.

To the best of my ability, I will protect you from harm, fear, loss, and deprivation.

I will *never* intentionally hurt you.

Ceremony of Acceptance

The husband should make the following declarations out loud, preferably in front of a witness. They should have equivalent emotional significance to a renewal of marriage vows.

> Because I love and respect you, I accept every aspect of you. I will never ask you to do anything that you believe violates your core value. I will, to the best of my ability, support your efforts to expand and develop whatever personal qualities you choose.
>
> I will never throw up to you anything about your past or in any way make negative judgments or criticism about you as a person.

Commitment to Growth and Development

The husband should make his declarations out loud, preferably in front of a witness. They should have equivalent emotional significance to a renewal of marriage vows.

> I will, to the best of my ability and within the constraints of our resources, support all forms of personal growth and development you wish to pursue, including education, training, exercise, and nutrition, as well as physical, emotional, and spiritual health care.
>
> I am committed to mutually solving all problems in the best interests of our family. I am committed to the gradual removal of all barriers to intimacy and connection.
>
> I will try to understand your core hurts, sympathize with any distress, and support you while you reconnect to the core value I recognize in you.

I will show love for you and will allow you to love me.

I will listen and try to understand and sympathize with all levels of your perspective.

I will tell you whenever I feel that I can't tell you something without fear of rejection or criticism.

I will negotiate with you to choose behaviors that help us both feel important and valued. I understand that sustaining interest in a relationship requires effort and openness to novelty. I agree to make that effort.

I will try always to earn your trust and understand that our past history means that genuine trust comes slowly and incrementally.

Ceremony of Respect for the Wounds of Your Heart

The husband should make his declarations out loud, preferably in front of a witness. They should have equivalent emotional significance to a renewal of marriage vows.

I acknowledge that you have removed the thorns from your heart and that you are trying to heal the wounds, many of which I caused. I will respect the lingering sensitivity of those wounds for however long it takes them to heal completely.

I respect the sensitivity of your:

I respect the sensitivity of your:

ognizes that any future hurt either of you does to the
other is only part of the total relationship interaction. It's an attempt to bring the focus of the relationship into realistic balance,
where the hurt is seen in a wider context of the good.

Repair has three components, all of which require utmost *sincerity*:

1. *Attempt:* I want us to feel connected so that we can see our hurt feelings in the wider context of our relationship. *I strongly reaffirm my value of you.*
2. *Reception (of your partner's attempt to repair):* I want us to feel connected so that we can see our hurt feelings in the wider context of our relationship. *I strongly reaffirm my value of you.*
3. *Consummation:* Because our focus is on healing hurt through the strengths of our relationship, we are connected.

The Repair Meter Exercise

Briefly describe an incident that resulted in hurt feelings between you and your partner:

Rate the initial hurt:

Mild				Moderate				Severe	
1	2	3	4	5	6	7	8	9	10

Rate the good things about the relationship independent of the hurt (if it had not happened):

Okay				Good				Very Good	
1	2	3	4	5	6	7	8	9	10

Rate your desire for connection independent of the hurt (if it were completely healed):

Okay				Good				Very Good	
1	2	3	4	5	6	7	8	9	10

Write what needs to be done to reduce the hurt one notch from its current rating.

Write what needs to be done to reduce the hurt one more notch from its current rating.

Write what needs to be done to reduce the hurt yet another notch from its current rating.

The Light within You

For Men

I have been privileged to witness thousands of men triumph over their resentment, anger, and abusive tendencies and become the husbands and fathers they've always wanted in their hearts to be. The process of change is arduous, and many resist it at first. Yet at some point, usually early in treatment, a transformation happens. They *find* themselves.

We usually end treatment with a group discussion of what finding himself was like for each participant. One man described the transformation this way: "It was like listening to music you think is okay, then, all of a sudden, you stop hearing it and start feeling it. Then you stop feeling it and start *being* it."

Another man said that it was a lightning-bolt revelation to him that he didn't *have* to feel resentful or angry.

Another guy pointed out, "You can feel resentment and anger, but you don't have to *be* resentful or angry."

Many others have used terms like "weights lifted from their shoulders," and "finally recognizing the face looking back at me in the mirror." They describe feeling, for the first time, genuine pride in themselves as husbands.

Have these men learned some magical formula of positive

change? Of course not. (HEALS is a useful exercise to strengthen core value, but it's not magical.) And they still experience destructive emotions, only now they see them as signals to value themselves and their wives *more* and to behave in ways that will make them feel like good and compassionate husbands.

Hopefully this awesome feeling of finding yourself has been your experience. Hopefully you understand the enormous power of your core value and your ability to do well by your family, even under stress. Your resentment, anger, and abusive tendencies were never the real you, any more than the runny nose you have when you have the flu is the real you. When you heal the flu the runny nose goes away, and when you heal your core hurts, your resentment, anger, and abusive impulses go away.

If you have done the work of the Boot Camp and the Resurrection sections, you should understand that *every* morning you wake up and decide whether to connect with your wife or disconnect from her, whether to value her or devalue her, whether to resent her or feel compassion for her. If you make the right choice, the light of your core value will shine within you and illuminate the most important relationships of your life.

For Women

You have suffered a great deal in the course of your walking-on-eggshells relationship. Hopefully these pages have helped you to heal at least some of the hurt.

You can outgrow the wounds of the past with a deep appreciation of yourself, your courage, sensitivity, resilience, and desire for a better life. You have enormous power and potential to become the person you were meant to be. Appreciate your strengths and resilience. Trust your inner voice—it tells you that you do not need to have value poured into you from outside sources. Your vessel is full and ready to "runneth over." As you feel the light of your core value within, you can make it shine out of you, to illuminate all your days.

Appendix I

When Your Relationship Doesn't Make It

No matter how hard they try, some of the people who buy this book will not able to save their marriages from the devastating fallout of walking on eggshells. Approximately 36 percent of the couples who go through the Boot Camp get divorced. That might seem like a high percentage, until you compare it with the 53 percent divorce rate in the general population and the nearly two-thirds who report that their marriage counseling failed. Here are the typical reasons why the approach to relationship repair described in this book does not succeed:

- He didn't do the work of the Boot Camp.
- He did the work, but there was too much damage done to the relationship.
- The passion is gone.
- The love is gone.

Leaving from Your Core Value

Just as you need to build your love relationship from your core value, so too, you need to end it in your core value. In fact, you need to spend more time in your core value when you choose to end a love relationship than if you choose to stay in it. You will need strength and peace of mind to overcome the guilt, shame, and anxiety inherent in breaking a deep attachment. Otherwise, you'll suffer prolonged resentment or anger that will impair your relationships with your children and inevitably spill into your next romantic relationship. Make no mistake, if you leave merely to escape core hurts or to get back at your partner, you will be attacked sooner rather than later by guilt, shame, and anxiety. These painful emotions keep us in attachment relationships, regardless of how bad they are. They developed in our brains at a time when to leave the protection of attachment meant almost certain death. Therefore, they are not rational and certainly not fair. Leaving while firmly in touch with your core value will give you strength and peace of mind to regulate the unavoidable guilt, shame, and abandonment anxiety with compassion for yourself, your children, and your self-destructive partner.

The best way to know that your decision to leave comes from your core value is by considering the self-building qualities of attachment discussed in Chapter 2. The crucial elements of *self-building* in attachment relationships are (1) unconditional safety and security for all parties and (2) high levels of compassion.

If a relationship consistently fails either element, it loses its self-building function and does more harm than good. If it falls below the threshold of safety and security, it becomes *self-destroying*.

Evaluating Your Attachment Bond

The following are questions you must answer from deep in your heart.

1. How much do you love this person?

2. Is the bond between you a strong one?

3. Or is it maintained by habit, convenience, or coercion?

4. Is the damage done to the relationship repairable?

5. Do you *want* to repair it?

6. How can it be repaired?

7. How will you know that it is being repaired? (There must be positive improvement, not just, "We don't fight as much," or, "He isn't so mean to me anymore.")

8. How will you relate differently when it is repaired?

9. How can you move forward and grow from the hurt of the past? (You must grow to heal, whether your loved ones grow with you or not.)

Use the following scale for questions 10–14
1—not much 2—some 3—quite a bit 4—a lot 5—highest level possible

10. I feel safe and secure _____

11. My partner feels safe and secure _____

12. Our children feel safe and secure _____

13. My level of compassion for my partner _____

14. My partner's level of compassion for me _____

Your answers to the above—or your inability to answer any of the questions—will help you decide whether you are leaving from your core value.

Grief and Tears of Growth

You might feel serene about your decision to leave your relationship. You might feel relieved. You might feel optimistic about the future. Hopefully you can feel all of these things. But even if you do, you will have to undergo a certain amount of grieving, not for the walking-on-eggshells part of your relationship, but for the love that existed before and during it. And that's not all you have to grieve.

Our brains tend to run all our losses of love and attachment together, in a process called state-dependent recall. What you learn in a strong emotional state is prone to automatic recall when you again feel those emotions. In other words, leaving your relationship will sooner or later invoke at least unconscious recall of every time you felt rejected by a loved one, as well as the sadness you felt when a loved one moved away or died. If these losses were unresolved in your heart, the welling grief will need to be expressed. Otherwise it will come out as prolonged resentment and may contract into a dull depression.

To paraphrase the German poet, Johann Goethe, it is not the tears we cry that hurt us, but the ones we struggle not to cry, for they drip within our sad and weary hearts. Crying may be the strongest act of self-healing and self-nurturing. Tears of grief nourish the seeds of growth. The direct opposite of self-pity, healthy crying is the natural method of self-renewal. (Have you noticed that children always feel better after they cry?) Some psychologists, noting that tears are almost entirely salt, believe that crying expels excess salt produced by the body in times of stress. Thus crying functions as a natural stabilizer in periods of stress.

But *how* you cry is crucial. Therapeutic crying should happen when you're alone and don't have to worry about how you look with your nose running or your eyes bleary or your lips swollen.

- Choose a time when you'll be uninterrupted.
- *Do not attempt to hold back the tears* or hold in what the natural grieving process tries to expel.
- Acknowledge the hurt that causes the tears; cry fully, broadly, and deeply.

The act of weeping can cleanse and heal. By allowing yourself such a deep expression of sadness, you put *value* on your emotions. Crying without inhibition (in private) confirms the *importance* of your emotions.

Invent Medicinal Rituals of Grief

A ritual of grief brings accumulated losses into the open, to be grieved and thereby stripped of their destructive power. (This, no doubt, is why virtually every formal grief ritual found in every culture in the world has an element of celebration.) The following is an example of a personal healing ritual. It should be adapted to suit your personal tastes and be performed as often as necessary.

- Take a hot bath and towel yourself dry as if in a kind of ceremony.
- Dress in freshly laundered clothes, as if they were vestments.
- Dim the lights.
- Play sad music especially meaningful to you.

Try to think slowly and deliberately of all the hurt you've experienced, every sad movie you've seen, every bruised shin, every loss that has sliced into your heart. As you think of these painful incidents, envision chips of corrosive, rust-like pain loosened from the walls of your heart and washed out by the cleansing flow of tears.

As the pain washes out of your body, as you are freed of the dead weight of leaden shame, *feel yourself growing.* Don't struggle to hold in the tears, for that is a message given to children, when their hurt is too much for adults to tolerate. Instead, encourage the tears, coax the sobs, always with the image of *healing* and *washing away* the core hurts, always with the image of *physical, emotional,* and *spiritual growth.*

Once you have completed the grieving and healing process, you are free to attain the ultimate peace. You will *find a good place for your former partner in your heart,* based not on your walking-on-eggshells experience, but on the love and positive experiences you once shared.

Co-parenting

If you have children, divorce does not end your relationship with your husband. Even when they are adults, you continue to share your desire for your children's best interests. Your children definitely have been harmed from your walking-on-eggshells relationship. So it is absolutely imperative that you make the divorce and co-parenting process as good for them as possible.

Research shows that drawn-out divorce and custody disputes are more psychologically damaging to children than the *death* of a parent. Although shocking at first, this finding makes perfect sense on further thought. When a parent dies, the child can idealize him or her and feel secure that the parent is "watching over me from heaven." But in a custody or protracted divorce dispute, the child sees both parents at their worst for a long time, feeling that, as more than one child I've treated put it, "It's all because of me."

Both parents must understand the following: *Anything you do to harm, put down, or in any way denigrate your former partner, no matter how true it might be, directly and profoundly harms your children.*

Children are so vulnerable to negative comments about their parents because of an otherwise adaptive psychological mechanism. Early in life they construct *internal working models* of both parents. Emotionally speaking, you *live inside* your children. Their

internal models of you help them stave off abandonment anxiety—
if you're within them, the threat of abandonment is lessened. They
quickly come to identify with certain attributes of their internalized parental images. This identity-building gets reinforced with
great frequency by the adults around them, who make statements
such as:

"He's just like his father."

"She has her mother's eyes and her father's disposition."

"No doubt about it, he's his parents' child."

In general, their identity with certain qualities of their parents
has a positive effect on their growth and development: they try to
emulate your good qualities and improve on your failings. But
when they hear either parent attack, insult, or put down the other,
they tend to see it as a fault within *them*. Younger children grow
sullen or get rowdy and teenagers fight back, as if they were being
personally attacked. Due to their internal identification with various qualities of their parents, they feel as if they *are* personally attacked. *The legacy of denigrating your former partner is self-loathing in
your children.*

You can protect your children from the damaging effects on
their internal identity by entering into the following Compassionate Parenting Compact.

Compassionate Parenting Compact

We the parents of _____
(name all the children) enter into this agreement to safeguard
our children's future development.

- We recognize the need to cooperate as co-parents for our
  children's welfare.
- We recognize that our children need to love and respect
  both of us and we agree to do nothing that would interfere
  with that need or divide the loyalties of our children.
- We will not talk negatively about each other.

- We will not convey messages to one another through the children.
- We will not ask the children for information about each other.
- We will not discuss our past or present disagreements with the children.
- We will each establish safe homes for the children and convey to them that they have *two* homes.

We each take responsibility for our own emotions and for avoiding and defusing power struggles between us, regardless of what the other does or does not do. We each take responsibility for discussing issues with respect, even if the other fails to do so, in recognition that power struggles are detrimental to our children.

Agreement to Be Compassionate

We hereby agree to work hard to resolve disagreements with my former partner in ways that are in the best interests of
_____ (name all the children). We understand that we will sometimes disagree about specifics of those best interests. When we have such disagreements, we will try to stay focused and agree on the best solutions for the child (children).

_____

Signature

_____

Signature

Anger at Your Children

The period of adjustment after leaving a walking-on-eggshells relationship can be as hard on you and your children as living in one. For the first few months you will most likely find yourself getting angrier at your kids than you would normally, and they will almost certainly get angrier at you in return. It will help you to cope with these higher levels of anger if you understand how the parent–child dynamic commonly produces irritation under the best of circumstances.

Every parent since the beginning of time has been painfully aware that children can do a great many things to irritate, frustrate, and turn your otherwise pleasant feelings into moods from hell. Those same creatures who look like little darlings when they sleep can, without a moment's notice, produce headaches, jangled nerves, strained muscles, aching bones, and overloaded emotional circuits. But there's one thing that even the most exuberant or obstinate of children *cannot* do. They can't *make* you angry. They cannot force you to give up *internal* regulation of your emotions. To understand this scientific fact, which seems to fly in the face of common sense, consider the psychobiological function of anger.

An automatic response triggered whenever we feel threatened, anger is the most powerful of all emotional experiences. It's the only emotion that activates every muscle group and organ of the body, and it exists to mobilize the instinctual fight-or-flight response meant to protect us from danger. Of course, our children are not predators. For the vast majority of problems in family life, anger constitutes *overkill* and *under-think*. Applying this fight-or-flight survival response to everyday problems of family living is like using a rock to turn off a lamp or a tank to repair a computer.

Modeling Anger Regulation for Children

Although their intellectual maturity is far less advanced than yours, your children feel anger for the same reasons you do, to protect themselves from core hurts. When you're angry, you both feel bad about yourselves. Making them feel worse can only produce more anger in both of you. What they need to learn from you is how to restore their core value, while respecting yours. They will *only* learn this by watching you model it.

Here is what you need to model for them:

- Acknowledgment of your hurt (feeling unimportant, disregarded, accused, devalued, guilty, rejected, powerless, inadequate, unlovable)
- Accessing your core value
- Recognizing their core hurts and their core value
- Solving the problem in everyone's best interests

The Sense of Self as Parent

Put a "Yes" or "No" next to each statement.

I learn from my children. _____	If you answered "No," what can you do to learn from them?
I understand their experience of the world. _____	If you answered "No," what can you do to understand their experience of the world?
I understand their emotional motivations. _____	If you answered "No," what can you do to understand their emotional motivations? (Are they trying to avoid core hurts or to feel valuable and lovable?)
I understand my emotional response to them. _____	If you answered "No," think in terms of the core hurts their behavior stimulates in you.
I enjoy my children. _____	If you answered "No," what can you do to enjoy them more?

I value them. _____	If you answered "No," what can you do to realize how much you actually value them?
I respect them. _____	If you answered "No," what can you do to respect them more?
I empower them—give them the right and confidence to solve problems in everyone's best interest. _____	If you answered "No," what can you do to empower them?
I teach them values. _____	If you answered "No," what can you do to teach them values? (Hint: Most of your values are based on compassion for others.)
I discipline them by helping them behave in their short- *and* long-term best interests. _____	If you answered "No," what can you do to discipline them by helping them behave in their short- and long-term best interests?

I give them enough affection. _____	If you answered "No," what can you do to give them more affection?
I express appreciation and interest, through eye contact, cuddling, cooing, soothing, and hugging. _____	If you answered "No," express more appreciation and interest, through eye contact, cuddling, cooing, soothing, and hugging.
I model affection with other adults. _____	If you answered "No," what can you do to model affection with other adults?
I allow them to be themselves. _____	If you answered "No," what can you do to allow them to be themselves?
I allow them to develop their fullest potential as individual human beings. _____	If you answered "No," what can you do to allow them to develop their fullest potential as individual human beings?

Dating

Many people who have ended walking-on-eggshells relationships are understandably reluctant to start dating again. While a certain caution in dating is a good thing, you want to be sure that your caution is proactive, rather than reactive—you want to base it on trusting your instincts, rather than distrusting love. Here's how it works: Trusting yourself stems from your core value. As long as you stay attuned to the most important things about you, you naturally gravitate toward those who truly value you as a person. This will make it less likely that you'll fall into another relationship where you have to walk on eggshells.

But even if you are firmly grounded in your core value, it's possible to be fooled by hidden resentment, anger, or abusive tendencies in the people you date. That's because it's easier for those prone to such tendencies to put on a false dating face. Not that we don't all try to put the best face forward in dating—most of us will exaggerate our good qualities at least a little. Sometimes this reaches the level of outright deception, as in, "Oh, did I tell you that I went to Harvard?" or, "Yes, I know some rich and famous people." But more often, we try to exaggerate some personal quality because we think the other person will like us more if we were more like that. "Oh, you're religious? Well, I've been feeling a bit more spiritual lately, so I'm going right home and read the Bible, or at least watch the movie version." Most of us have enough of a sense of self to keep these kinds of distortions within reasonable limits. But those prone to resentment, anger, or abuse have a more fluid sense of self. It's easier for them to pour it into any container they think you might like. They can pour themselves into a nicer container just fine, but they can't and won't *stay* in it once you start living together. Then the resentment, anger, or abuse emerges in full force.

Why Compassion Is Your Best Defense

Research shows that if a woman has been mistreated in the past, there's a very high probability that she'll be mistreated in her next relationship as well. It's a troubling phenomenon called multiple-victimization. I have heard far too many women clients say things like, "I could walk into a room full of doctors and therapists and fall in love with the one criminal." Or they ask with sad and bewildered eyes, "Why do I only attract resentful, angry, and abusive partners?" They wonder if they put out signals that say, "Please abuse me!" This misconception has even infected a few professionals who have ridiculously theorized that some women "*want* to be abused."

Please get this straight: The problem is not that you attract only resentful, angry, or abusive suitors; it's that, by and large, you have not been receptive to the gentler, more respectful ones. But this is *not* due to your temperament or personality. It's a *normal* defensive reaction. Here's how it works. After you've been hurt, of course you'll put up subtle barriers for self-protection. Nonabusive men will recognize and respect those barriers. For example, suppose that you work with someone who's attracted to you. But he senses that you're uncomfortable with his small gestures for more closeness. He will naturally back off and give you time to heal, or he'll settle for a platonic friendship. But a man likely to mistreat you will either not recognize your barriers or completely disregard them. He will continue to hit on you, until your hungry heart breaks down the walls that surround it.

Make no mistake: if you have lived in a walking-on-eggshells relationship, you have a hungry heart. On some level you're quite aware of it, which is why you try to protect it behind defensive walls. It's a natural reflex, but not a wise one. Starving your hungry heart cannot make it stronger—nothing that lives becomes stronger through starvation. Furthermore, I don't believe you can starve the hungry heart to death, anymore than you can hold your breath until you die. Reflexes eventually take over and make you breathe, and the hungry heart eventually kicks its way through your defensive walls to feed on the first bit of affection it finds. Because only a certain kind of person would disregard your boundaries, you will most likely find abusers waiting by the ruins of your defenses.

As you become comfortable in your core value, you will feed your hungry heart with more platonic friendships and by making more investment in other areas of value; you will build up your Core Value Bank account. This will make you more sensitive to the concealed emotion beneath the manipulative behavior of a potential lover. Many people will be able to fool you with words, but the basic attachment mechanism works through *nonverbal emotional signals*. (We bonded for thousands of years before we developed language.) Our emotions give definite internal signals regarding the viability of potential attachment figures. You almost certainly got warning signals early in your relationship with past resentful, angry, or abusive partners. You either doubted them or chose to ignore them.

The following intimacy test can help you become more sensitive to and trusting of the nonverbal signals about attachment that ultimately rise from your core value.

Intimacy Test

Can you disclose *anything* about yourself, including your deepest thoughts and feelings, without fear of rejection or misunderstanding? _____

Is the message of your relationship, "grow, expand, create, disclose, reveal?" Or is it, "hide, conceal, think only in certain ways, behave only in certain ways, feel only certain things"? Grow _____ Hide _____

Does this relationship offer both parties optimal growth? _____

Can you both develop into the greatest persons you can be within the parameters of the relationship? _____

Do you want to accept that your partner has thoughts, beliefs, preferences, and feelings that differ from yours? _____

Can you *respect* those differences? _____

Can you cherish your partner despite them? _____

Can you accept them without trying to change them? _____

Red flag of a potential for walking on eggshells: A *blamer*.

Those who blame their emotional states or behavior on someone or something else in dating will eventually turn the blame to you.

Is he or she a blamer? _____

Avoid Blamers!

Despite their apparent negativity, blamers can be especially seductive in dating; their blame of others will make you look awfully good, perched high on the pedestal to which they can elevate you.

"You're so smart and sensitive and caring and loving, not like that bitch I used to go out with."

"Why couldn't I have met you before that self-centered, greedy, unfeeling woman I married?"

"You're so calm and together, and she was so crazy and paranoid."

Hearing this kind of thing might make you think that all he

really needs is the love of a good woman. That mistake has caused so many sisters to walk on eggshells because it flies in the face of the *Law of Blame.*

The Law of Blame is that it eventually goes to the closest person. When you become the closest person, it will certainly fall on you.

A greater sense of your core value will give you more confidence in your internal emotional signals and guide you through the dating maze until you find the caring partner you deserve. Listen compassionately to the faint messages of your hungry heart. Then it won't need to make the desperate outcries that suspend your best intuitive judgment, scare off appropriate matches, and attract resentful, angry, or abusive partners.

Appendix II

Resentful, Angry, and Abusive Women

Just as the number of men requesting help to change their resentful, angry, and abusive behavior has radically increased, so has the
number of women suspecting that they too might be emotional
abusers. This chapter outlines some of the similarities and differences to look for if you're unsure about your own behavior and
your reactions to your partner.

Women who make their partners walk on eggshells are just like
men in their addiction to blame. Like men, their chronic *blame—*
not the *stress* they're under—causes resentment, anger, and abuse.
It's certainly true that our culture places women under enormous
stress in balancing careers and motherhood. But the vast majority
of women walk this tightrope without resorting to chronic resentment, anger, or emotional abuse of their partners.

Resentful, angry, and abusive behavior by women, like that of
men, attacks their partners' deepest vulnerabilities, although the
deepest vulnerabilities of men and women differ. As we have seen,
behavior that makes women walk on eggshells invokes fear of
harm, isolation, or deprivation: "You're going to hurt me, ignore
me, reject me, make me feel unlovable, or leave me without comfort, help, money, resources, or power." Behavior that makes men

walk on eggshells invokes the primary male vulnerability of
shame—dread of *failure* as a provider, protector, lover, or parent. Although it rarely causes fear in men—most male victims are not
afraid of their abusive wives—the behavior is nonetheless dreadful
and psychologically damaging when it says or implies:

"You're not a *real* man!"

"No woman could love you."

"You don't make enough money."

"You don't get promotions because people don't like you at
work."

"You're lousy or disgusting in bed."

"You're a loser—compared to the other guys I could have married."

"You're a wuss."

"Your own kids don't like you."

Men who bear the brunt of their wives' resentment, anger, or
abuse have the added social shame of cowardice, for letting her get
away with it. If he fights back, he becomes the primary abuser, and
if he takes it, he's "pussy-whipped." (Our culture does equal harm
to both sexes when it encourages women to think of themselves as
victims and shames men for being victimized.) He's damned if he
does and damned if he doesn't.

They're the Same on the Inside

Men who walk on eggshells to avoid feelings of failure suffer the
same self-doubt, self-editing, and loss of self as women who walk on
eggshells to avoid fear of harm, deprivation, and isolation. Their
partners equally suffer the tragic substitution of power for value. Resentful, angry, and abusive men *and* women want to feel valuable
and lovable but instead opt for the power to control, devalue, or
emotionally harm the people they love, which can only make them
feel more inadequate and unlovable.

But Look Different on the Outside

Men who walk on eggshells tend to be calmer by temperament and more internalizing by nature than their female counterparts. On the whole they appear less emotional and quieter, and often become sullen and brooding as their relationships deteriorate. Women who walk on eggshells tend to do more to accommodate and try to please their resentful, angry, or abusive husbands, at least until they understand that they're attempting the impossible. They also make more emotional demands on their partners: "Why can't you love, understand, sympathize, or care about me?" Men who walk on eggshells may complain about their sex lives but more typically drag a silent emotional cross through life. Eventually they disengage from their wives and become like boarders in the house.

Imelda and Mark illustrate the differences between the sexes in walking on eggshells when they fall into a common trap of courtship. Too many men and women try to rescue partners they perceive as needing them. Men do it with exaggerated (and usually unrealistic) protectiveness—they'll take care of everything you'll ever worry about. This appeals to women who fear harm, isolation, and deprivation. On the other hand, women like Imelda tend to rescue with nurturing, care, and support, which alleviate the male dread of failure.

Imelda first fell in love with Mark because he was "sensitive and caring." He was the complete opposite of her Type-A, hard-driving father, who, as she put it, would "Step on anybody (including her) to get what he wanted." She was attracted to Mark's reserve and gentleness. They seemed like a perfect match, since he was just as enamored with her energy and assertiveness.

After about a month of dating, Imelda began to interpret Mark's reserved nature as a lack of motivation. She thought he had a confidence problem. Although she was wrong about that, her misconception had the effect of making her more nurturing, as she tried to increase his confidence. As it turned out, she *was* right about one thing, Mark was hungry for nurturing. His attachment history before meeting Imelda included an absent mother and a string of aloof women who dumped him after just a few months of dating. Imelda's nurturing and support gave him what he'd been looking for all his life, and he quickly fell head-over-heels in love with her. Although their walking-on-clouds state of euphoric love was less than two years old, it had been obliterated by the cruel drudgery of walking on eggshells by the time they came to see me.

Mark was visibly irritated by "Imelda's same old refrain," when the first thing she told me in our first session was that he "*always* had a confidence problem."

"I have one *now*," he said sarcastically. "But I used to be confident, before we were married."

"You were never confident in your life. I should have known better than to marry a man whose own mother rejected him."

Mark looked away from her, glancing on the floor first then at the opposite wall, before settling his gaze on his lap. His face showed neither disgust nor dejection. It was almost as if he were reading an imaginary magazine. That quickly, he had dissociated, as if she'd made her remark about a stranger in whom he had no interest. Dissociation—turning off emotions and attention—is a common response in men who walk on eggshells. Quite suddenly—on a dime, some say—they can zone out or mentally leave the scene, as Mark did. But it's not stonewalling or any intentional effort to shut out their wives. It's a purely reflexive defense mechanism to relieve pain for a little while. Imelda didn't seem to notice.

"Why *did* you marry him?" I asked her.

"I was one of those women who are stupid enough to think that all he needs is a little love and a little support to grow a backbone."

"So you gave him a little love and a little support?"

"No, I gave him *a lot*," she said defensively. She even cited a book about "women who love too much."

I corrected myself: "You gave him a *lot* of love and support for the sole purpose of giving him a backbone?"

"Yes," she said, with a little less conviction under her still-defiant tone.

"Well, let me get this straight. You loved and supported him so he would be able to send his steak back in the restaurant if it wasn't just right?"

"No, of course not."

"Then I'm confused. Mark, I'd like your thoughts on this, too." It was time to pull him back.

"On what?" he asked, as if closing his imaginary magazine. It was obvious that his thoughts were not often solicited.

"I'm trying to get a sense of a timeline here. Did you feel that she loved and supported you at some point in your relationship?"

"Sure she did. I'm stupid, but not that stupid. She used to say she never loved anybody like that before. Now I hear about all the men she could have had."

I shook my head and turned to Imelda. "You have to help me out a little. Why *did* you give him a lot of love and support?"

"Because I wanted to."

"You liked doing it?"

"Yes.

"When did you stop liking it?"

"He was such a disappointment. Just *look* at him. He can't even focus for five minutes. I even had him tested for adult ADD, hoping he'd have an excuse. No such luck."

This was my mistake. I should have known that she would rev up her attack of him if I made her feel threatened. She was already getting flustered, her face reddening ever so slightly.

"He looks okay to me," I said lamely. But she wasn't through.

"Sure, he's a therapist's dream—why would *you* be disappointed?"

"You're disappointed in him because he didn't *become* confident, despite all your hard work?" Finally, I hit the right nonconfrontational tone, enough to take some of the wind out of her defensive-aggressive sails. She hesitated a long time, but would not look at Mark or at me. "What *first* disappointed you?" I persisted. "You wanted him to become more confident and he didn't?"

"I *was* confident," Mark quietly protested, more out of habit than assertion. But he no longer had to protest. She finally got the point.

"I guess because he started to *lose* it?"

"Lose *what*?" I asked, because she had to hear herself say it.

"Lose confidence." She said softly, with palpable regret in her voice.

"So he *was* confident. When did he start to *lose* confidence?"

"I wasn't abusive to him *then*," she insisted.

Mark leapt on this statement as an admission that she was abusive *now*, but she didn't seem to hear. It was unnecessary to respond because she was no longer resisting the charge. Instead, she offered a meager excuse.

"He got so whiny and complaining all the time. I just lost respect for him."

"He whined and complained after you stopped being loving and supportive?"

"It's not my fault he's a failure."

"I doubt that he's a failure. But even if he were, do you think your negative emotions are about *his* failures?"

"Who wants to live with a failure?"

"Do you feel guilty because he's a failure or because you feel that you are?"

"I have a better job than he does. I don't have any trouble making friends. . . ."

I interrupted because she was prepared to go on for quite some time with this defensive attack, and I couldn't let her do that to Mark yet again. I purposely pressed her: "So why do *you* feel guilty? How have *you* failed?"

Something happened then that I have seen only a handful of times this early in working with couples who walk-on-eggshells. With tears in his eyes, Mark touched Imelda's hand. He no longer felt like a victim. He realized that all the hurtful things she said and all the lost weekends in which she either ranted at him or refused to speak to him were not because he was unsuccessful, or didn't have a backbone. It was due to the simple fact that she couldn't *sustain* her loving and supportive behavior. His touch had the same meaning for her.

"Why is it so hard?" she asked me, like a frustrated child learning to ride a bike. It was so hard for her because, like everyone else in walking-on-eggshells relationships, her sense of inadequacy about love had cut her off from her loving nature. Many female abusers are like Imelda. They need an excuse to start loving and an excuse to stop when it gets hard to sustain—and it always gets hard, if you need an excuse to start in the first place. She imagined that Mark was unsure of himself, which meant that he needed her. As long as he needed her, it would be safe to love him. But if he only *wanted* her love, it was too risky—you can always change your mind about *wants* but not about *needs*. That's how it seemed to Imelda. The more she withheld the affection and care that Mark so wanted the more inadequate she felt.

"I used to ask her all the time, before the criticism started, 'Don't you love me anymore?'" Mark said this with a strange combination of relief that he wasn't to blame and sadness for what they'd missed in their life together. To have answered him honestly when he first started asking would have required that Imelda own her guilt and sense of inadequacy. Instead, she blamed it all on him, on his lack of a backbone.

At least Imelda's newfound ability to ask, without blame, why it was so hard for her to sustain love and support signaled that she was ready for her Boot Camp. Once she reclaimed her core value in treatment, her natural compassion made her feel adequate and lovable and immediately stopped her resentment, anger, and abusive behavior. She let herself once again love the man she married.

Imelda and Mark were equally invested in their relationship before her resentment, anger, and abuse started, and they were once again equally invested after reading and working the exercises in the Boot Camp section of this book. Some marriages start out at the polar opposite from them in equality of emotional investment but end up playing the same painful song.

Unequal Investment of Love

One kind of walking-on-eggshells relationship that is more common when women are the offenders results from *unequal* investment of love. It happens when women marry men they don't really love but who very much love them. These ladies often have been hurt by someone in the past and now want a less intense emotional connection. The reasoning—to the extent that it's reasoned-out at all—is that it won't hurt as much if a weak connection fails. Others fall into the trap in pursuit of financial security, children, or companionship, without the high risks of love.

The contribution of our "dating culture" to this kind of walking-on-eggshells relationship cannot be underestimated. Men are *supposed to* pursue potential partners until they wear down their resistance. Think of how many romantic comedies you've seen with this theme, featuring some of our most beloved actors and actresses. And there are at least a dozen books written about how women can play "hard to get" and otherwise manipulate the cultural imperative for men to pursue and women to resist. These only reinforce the male feeling of, "I pursued her until she caught me." While some women enjoy being wooed and pursued, many others really do get worn down by the praise, gifts, flowers, and promises of endless love. They end up thinking, "If he loves me that much, maybe I'll start to love him too." This is a formula for disaster if she's also addicted to blame.

Bella was a tall and beautiful Eastern European woman with long blonde hair and striking, jade-colored eyes. Her husband, Jose, was a wealthy investor, short and stocky, a bit overweight, and much older than she. It was obvious from the moment I met them that Jose adored his wife. Even in the depths of their walking-on-eggshells relationship, he couldn't keep his eyes off her. He lived to see her smile, which, these days, she did only in public. She smiled warmly at me as I introduced myself at the beginning of our interview.

Jose tried to explain his intense attraction to the statuesque woman sitting next to him. "I've had a lot of women in my 55 years, but no one ever turned me on as much as Bella. She's the love of my life." At this point in their five-year marriage, they slept in different rooms and hadn't had sex for at least two years.

"He thinks he can ignore me all day and then I'll want to jump into bed with him at night," she said.

"Why do I ignore you all day?" he asked her.

"You're never around," she said.

"Why am I never around? What happens when I am around?"

"You're annoying," she said.

"You tell me to stay out of your way."

"Because you're annoying."

"But then you're annoyed when I'm not around. So how can we make contact? How can I let you know how much I love you?"

She cut him off in a sarcastic, sing-song voice, "I *know*, you love me so much because you give me so many nice things."

"I give you my heart. Apparently that's not nice enough. You don't respect me, I'm just a paycheck. A very *large* paycheck."

"You don't know the difference between love and groping. You're uncouth, unmannered, and, worst of all, you just don't *get* me."

"How can you help him get you?" I asked her.

"Why should I bother? He's hopeless. This isn't the first marriage he's failed at, you know."

"I thought you wanted him to get you," I persisted.

"It's too late."

"Too late to get what you want?"

"I don't want it from him anymore. Do you know what it's like to live with a man you can't stand to look at? Even his own kids (from a previous marriage) can't stand him. The only time he hears from them is when they want money."

"You won't let them in our house," he reminded her.

"Because they don't respect me."

Jose apparently felt that he had to explain this to me: "They had a little trouble with the idea at first—she's *younger* than they are, for

Christ's sake. But they know how much I love her, and they've tried
to—"

"I won't have anyone in my house who doesn't respect me," she
interrupted.

"They *act* respectfully to you."

Once again, she interrupted, "But they don't really respect me."

Jose sighed deeply and looked at me with defeat in his eyes. "I just
don't know what to do anymore. I've tried all kinds of changes—
jumped through every hoop she put up. It doesn't matter what I
do, she just wants to be with somebody *else*. She obviously doesn't
love me. I could even live with *that*, because I love her so much. But
these constant put-downs, I just can't take it anymore."

Bella shook her head with a disgusted look on her otherwise
beautiful face.

"Well, I guess you'll have to leave her then," I told him. Now she
looked surprised.

"I thought you were supposed to help," she said sarcastically,
transferring a little of the contempt she'd been directing toward
her husband onto me.

"Well, it does seem like you want him to be someone he isn't.
He's uncouth and disgusting after all. How do you become
couth?" I asked.

"Are you trying to be sarcastic?" she challenged.

She was right, I needed to be more compassionate. "I know this
is painful. But you said that you don't want him to get you anymore and you don't want to get him. So what's to be done?"

"*You're* supposed to know that!" she shouted in sheer exasperation.

"He's not a magician," Jose said. "Neither were all the other
marriage counselors. They can't make me into a different person,
and that's what you really want."

"Oh, but I *am* a magician," I said with a stupid grin. "If all you
want is a magical change in Jose, I can do that. What kind of magic
do you want?"

"Can you make him taller?"

"No, I can only do psychological magic. But he hasn't gotten any shorter since you married him," I felt obliged to point out.

"I want him to be more sensitive," she said. "He *has* gotten less sensitive since I married him."

"Oh, I can make him more sensitive," I assured her, "because that's in his heart. But then he'll be more vulnerable to rejection. And you don't want that because then you'll feel worse about rejecting him."

"I wouldn't reject him if he were more sensitive."

"You never reject him when he's sensitive?"

"Only when he's not sensitive enough."

"How sensitive does he have to be for you not to reject him?" She was looking at me suspiciously. "Think about it, how sensitive does he have to be for you not to reject him?"

After a long silence, she felt she had to insist: "I *do* love him."

"Of course you do, that's what makes it so hard for you to keep rejecting him."

"I make her sick, that's all," Jose sadly declared. "Physically, psychologically, the way I eat, the things I do. It's not her fault, I just make her sick."

"I could go on making allowances," Bella said. "I'm a compassionate person at heart. But I don't know how much more I can do."

"You *are* a compassionate person at heart, that's why you feel so bad rejecting him. So *whose* values are you violating?"

Jose seemed surprised that this so abruptly stopped Bella's blame. For her part, she felt more isolated than ever.

"*Mine,*" she said softly. She was ready for her Boot Camp to begin.

Relationships like this one, where emotional investments are unequal, begin with two strikes against them. By "unequal," I mean sixty-forty. You can love a *little* more and have *somewhat* more compassion and interest than your partner, but once it gets around sixty-forty, a built-in mechanism starts making you both miserable. The one loving *more* feels *unworthy* (of getting back the love that he or she gives), while the one loving *less* feels *guilty* for getting more than he or she can give. Both feel inadequate. If they can appreciate and sympathize with the core hurts inherent in unequal investments of love, their increased compassion gives them a chance of making it. But as we have seen, too many people blame their core hurts on their partners, as Bella did, which produces resentment, anger, and abusive behavior.

You might wonder why men who give a lot less love than they get are not quite as likely to be resentful, angry, or abusive as women who do the same. The reason is simple. A man who loves significantly less than he is loved has a chance of holding onto his core value, as long as he can protect, provide, and perform sexually for his wife. That gives him less personal failure to blame on her. But a woman's core value is more likely to emphasize attachment, care, and emotional support. When she fails at any of these, she's a bit more likely to blame her husband.

The Same Treatment

The treatment of resentful, angry, or abusive women is the same as that for men. They must systematically connect core value to core hurts so that they convert their resentment and anger into compassion for loved ones. Both Imelda and Bella developed far more compassion for their partners in the course of their treatment. Imelda's marriage improved spectacularly. In Bella's case, her enhanced Core Value did not increase her love for Jose, though it raised her respect for him. As it turned out, respect was not enough for him. Understandably, he wanted a partner who was not disgusted by making love with him. They eventually divorced, but became good friends, which probably would have been a better choice for them to have made in the first place. Relieved of the guilt she felt by constantly rejecting her husband, Bella even became friends with Jose's adult children, the same people she could not abide and would not allow in their house while she and Jose were married.

Are You One?

The usual defensive-denial aside, it's harder for women to assess their resentful, angry, or abusive behavior than it is for men. Male partners who receive the brunt of such behavior do not show the same kind of fear and anxiety reactions to walking on eggshells. So the feedback you get from them may just seem like complaints. The best way to know if your behavior crosses the line is to talk to your partner frankly and openly. Try to identify his core hurts and your own. Try to recognize his core value and your own. The following questions might also help.

- Does he tell you that you sometimes yell and scream or lash out at him?
- Do your girlfriends ever remark that you might treat him badly?
- Do you automatically blame him when things go wrong?
- Do you resort to name-calling, swearing at him, or putting him down?
- Do you demean or belittle him in front of other people or your children?
- Do you threaten him physically?
- Do you threaten to take his children away so he will never see them?
- Are you often jealous and want to know where he is at all times?
- Would your family and friends be surprised to know how you treat him behind closed doors?

If you answered "yes" to any of these, be sure to work the Boot Camp section of this book carefully. In your heart, you are not a resentful, angry, or abusive person, and you do not deserve to bind yourself and your family in the chains of resentment, anger, and abuse. It is time for everyone in your family, including you, to stop walking on eggshells and enjoy the compassion and love you deserve.

Appendix III

Statistical Foundation of the Program

Developmental Evaluation

The foundation of the Boot Camp treatment was developed page-by-page with ongoing experimental groups of mostly court-ordered domestic violence offenders and child abusers. The treatment was then called, The Compassion Workshop and was later changed to The Core Value Workshop. The following are follow-up results from those developmental workshops, based on a sample of 285 randomly assigned court-ordered abusers from Prince George's County, Maryland.

Compassion Workshops for Spouse and Child Abusers

The violence is defined as a push, grab, or shove as measured by the Conflict Tactics Scale. Of those ordered into the program, 74% completed it. Group completers are:

- 86% violence-free (push, grab) after one year, based on victim report

- 71% verbal aggression-free after one year, based on victim report
- 92% free of serious violence (at least one instance of beating up, choking, or threatening with a weapon) after one year, based on victim report

The following represents change from pretest before treatment to posttest at the conclusion of treatment. On average, group members show:

- 250% increase in strategies to resolve anger and violent-situations***
- 36% increase in compassion***
- 49% reduction in anger-hostility***
- 33% clinical anxiety reduced to normal level***
- 13% improvement in well-being***
- 5% improvement in self-esteem**

$* = p < .05$, 1-tailed; $** = p < .01$, 1-tailed; $*** = p < .001$, 1-tailed; $**** = p < .0001$, 1-tailed

Former Victim Data

The following represent changes from pretest scores of female victims of domestic violence at the beginning of treatment to posttest at the conclusion of treatment.

- 49% reduction in anxiety* dropping clinical levels of the entire group into normal range
- 54% reduction in anger-hostility* dropping distressed levels of entire group into normal range
- 21% improvement in well-being* raising below normal levels of entire group into high range

For a full report see *Treating Attachment Abuse: A Compassionate Approach,* by Steven Stosny, published in 1995 by Springer Publishing Co.

- 41% improvement in self-esteem* raising slightly below normal levels of entire group into high range

* = p < .0001, 2-tailed

Aggressive Driving Linked
to Family Abuse

The Maryland Motor Vehicle Administration analyzed the driving records of 300 persons court-ordered into treatment for family violence and found that:

- 2/3 had multiple aggressive driving violations (M=3.4 for the whole group) the year before domestic violence intervention.
- The Compassion Workshop reduced violations by 98% the year following treatment, which was *three times* better than standard driver improvement intervention. 86% of the same group was free of family violence after one year, based on report of the victim.

Making the Home and the Road
Safer at the Same Time

These data suggest that:

- People who use aggression at home are likely to use it on the road as well.
- Making other drivers angry on the road can lead to family violence.
- Aggressive driving, unlike careless driving, may require conditioning in impulse-control to regulate.
- Stricter enforcement of traffic laws with impulse-control intervention as a consequence of violations may prevent family violence.

Note: Though very promising as a beginning exploration, these statistics are not presented as definitive proof of success of CompassionPower programs. That would require an experimental design with double-blind comparisons done by independent evaluators, a gold standard of research as yet nonexistent in this field.

Acknowledgments

A book like this one, inspired from the suffering of so many women, children, and men, does not come gently into the world. I am grateful to Leslie Meredith for her insightful editing and patience in shaping what was essentially workshop material into a readable text. She labored intensively under an amazingly tight deadline.

My agent, Jim Levine, put more effort into making this project come to fruition than anyone I have known in his profession. All the while that he was working so hard for me, he was also engaged in the chaotic process of moving his Manhattan offices. In the process, he moved into my heart.

No one has helped my career more than my dear friend, Diane Sollee, who came to observe our abuser groups several years ago and made it her mission to bring the core value message to national prominence. And she did so, despite early critics who adamantly opposed a compassionate approach to family suffering.

The Core Value Workshops flourished for 12 years in Maryland, Virginia, and Washington, DC, before gaining national recognition. Helping to bring about their success almost from the beginning were my colleagues, Diane and Bob Nicholson, Eunice Proctor, Tom Crepeau, Jackie Clark, and Cynthia Crockett. An inspirational pastor, the Reverend Dr. Lee P. Washington, of a very special church, Reid Temple AME, supported us from the start by giving us rent-free space in which to hold our groups. This allowed the poor people of Prince George's County, Maryland, access to this treatment. Catholic Charities of Prince George's County soon followed with the same generosity. Also instrumental to the ongoing success of the program were Therese Harrigan and the Family Services Division of the Seventh Judicial Circuit of Maryland, and the honorable Theresa Nolan and Patrice Lewis, outstanding judges and chairs of the domestic violence coordinating committees of Prince George's County.

I could not have found the emotional strength to write this book without my mother, Barbara McCrocklin, who taught me compassion, my stepfather, Richard McCrocklin who gave my mother a better life, Christine Parcelli, who taught me basic relationship values, and my stepdaughter, Carmen, who taught me unconditional love.

My greatest debt for the insights and methods presented in this book is owed to thousands of my clients who were able to overcome sometimes outrageously hurtful pasts and heal the great wounds in their hearts. Without their courage and determination to make their lives and relationships more compassionate and loving, I could not have persevered for very long in this often difficult work. They are my continuing purpose and inspiration.

Steven Stosny
GERMANTOWN, MD
2005

Index

About the Author

Well-known and respected among his professional peers, Steven Stosny, PhD, has treated more than 4,000 people for various relationship problems through CompassionPower, the organization he founded and has directed for more than 12 years. Dr. Stosny has also trained more than 1,000 therapists all over the world. Compassion-Power runs successful programs to eliminate resentment, aggression, and violence in its primary breeding grounds: schools, work, highway, and home.

His textbook, *Treating Attachment Abuse: A Compassionate Approach* (Springer, 1995), set a new standard for understanding and treating family abuse and is widely used in therapeutic settings in the United States and abroad. Dr. Stosny has authored many articles and chapters in professional books and has been quoted by, or the subject of articles in, *The New York Times, Washington Post, Wall Street Journal, Washington Times, Chicago Tribune, U.S. News & World Report, Esquire, Cosmopolitan, Seventeen, Mademoiselle, Women's World, O, The Oprah Magazine, Psychology Today,* AP, Reuters, *USA Today,* and many syndicated columns and foreign newspapers. He has also appeared on programs on the major networks, CNN, local TV, *The Oprah Winfrey Show, Talkback Live, The Anderson Cooper Show,* and numerous radio shows here and abroad. Dr. Stosny has been a consultant for several mental health, social service, and motor vehicle agencies and is a behavior expert on the steering and advisory committees of four national task forces: Smart Marriages; The National Fatherhood Initiative; Smooth Operator; and the impaired driver task force of the National Association of State Courts.